D1128902

Michelle may crack!

A Personal Memoir of Bipolar Disorder

Michelle May Krack

Copyright ©2014 by Michelle T. Krack

Park Heights LLC

All rights reserved. This book or any portion thereof may not be reproduced or used in any manner whatsoever without the express written permission of the author except for the use of brief quotations in a book review.

ISBN-13: 978-0578451732

ISBN-10: 1502368595

Library of Congress Cataloging-in Publication Data has been applied for.

In loving memory of H. V. and those like him, living and passed, whose struggles are not forgotten, whose dreams are only deferred to those they inspired. May these stories provide solace in time of need, resolve during personal transformation, and hope for a better day.

Foreword

By: Carrie Harris

My mom can do no wrong. This is what I believed as a seven-year-old who had just finished second grade. It was a school year of epic proportion. My teacher, Mrs. Ballard, was one that every child dreamed of having: gentle, beautiful, fun. I was proud of the fact that MY mom was one of those parent helpers that Mrs. Ballard wanted involved in every classroom event. This perfect year was made even better by my mom being knee-deep in every glory I experienced as a second-grader: the farm field trip to Illinois, her hand-painted cafeteria murals, her hand-created, lined cursive paper to help me practice my penmanship, the homeroom Christmas party where I won Mrs. Ballard's coveted homemade gingerbread house, and numerous after school Girl Scout meetings. Although I was sad when the year came to an end I looked forward to the summer adventures ahead. I knew Mom would not let us down; she never ran out of imaginative summer activities to keep the four of us kids entertained.

However, that particular summer would be memorable for reasons beyond the water balloon fights, craft projects at the kitchen table, and late-night neighborhood flashlight tag. This summer Mom would have her first manic episode. At seven years old I did not know what it meant for someone to be manic, but I did know that my mom could do no wrong. So when Mom woke up my sister and me in the middle of the night for a tea party I was excited.

My mom could do no wrong.

When she had all four of us kids cornered in the kitchen, arms stretching behind her to protect us, screaming at our father asking him not to hurt us while convinced he was the devil, my thought was Dad must have done something horrible.

My mom could do no wrong.

This is what I believed as a twenty-year-old. As a college student I was able to reflect on the countless hours my mom gave up for my siblings and me: planning for and creating prom decorations, teaching me how to create grocery lists and cut coupons, hours and food wasted allowing me to experiment in the kitchen, creating beautiful flower boutonnieres and corsages for each special high-school dance, countless occasions of rescuing me from last minute "emergencies" I had to tend to as student government leader, various apartment packings and moves during college. The list goes on.

As I came closer to graduating college, and would soon after begin my teaching career, I yearned for the Mom who could do no wrong. During these monumental times in my life my mom was experiencing her most unstable episodes of depression and mania. I started to question the perfect relationship I had once had with my mom. I often asked myself, Who is this person? My heart would drop when my gentle, selfless dad, a man of few words, would call on the telephone. His calls were usually prompted by something interesting he had seen on the History Channel or to deliver news that Mom was not well. I dreaded those first few seconds on the phone where I could hear in his tone the news about to be delivered. He never had to say the words. I would know. "How's Mom doing?" He would sigh deeply and I would then ask, "How bad is it? Do you need me to come home?"

I wanted that Mom back that I had in second grade. I would do anything to get her back. I would halt my life at work or school, each one now blurring together, to lend support to my mother and father. These visits home were often heartbreaking. Her illness had taken control of her mind almost as though she was possessed. This person looked like my mom but in no other way resembled her. Not her words. Not her temperament. At times not even her voice. I began to lose faith in my relationship with her. But my perspective on Mom's illness changed one very fateful spring day.

During one episode Mom's mania was so out of control that she physically pushed my sister and said very hurtful things to both my sister and me. So startled with my mom's behavior, my sister wept on the living room floor. I held her as Dad took Mom to the hospital. Later that day my sister, still hurt and enraged by what had happened that morning, asked my dad, "How can you go through this time and time again? How can you stay with her?" Dad, without hesitation, said "Because I knew her before the illness. This is not your mom. She is not the illness." Dad knew that Mom could do no wrong. It was not Mom who was doing these things. It was the illness. My mom has been in recovery now for seven years and as a thirty-seven-year-old I have come to realize that my instincts as a seven-year-old were correct.

My mom can do no wrong.

I

Now is the Time

❧

It is quite a miracle that I have lived this long. I share a deep, close secret that for many generations was unknown, untreated, and especially unspoken. Two weeks shy of my thirty-first birthday, I became aware of a genetic illness that would turn my life upside down and inside out. My mood at any time may push me to be whimsical, down-trodden, practical, and sometimes philosophical. My mind is loaded with ideas all jumbled, ready to jump forth and be seen. My life has been a tumble of sorts, with many talents, jobs, and opportunities all struggling to find time in this circus called life. Also present is the ever-changing regimen of medications that, until recently, had not been remedied. To speak about myself I have to include others including family members and those closest to me. Yet, it remains *my* story.

To know ourselves and understand who we are originates from memories and experiences that we create in the present. I have always longed to write or teach and my life experiences have allowed me to do both. So, upon rising today and making time for a moment of prayer, I realized now is the time. I have promised myself this for far too long. For at least the last decade, there has been a sense of longing and eagerness to write for my children and anyone else willing to listen to the unusually lively stories from my life. This includes the good, the bad, and the ugly. Some names have been changed. All of the following is true.

Many times I have started and restarted writing my story, or at least put thoughts to paper, only to allow other distractions or life events to interrupt. Please have patience with me in my writing style as I may jump from past to present and back again in order to convey a point or message that otherwise would be like a thousand piece jigsaw puzzle with crucial pieces missing. Certain events propel me to get it out of my system and on to paper to provide at least a few laughs at my expense in even the most unlikely of times. It has all been a matter of survival as I hope to enjoy the longevity similar to that of my grandparents who lived into their eighties and nineties. Much have I learned from them and I thank them for being a part of my life. However, I must implement a disclaimer for the various types of self-treatment mentioned in this story: This book is not intended as a substitute for the medical advice of physicians. The reader should regularly consult a physician in matters relating to his or her health, particularly with respect to any symptoms that may require diagnosis or medical attention.

II

Family Photo Album

Stories of long-gone family members are important as the decorative nature of my home reflects their memory. One could safely assume that my nostalgic tendencies and constant battle with order in my writing have kept me from it for so long. I have decided to put these events in a hat, so-to-speak, and draw out what will hopefully be a worthwhile bit of expository pulp-*non*fiction. Life is sort of jumbled and tumbled in this manner anyway. My stories are sometimes not for the faint of heart and happen to be too unbelievable to happen to just one person who normally was just minding her own business.

Numerous photo albums of family members and friends have been added to my library waiting to be shared with future generations. In this sense, I have indirectly authored books by filling volumes with personal notes and identifying parents, grandparents, aunts and uncles, cousins, and friends. I can recall blessing these family members through prayers we said with Grandma and Grandpa Koressel as we laid our heads to sleep. I hope you also have volumes of stories to tell, not only to keep the memory of your family and friends alive, but to first bring them to life by labeling them in whatever photos you may have. Use a three-ring binder with sheet protectors and fill them with photos that have long been placed in boxes and stacks. Use typing paper to place between the protector sheets. Glue the photos into place on these sheets. Write on the paper right next to the photo with a black Sharpie so the books may be scanned or identified with a quick glance. The family marvels and looks at each and every page this way, looking for how they fit into the family tree. Our roots are so meaningful and if it is important enough to take a picture, it is important enough to label. Few are the items that humble the heart like that of a book with pictures and writings of loved ones. It is always easier for me to have visual aids in telling or learning a story, especially my family story, which starts with Tom and Mary May.

My parents were a beautiful young couple. After falling in love in grade school, they stayed in love and were wed just barely out of high school. It only seemed natural the two would marry one another. This love would eventually foster into my birth, the eldest of three other children. My parents are Thomas Benedict May and Mary (Koressel) May. The following note remains posted in my baby book; my maternal grandmother, Lucille Koressel, slipped it into my mother's hand during her labor and it reads: *Hope it's a boy*. Back then it was favored to have a boy first. Doctor Walter Dycus slipped another piece of paper in my Dad's hand as he slept. However, this one read, *It's a girl*. I guess I have been a surprise ever since. The next two years were quite enjoyable until I had to share the spotlight and the oohing and ahhing with my brother Michael. My next two siblings, Christopher and Martha Jean (Marty) came two years apart.

My first memory was clambering up the inside of my baby bed, with quite a struggle I might add, and standing there. I could not open my eyes for they were crusted shut. I tried picking at them. I cried for Mom who relieved my discomfort with a warm, wet washcloth. I was slowly able to open my eyelids. It must have been pinkeye or something of the sort. Many have noted that I have an uncanny way of remembering the slightest of details from my early childhood. This is quite helpful, as I am a stickler for detail. Looking at life that way makes it intriguing to say the least. Despite the *pinkeye situations* in life, I felt loved and remember laughing like any youngster should. It would show in all the black and white, and then eventually colored, Kodak-moment pictures that were taken.

Our first home was a double tenant house across from what later, I believe sometime in the seventies, would be known as the Country School Restaurant. Today it is a church. Our address was 3119 Mt. Vernon Avenue, Evansville, Indiana. The house has long been torn down and a few concrete steps are all that remain. Memories of those days have not quite faded. My mother tells me the old wooden dwelling had two small rooms with a tiny kitchenette. An elderly woman, the owner, shared not only the other side of the house, but also the bathroom. She was a respectful lady and quite gentle. Mom and Dad did not live there long because they were building a house on the same street. The property and the foundation that were being built was a wedding gift from my grandparents. My mother's parents, Rudolph and Lucille Koressel lived on the west side of the property and we were building a home next door. They graciously decided to give the foundation and plans to their only daughter and son-in-law; my parents were very thankful. As the building progressed, Mom and Dad were sure to chronicle it in our family picture album.

The house sat down from the road with a wooded area just east of it and my grandparents' large yard to the west that separated the two. Grandma and Grandpa's house was a grey, shingle-sided shotgun with rails along its steps. These rails would later be my playground. The backyards shared a large, grassy, flat, regulation-size tennis court which today is a large vegetable garden. In the middle of the two properties, Grandpa planted a Hawthorne tree that grew to an incredibly beautiful size over the years. He had quite the green thumb and owned Koressel Nursery. Even to this day I see his evergreen plantings at west-side residences and businesses. When I grew to about age twelve or so, I would go with him to help with trimming or planting. Grandma Lucille was a very short and petite woman and shared the same diligent work ethic as Grandpa. They learned it early on in their respective childhoods.

Grandma was the eldest of she and her two brothers, Marvin and Harold Morris. Their mother, my great-grandmother, Mary Morris was very strict and would spank Grandma if she returned home to one of the boys with a messy diaper. In such instances, there would be hell to pay. Little did I know how much time I would spend with this Dutch woman or her son Harold in latter years. Grandma Lucille was described as little but mighty jokingly by her friends, and she lived up to her nickname quite well. She worked in the cafeteria at Mater Dei High School and when at home she would iron and starch anything that needed it such as the white hassocks, priests' whites, or crisp linens for the altar table at Sacred Heart Catholic Church. I can remember her drinking Skis and smoking Camels as she ironed on the old, creaking ironing board. Playing on the floor near her I could feel the spray starch mist blanket me as she guided that iron smoothly over the stack of wrinkled church laundry. She would, at times, give a little spit. I found out later when I could read that she smoked filterless Camels and small pieces of tobacco would catch on her lip and she would expel it with a quick *"phew."* It is funny the things you remember as a kid.

Grandma and Grandpa rose early every morning around 5:00 a.m. Grandpa would bend and stretch in the living room while Grandma would start a breakfast of toast, coffee, and eggs that were partially fried with a little water and covered to finish off the cooking. Grandpa liked his toast so dark it would practically make your gums bleed when you bit into a slice. I never could recall why a bowl of plastic fruit was put on the table. To this day, I have a bowl of real fruit in the middle of my kitchen table that pays homage. The grandkids had our own special bowls, spoons, and plastic cups. They were so soft you could bend the cup if you squeezed them hard enough. How did they get those sparkles in those cups anyhow? After breakfast- weekend or not- the doors of Sacred Heart would be opened by Grandma and Grandpa, always the first to arrive.

Grandma and Grandpa were always loving to their grandchildren. This was even despite Grandma who, at times, would be so annoyed with the most miniscule of disruptions by Grandpa, or his way of thinking, that she would holler out *"Rudy!"* He always seemed to be in trouble with whistling a tune or telling of stories like the rhyme of the *Wobbly I.W.W. (I Won't Work)*. He would rattle it off so fast that in later years I took pen and paper and had him recite it to me. Please take the time to write down stories, poems, or sayings from your family. You will never regret it and the up-and-coming family members will be ever-grateful. I do not know where this poem originated, but it was embedded deeply in his brain and swift on his lips. Here it is:

The farmer stood on a hay stack,

The wobbly stood on the ground,

And to the farmer said the wobbly,

"Do you quit when the sun goes down?"

"No," says the farmer, "we work from day to dawn."

"Well," says the wobbly, "I guess I'll pack my

turkey and tramped the wide world over

'til I find that hard shelled scissor bill

that quits when the sun goes down."

Grandpa said this was from his 1920s western-era cowboy days in South Dakota. Grandpa would always make you jump when he would let out a loud *yelp* or even belch– outside mind you. I guess I know now why Grandma would holler out *"Rudy!"* I shall always remember his smile, that shine of a gold tooth in the left of his mouth, and the twinkle in his eyes when he was with his grandkids. There will always be a place in my heart for my grandparents – all of them, who showed me unconditional love and to have a great work ethic. We worked and loved together.

My dad's parents were always called *Grandma and Grandpa (May) Up the Hill*, due to the location of my grandparents' homes. Grandma and Grandpa Koressel lived on a lesser hill on Mt. Vernon Avenue whereas Grandma and Grandpa May, Joe and Bennie (Benedicta), lived a hill atop a breezy Maryland Street. Their home sat on a once coal-mined area. They both worked hard raising a family. My dad was second of four children. As a young girl, Grandma Bennie worked at Fendrich Cigar Factory, then later at St. Mary's Hospital in housekeeping. She spent her latter years raising the family, gardening, and canning. She was quite the quilter and one heck of a cookie baker. The first generation of grandchildren enjoyed receiving a made-with-love quilt by Grandma as a wedding gift. She also had a knack for making pincushions out of tuna and sardine cans and pot scrubbers that were made from netted fruit bags folded over themselves and topped off with a plastic or silk flower. They would be included in a thoughtful shower gift of kitchen towels and always a set of slotted spoons. You could never really find those at the time, but her trip to Baum's Grocery on Fulton for quilting supplies provided those handy utensils. She always kept Juicy Fruit and Double Mint gum in the top drawer of her dresser for all those twenty grandkids that would visit. Whoever has that piece of furniture today probably has the essence of both gum flavors.

Grandma Bennie and Grandpa Joe hosted many Christmases at their house. Grandma would set her dining room table to the nines for the adults. The lace tablecloth, china, silverware, napkins, and her delicious iced-tea served in hand-cut glasses were beautiful. She too had a bowl of plastic fruit on the table usually replaced with a fresh bouquet of flowers or a planter provided by her daughter and daughter-in-law Mary May. The Christmas tree had bubble lights and proudly displayed every ornament any grandchild ever made. Her baked oatmeal-raisin cookies were to die for. She took great care in making sugar cookies. The coveted delicacies were either Christmas tree-shaped or circles with scalloped edges. When she was not baking for the hordes of hungry hands and mouths at Christmas, she would bake all year-round and freeze those cookies. A visit in the summer would lend Grandma a dip into the freezer for a savory cookie we enjoyed so much.

She did not babysit my siblings or me much, but one time my parents went out of town leaving Grandma in charge. Just a few years ago she told me a story about that visit. About the age of five, I told Grandma with hands on my hips that she was *"not the boss of me!"* I have no idea what the altercation or disagreement was about;

it was probably time to come in from play and get cleaned up. There were many places to hide in Grandma and Grandpa's yard, primarily in a tool shed that resembled a small house. A pear tree for eating and climbing was near what the cousins called the *gorilla cage* which was nothing more than a piece of fencing in the yard, but it looked the part. I never knew if it was a root cellar in the hills, something to do with the former mine, or just a place to keep wild gorillas! The porch provided wooden rails on which to sit and, more importantly when Grandma's eyes were occupied, an even better place to practice the balance beam. There were few toys, a multitude of coloring and drawing books, and an overwhelming amount of imagination from Dad's childhood wooden rocking horse.

Too, there were always plenty of crayons and blank canvas of paper. Grandpa was quite the free-hand artist as a sign and graphics painter and was a self-taught genius in the mediums of pencil and paint. In my own home, I still treasure some of his artwork as any visitor of our westside home can see. He never really told or taught us how to express ourselves through art, but there was great respect for his tinkering and creative space in the small basement that shared a shower, washer and dryer, and root cellar. This area was pretty much off-limits mainly due to the steep steps that led there. Grandpa usually smoked a pipe of some sweet tobacco and shared his home brew when an occasion would arise, like when the sons arrived for holiday or for a good card game of Clabber. Never could figure that game out until I had to learn it to marry my husband. It was a necessity to acquire my new name. A sip of Grandpa's home brew left a very salty taste in your mouth with another undecided and unlikely twinge of what, I would have guessed, resembled beer. It helped me decide I did not have the palate for beer, much less homebrew. It did get some use as the uncles and Dad just marveled over it.

Grandpa was a hard worker, working the tool and die trade at the Chrysler plant in Evansville. He worked the same trade at International Harvester. Fate would cause a special event while working at Faultless Caster. Grandma tells that while she was packing casters across the hall she caught the eye of handsome Joe

May and the rest is history. Her maiden name changed shortly thereafter from Vowels to May following a very conservative wedding. I am not sure why Grandpa changed jobs so often. Maybe it was a sign of the times or due to some other reason that only he knew. He followed with jobs cleaning at Evansville Sheet Metal and later worked at Electric Plating that, I understand, was a very horrific and dirty job. Grandpa May was a staunch believer in labor unions. In his day he attended a labor parade just days before his wedding and was fired as a result.

Grandma and Grandpa never owned a car. They walked to the grocery at the bottom of their hill and to Franklin Street that offered shopping for all their necessities. If need be, they would catch a bus for longer travels. If you ever saw them walking, they would usually decline the ride saying they needed their exercise, unless of course the weather was inclement. My grandpas May and Koressel enjoyed beer and horseshoes. Sterling Beer was a staple in both households. Grandpa Koressel worked at the brewery and much of his hearing loss was due to the clanging of all the beer bottles in the assembly line.

Memories of both sets of grandparents are quite vivid as I spent much time with them. Extended families today are not quite so lucky to have had the everyday presence of this great generation. I was even blessed to have access to two great-grandmothers during my childhood; Great-Grandma Elizabeth Botzum May and Great-Grandma Mary Lutterbach Morris.

Elizabeth was Grandpa Joe's mother, a petite woman whom my mother says always wore a flat hat upon her head. She was a soft-spoken woman that showed love for her grandchildren by keeping every single coloring book page and child school photo ever drawn or shot. She lived in a shotgun house on West Indiana, east of the library but a now empty lot. As you would open her side door, the artistic creations from her descendants would flutter and welcome you as you entered. She spoke few words, but come Christmastime, she would pull a harmonica out of her apron pocket and play the quickest tunes you could imagine. I remember dancing, giggling, and laughing to this solitary musician who could play melodic childlike tunes with what seemed like great ease. Grandma Elizabeth was a crafty lady indeed. She was able to make a small stool for the grandkids which was put together from all sorts of things like tomato juice cans and heavy fabric she had gathered from her son who had an upholstery business. She would cover five cans with the heavy-duty scraps and somehow sew them together making the most perfect little seat for the kiddies. She was quite frugal and had to be raising four children by herself. Her husband left her during her children's formative years. I never heard her raise her voice or say a cross word. Such was Great-Grandma May.

On my mother's side was Great-Grandma Mary Morris. She too raised her children mainly by herself. From stories from her only daughter, my Grandma Lucille, she was said to be quite strict. She was pretty stern and you had to work hard to even get a smile out of her. She lived at least thirty of her years at the Little Sisters of the Poor in Evansville. There was not a Sunday that passed that we did not load up the family and visit my great-Grandma with my mother, siblings, and Grandma and Grandpa Koressel. You knew you would always receive a pat on the head or even a kiss from the nuns that sheltered the elderly. The original Little Sisters Nursing Home had huge hallways with heavy wooden trim and black and white tiled floors. We usually visited Great-grandma in the dining room where she had a drawer built into the table to sit and dine. I always thought that was pretty clever. There was a caged parakeet named Pete who took up residency near the sunny porch that had every plant imaginable. It was like a miniature jungle, a perfect place to hide. The only games we played were cards, lots of them. She would show us many styles of solitaire and would painstakingly teach us every part of every game.

Before I was married in 1978, I worked at the Little Sisters and Great-Grandma was one of the twenty or so residents who were in my care. I had just graduated from LPN Class No. 32 through North High School's Vocational program and started to work as a nurse. I enjoyed the busy schedule on second shift and enjoyed even more the chance to tuck my granny in at night with a goodnight kiss. She spent many an hour crocheting and making all sorts of doilies and hot pads, even some pillowcases. Some of these handcrafted items and the tools that made them are in my possession still. Some of her beautiful handiwork is framed and hanging in my home in prominent places for all to see. Great-Grandma Mary Morris lived to be ninety-three. So much of my creativity and patience is derived from this generation of precious grandparents and great-grandparents.

In today's *Westside* newspaper, I came across an article concerning collections. I have been an avid collector, and creator in the process, of family photo albums. I have already given some to my four children which mainly consisted of their baby books and adolescent years. They never grow tired of perusing the illustrations and footnotes of their early lives. My albums may seem obsessive but at least they are not currently tucked away in some computer file without personal notes or names. When there is a death in the family I take those books to the funeral home. Amazing is the dialogue and family connection the albums bring. If you miss a picture or a page of information, you can easily flip back and forth to share that memory immediately with an interested aunt or cousin. No digital slideshow can conjure that type of nostalgia. As the years progress, so do the family members, added pictures, and captions. I only hope that they will someday be preserved and kept as a precious family tree.

Maybe I always needed a special place to write, to have peace and no interaction with the outside world in order to release and express this story. I believe I have found it in the sunny, well and naturally-lit sunroom that has been added onto our one hundred and thirty-two year old home. We have needed and wanted this addition for many years. I am certain the kids would have liked it too. Raising four of them- especially when two are girls and two are boys- indeed tested our patience. We are blessed to have this new space especially when they all come home.

The sunroom has a large, long, heavy oak table upon which I write. Once belonging to one of the Sacred Heart kindergarten classes, the legs of the table were sawed off to match the children's height. It was refinished and six inches were added from four round kitchen table legs found at Trader Bakers. This table is an extension of my kitchen and will allow ten family members to dine at its sides. I love the feel of wood and am fortunate to have received this castaway fifteen years ago. I imagine my parents and children probably sat at this very table. History reveals itself by the hundreds of pieces of gum that were stuck on its underside. The carvings on top sanded out pretty well except for some guy named "Joe" who apparently wanted to be remembered for all time.

My mind turns back to my genetics and how I express myself. Two days ago, I was awakened to an anxious state of mind along with crying and a desperate depression that rendered me, mercilessly, to the couch most of the day. It took half the day to arise from that couch, and the funk that seemed to hit me from all sides. By evening I was driving my mother's barbershop singing group, The Sweet Adelines, to Lincoln State Park for their sing-out during a preshow dinner. I have lived but a dream, not knowing what I want to be when I grow up. It is never clear to me other than through writing what I am adamant about or determined to accomplish. Hopefully, I find my dream and can believe that you are ready for the journey into my world.

Not every day do I feel like writing. My best and most productive time is 4:30 a.m., even before the birds start greeting the day. By then I have set my brain to a focus only until my husband's alarm clock goes off. I am usually an early-to-bed and early-to-rise type person. I work best that way. Secretly, I enjoy the mornings when my husband returns home at 7 a.m. from his twenty-four hour job with the Evansville Fire Department as a District Westside Chief.

∽

Tim and I will be married forty-one years this October 2019. He has stood by me and taken his marriage vows very seriously, especially *in sickness and in health.* The roller coaster ride, the expense, the turnover of doctors, trials, and letdowns of medications, has been trying and testing to our marriage to say the least. The better days, the creative days, the loving and laughing days, the understanding days, have all made it worth it. He wrote a poem for me while in a writing class at the University of Southern Indiana. I wood-burned it on a large, rectangular piece of driftwood and presented it several years after he wrote it. I thought he picked it up somewhere only to find out at that time, embarrassingly, that he wrote it especially for me. It hangs in my kitchen where I can see it no matter my mood. Still untitled, it reads:

Friends we are,

Always listening to each

other's problems.

    Helping each other

understand ourselves.

    watching the stars.

wondering how we

relate to them and ourselves.

We are confused but

I pray we will find

the right road.

Lovers we are, traveling

the road to freedom

and openness with each

other. always there to

help the other.

THIS IS THE ROAD TO LOVE

I presented this wood-burning on Valentine's Day 1975. I guess at this time it could have very well been a wedding vow. We were married after nearly five years of dating on October 14, 1978. We shared our wedding date with, Tim's father, Ted Krack's birthday. It happened to fall on a Saturday that year. We wanted to get married in the fall, but thought about having a summer wedding because Tim's mother had contracted ovarian cancer. She insisted that we keep our original plan for a fall wedding. I wish now we would have moved the date up. She may have enjoyed it more and would not have been so ill from the cancer treatments. By this time she was wearing a wig, but it did not change her positive disposition.

Our wedding day was on a crisp, semi-cloudy day. Even the weather seemed like a blessing; we experienced rain, snow, and sunshine all in one day, a sign of good luck. Earlier in the day, before our two o'clock ceremony, the altar was being painted. Just six weeks prior to the wedding, literally every pew was removed from the church for a remodel. Mom said, *"This will never be done in time for the wedding!"* We were concerned about the backdrop behind the cross that hung prominently above the altar. There was indecision within the church congregation about what colors to paint the backdrop. At that point in time, it had several colors painted across it. Father Dewig asked us what color we thought it should be. I said, *"Blue would be nice. It would match the blue cushions on the chairs around the altar."*

With that, the painters arrived early that Saturday morning and tip-toed over the yellow mums for the wedding and painted it the chosen blue color. The hue was perfect as it also matched the color of dresses my bridesmaids wore during the ceremony. My maid-of-honor, sister-in-law Ann, wore yellow. I made all the flower bouquets from silk flowers that I purchased from K-Mart and Woolworths. I carried my Grandma Koressel's First Communion book which had been covered with white velour, tipped with a blue and yellow rose and flowing white ribbons. I also carried her mother of pearl rosary. All of these details and more would be written up with a picture of me in my gown in the *Westside Story* newspaper. My gown was borrowed from a second cousin and I altered the full-length veil that was also the train. My sister Martha, sister-in-law Barb, and neighbor friend Carol served as bridesmaids. My sister-in-law Ann was my matron-of-honor. Tim's brothers, Paul, John, and Larry were groomsmen with best friend Rick as best man.

As we knelt in front of the altar, Tim whispered to me that the guys used masking tape to spell out "HELP" on the bottom of his shoes. He tried his best to keep his toes curled under his shoes so no one could see the message. You could just barely see it in one of our wedding pictures. This is same group of pranksters that would harness Tim with a ball and chain at the reception. The ceremony was as beautiful as I had dreamed. The guitar and organ music was special as it had been a gift from the St. Philip Choir.

I was happy to be marrying my best friend.

There were two hundred people in attendance at our wedding. Our large families allowed us only a few friends to invite. A wedding gift from my friend Nancy was the making of the cake. At that time, Posey County roads were treacherous to drive on. There were even t-shirts made at this time that brandished a roller coaster ride with the words, "Have a Thrill, Ride Posey County Roads." Poor Nancy was a nervous wreck trying to transport our decorated cake over the deep, pot-holed miles to church. The cake was three-tiered and beautiful with steps encircling one side and blue-lit candles on each tier. A cascade of blue, silk flowers lay down the stairway. The top of the cake had a blue satin bell.

Everyone enjoyed a sit-down chicken dinner with sides from the Saveway Market. There was, of course, plenty of beer. A Catholic wedding reception would not be complete without a few adult beverages. Later we would learn we had two wedding crashers. They had come for the booze.

When it came time for the best man to retrieve the garter he quickly pulled a pair of scant panties from his cuff as he held up the garter. It appeared as if he had gotten a little more than the garter! I am glad my grannies were not paying attention.

We would take a picture of our four generations of women in the family: my mother Mary, her mother Lucille Koressel, her mother Mary Morris, and me. Pictures at the wedding were a concern. The deposit I had secured for the wedding resulted in the photographer's assistant taking all the pictures. I was told the photographer had left town and had suffered a nervous breakdown.

We had planned a honeymoon to Orlando, Florida to Disney World. Epcot was just being built. We said goodbyes to our guests and headed south by car with "Just Married" scrawled in paint across the back window. Tim had decided we would travel with a Citizens band, or CB, radio. It was fun listening to and answering the truck drivers. They congratulated us on our nuptials. Some asked, *"Can she cook?"* We drove for miles into the night unable to stop in Nashville because all the hotel rooms were full. We finally had our honeymoon in a town called Winchester, Tennessee. We should have gotten a room in Henderson instead of driving for hours.

We arrived in Orlando and enjoyed our honeymoon package that included Sea World, Disney World, Ruby Tuesday's, and the Barnum & Bailey Circus. Unfortunately, we did not have or make time for the circus. I recently came across the tickets that I had still saved all those years ago. The ornately decorated tickets always stand out in my memory. We were given a complimentary five-day supply of champagne. We decided to ice it down and drank only one bottle during our stay. We bought our first cooler to keep the bottles cold. We did not want the bottles to pop prematurely on our way home. We enjoyed ourselves at all of the sights and before we knew it, our honeymooning days came to a close. We looked forward to getting home and opening our wedding gifts with our immediate family and wedding party.

As we approached Atlanta, a voice came over the radio *"Congratulations! Where are you from?"* We responded, *"Evansville, Indiana."* We learned the voice belonged to a professional baseball player from Atlanta and he saw the "Just Married" sign still painted on our window. He told us he would guide us through Atlanta and tell us about the skyline as we passed under the tangle of overhead highways. After we passed through Atlanta, we exited and shook hands with Lightning- as was his radio tag. We never learned his real name. He wished us well and waved goodbye as we continued on our journey home. Who knew how much fun one could have on a CB radio!

Now through Atlanta, we passed a large truck with an open backdoor. Inside the truck we could see the backend of a large elephant. His rear end swayed back and forth as the truck sped down the highway. We hoped that he would reach his destination safely too.

We returned home and shared the champagne with our family and friends. Rick christened our living room with one of the bottles as it popped open and everyone, perhaps reluctantly, received a champagne shower. Tim returned to work at A & F Fire and Safety and as assistant manager of sporting goods at the K-Mart on St. Joe Avenue. I returned to work at the Little Sisters of the Poor as a Licensed Practical Nurse. I continued to tuck Grandma Morris in bed at night while I administered her evening medicines.

Tim's parents are and always will be special to me. While growing up in my teen years, I made a loud thundering claim walking up my parents' long cinder and brick driveway: *"I am not going to live like this!"* I took any opportunity I had to get away from home. Being snowed in town at Tim's parents' house was always welcomed. I only hoped there could be snow days in the summer. Any excuse would have done. Ted and Alberta welcomed me into their home for meals and overnights when possible. I loved their couch and warm hospitality. Always was I eager to help with chores or errands to run next door to Jim Seib's Market to purchase a day's worth of groceries. Alberta had to get around with a little more difficulty than the usual person. She was born without hip sockets and as a result was much shorter than most in her family and had a swinging gait to her walk. I never knew how she managed to have five children after the doctor told her she could have none. I married the baby of the family. Maybe that is why Tim and I got along so well, me being the oldest in my family. Opposites do seem to attract.

On top of just being great souls in general, Alberta and Ted were also hard workers. Ted worked for years at Bucyrus Erie on Claremont Avenue and took an early retirement due to Alberta's unfortunate ovarian cancer diagnosis. Alberta was a stay-at-home mom and prided herself in making her family comfortable. She fed them well and supported all their ventures, from Fall Festival float making for the pet parade to Red Cross and Civil Defense operations. She was a very fine seamstress that I do not doubt she learned from her mother Carrie Zanella Logel. Alberta, sometimes called Bert, had an embroidery machine. You were lucky to receive her monogrammed towels or a jacket or purse with her artful embroidery. I recall she did work for some years at the Shane Uniform Company on Maryland Street which is now the building of an industrial contractor. She pieced together a baby quilt top with scraps of material from her work. Years after she passed, I had my great Aunt Lucy Morris, who happened to live next door to us, put a backing on the quilt top. She quilted it beautifully. The fabric was so fragile on the patches that I could not use it for an actual family baby quilt so I had it framed at Ben Franklin on Weinbach. The colorful framed quilt hangs in our living room for everyone's enjoyment.

It is interesting to know that Ted and Alberta were actually neighbors as they grew up in the neighborhood of West Iowa Street and Tenth Avenue. Much time was spent at the Logel home. There was a beautiful trellis along the side of the porch where a viney plant flowered along the wooden lattice. Any important family pictures were taken at this location in the family yard. Ted and Alberta's wedding picture was no exception. She was thirty and he was twenty-seven years old. Their wedding date was January 2, 1943. They raised their family at 503 North Tenth Avenue, which was across the street from where Ted grew up, also on Tenth. I much appreciate Alberta's sister, Leona Logel, for keeping records of birthdates, marriages, divorces, deaths, and names of the Logel family. I refer to her notes frequently. Aunt Leona never married but enjoyed her nieces and nephews and even the next generation making her Great-Aunt Leona. She lived at 2218 West Iowa all her life. She always offered food to any of the family kids that would drop by. Their favorite was a *Nony* sandwich. Nony was a slightly shorter name for Leona. The sandwich consisted of bread, jelly, and bacon. My kids still call them Nony sandwiches and the recipe is in the West Side Catholic cookbook as a testament to their fame. Aunt Leona was also a self-taught artist. Her medium was water color. She would make flowery pictures or paint winter scenes. I have kept all of her painted ones and some are framed and decorate my walls. Leona shared the genetic trait like that of her sister Alberta; she lacked a formed hip socket to her left leg, whereas Alberta had none to either leg. As a result, Alberta was slow to walk as a young child which lasted until age three.

Learning the names of some of Tim's family members was comical to say the least. I thought he had so many uncles that I would never be able to remember all of their names! There were actually only five uncles: Carl, Alvin, Julius, Cornelius, and Henry. Little did I know Alvin was also known as *Dick* and Julius was better known as *Snottus*. He always had a runny nose and used his sleeve a lot. Cornelius was *Noodles*– he was quite a genius child-mechanically speaking– until he was given too much ether for an operation. He was never the same again. Henry was a.k.a. *Hiney*. Whew! It took me years to figure this out, which was nearly as long as it took me to learn Clabber– my initiation into the Krack family. For anyone knowledgeable on Clabber, one day I led out a bare jack and side ace with my father-in-law as my partner. I had no idea who had the remaining trumps. Luckily he did and we won the hand. This was a serious game and was not to be played so fool-heartedly.

I suppose I write about all these people and events now because for the most part, they were happy. They formed a ritual in my life that was normal. My early days of growing up seemed normal to me in all outward appearances. This would soon change drastically. What was once routine, pleasant, warm, and welcoming was soon to become an often-present nemesis that would grow to monstrous proportions. It grasped ahold of us like nothing else. I speak of two separate nemeses. Unfortunately, they could rarely be sated in the closet of my childhood like so many bad dream.

III

New Adventures

My most vivid recollection of early childhood days began with the new adventure that was kindergarten. What a lovely place to be! My mother chose for me to attend the morning session. Soon after my arrival to this particular time slot, something beyond my control moved me to the afternoon session. I had just barely learned where to hang my coat and put my boots away and sheepishly utter a *"hi"* to what would be my new friends and classmates. The name of the school was Marrs Elementary and to me might as well have been the fourth rock from the sun.

Mrs. Nickels would have to take me to this new time slot. The afternoon bus was my ride home. My new chauffeur had a kindergarten-aged daughter named Sally. My mother recalls how happy and relieved she was for the travel arrangements to work so well. We did not live far from Marrs at that time. The house was a huge, white, two-story farmhouse on Carson School Road and still stands majestically today. It was a perfect place to play and hide at the age of five. Of course, the downside was the fact that now I had to meet all new faces of the kids in class. Despite this, I was more intrigued by the new playthings at my disposal. The largest stack of cardboard bricks I had ever seen caught my eye until I saw the neatly kept rows of toys and other items on the long shelves. Who could have imagined a grocerette to play with too? Believe it or not,

I could even enjoy a slicky slide right there in the middle of the room. I soon learned to tuck my head while climbing to the top as to not hit it on the metal grates that covered the fluorescent lights. What a thrill it was to be in this place! Even more fascinating was the beautiful fish tank which had so many fish, they could not be counted. I mean, come on, I only had ten fingers and ten toes after all.

It would soon come time to find a seat with my own name printed atop the table. Enthusiasm ran through me as I hunted for my name although I was not totally sure what I was looking for. Miss Martin introduced herself and told us where the bathroom was and proceeded to help us find our place. What pride I felt knowing that this was all mine- my very own name card! The room was explored further and at some point during the day we had a session with instruments and singing. I hoped the fun would never stop! But it did.

It soon became time for a nap, which I faked sleeping with one eye open as to not miss anything that might happen at this place called Marrs. A snack soon followed of graham crackers and a cool glass bottle of milk with a cardboard lid. It was more than anything a young brain could dream up. As days passed so did the skills of learning to print my name, learning my colors, taking turns at the calendar board, getting in line to go outside for, you guessed it, recess! What fun! Play time on top of more play time! This place was great! The calendar board was the coolest thing since the inception of crayons. The colorful blue board was made of felt and had the monthly calendar on it; each child took turns placing the date in the corresponding square. Another child, and this was my favorite, would determine the weather for the day and would place a sun or rain cloud atop the calendar. I fell in love with felt the minute I touched it. There were many things I would fall in love with like Miss Martin. She was pretty, smart, and loved by her brood of kindergarteners. I even enjoyed playing school at school, taking turns being the teacher on occasion, and the cashier at the grocerette.

While I was living a great life and catching the bus to go home for the first time, Mom was about to experience her worst nightmare. She longingly waited for my arrival from my exciting day at school. The time slowly ticked by and by until it was almost five o'clock. She became concerned that something had happened to me. She called the school and was told that my bus had to wait for the Mt. Vernon High School bus before I was dropped off as the last stop. She was so worried so I got extra hugs and kisses that day. While practicing my flip flashcards of the colors that were to be learned, I quickly put to memory the color and its spelling. I always recognized yellow in color but the spelling just never seemed to fit the color; I always had trouble with that, even through the first grade.

Before I knew it, it was time to start first grade. I was excited to know I would soon be seeing Miss Martin and my classmates again. The excitement of starting first grade just bubbled up inside me with pure joy. There was talk of St. Philip, a change in the location of my schooling. A bus could take me there and soon, I was dressed in a white blouse and a blue uniform with front panels and a solid back. New shoes and socks completed my back to school wardrobe. It felt odd wearing it, but it was just first grade.

Before school started, it was decided that I would meet a neighbor girl two years my senior named Carol, who would look after me and make sure I would get off the bus at the right time. God forbid my mother lose me again. My mother drove me to her house about a mile down the road. In all outward appearances, she dwarfed me and looked like she could easily be the boss. The first few days Mom stood at the top of our winding, football field-length, brick and cinder driveway. I would later learn being late for the bus made a furious, uphill hundred-yard dash a challenge. Mom and I met the bus driver. He was an older and kind man named Mr. Williams.

As we pulled into the dusty drive, there was a myriad of yellow buses. I panicked as to which one was my ride to St. Philip. Luckily, Carol appeared. Catching the bus on time was key, especially for a shy first-grader. My wish was that she would take my hand and guide me to the big yellow number B-12 bus. I did not have a sister at that point in time, but I hoped Carol would be. With her arms crossed she said *"follow me"* with as much authority as a third grader could muster. We got in the bus and it was my first encounter with Mr. H. He *seemed* friendly enough. I already missed the familiarity of my first bus driver, Mr. Williams. Mr. Williams was soft spoken, but had a green willow switch above his long mirror that hung above his head. While waiting for the high school bus exchange, he would offer the waiting children either a butterscotch, or a Brach's brand red hot, hard candy. It was against the rules, but he would let us off the bus to play in a hillside where we made a house and etched the steps out with sticks we found and bark that held berries we gathered for play food. My brother Mike would scale a large sycamore tree to hail the high school bus coming, as it would leave a large dust trail as it approached. There was a small county bridge nearby and a cemetery across the road. They were both off-limits, yet every once in a while one of us would sneak down to the bridge and be quickly called back. He never raised his voice, nor that green switch. He was a nice man who had chickens and would sell eggs to my mom and others on the route. Some days I would pluck two dozen cartons of eggs carefully wrapped with string from under the cubby hole near the front door of the bus. There was always a polite exchange of thank yous. Shortly after, the egg sales progressed and the school found out Mr. Williams was selling them from the bus and it had to be stopped. The eggs were the best and little did I know I had the best bus driver ever. As I climbed aboard good ole B-12 one day, something just felt different. The kids were rowdier and there seemed to be more chaos on the bus than ever before.

The trip to St. Philip's School seemed exciting, new scenery with my head pressed against the window. All of a sudden we hit a large hump and the kids in the back of the bus jumped and almost hit their heads on the roof. They let off screams of joy and excitement from the incident. As I turned to look back to the road, I saw that we had just flown over a country bridge. Mr. Williams sure had not driven like that. Soon we approached the church on a hill called St. Philip and us kids scrambled to get our bags of lunches and stacks of books. The girls had to wear something on their heads before entering church. Usually a lace doily of sorts was pinned on, but in a pinch a Kleenex pinned in the same manner would often suffice. As we fumbled to the front door I noticed a lot of commotion with the girls slapping the bus driver and saying mean things to him like *"stop it stupid"* and *"you freak"* and *"you dirty old man."* As my turn came up to leave the bus I saw that he was flipping the girls' uniform skirts. I was petrified. He did it randomly so I was spared his hand that day, but there would be others to come.

My first experience with alcohol came with this same bus driver, Mr. H. After school each and every day you could smell a strong odor on his breath. I soon learned it was alcohol, lots and lots of alcohol. He acted normal when the sisters or teachers stood near the bus, but as soon as he got down the road, there was a need for speed and he would cajole and harass by yelling loudly to the kids in the back who had the best seats for joyriding. I was never so happy to get finished with this final ride with Mr. H, as I felt safer and closer to home. As days went by, I needed Carol's help less and less to find the right bus, but she still spoke to me in an authoritative tone. *"I am the boss of you"* she would say. There was no one else there to really convince me otherwise.

Not long after riding the bus and going to school together, she would come up to my house to play. Except by this time there was not much play. My dad began drinking Sterling beer or whatever was on sale at the time. The ravines around our home would reveal as much, as there were spent cans everywhere. Carol always had the latest kids' gadget or toy and liked showing it to me on her visits. I really did envy her because Mike and I never got many new things. We relied on our imaginations and the woods surrounding our home for most of our play. The first stop was a climbing tree in the shape of a y that our rear ends filled in perfectly while our feet touched the trunk. A few feet further up were the *pedals*- two branches at equal levels were pushed with your feet up and down like pedals for gas and clutch on a car. Carol's size kept her from climbing our prized tree, but that did not stop her from visiting.

I only remember the most grandiose and silly things about first grade. The first thing I noticed was the huge, wall-filling blackboards with long, green lines. Gone were the bright and cheery decorations and fun things from kindergarten. The desks were in neat rows; they looked like sleigh chairs one right after the other on runners made of wood to keep them neatly planted together. To match the dark blackboards a woman appeared in black... everything. Her hat and, what I thought was a veil at the time, were black and her long dress covered every inch of her frail white skin. For a while I thought she did not have arms for she had them tucked somewhere inside her garment. She had the longest skinniest fingers I had ever seen and behind her wire-rimmed glasses was the stern, no nonsense face of Sister Mary Dominic.

She clapped her hands at every command *"Sit down."* CLAP. *"Stand up."* CLAP. You can imagine how this continued, day in and day out. She kept a ruler close by and with further inspection one day she had it in her hand and was waving it in the air at the boy sitting next to me, Randy Flick. She told him, rather unsympathetically, *"Randy, quit blinking your eyes."* Poor Randy was so shy he was afraid of himself. One more time, *"Randy, I must demand you quit blinking your eyes."* With that he blinked twice as fast and ever more nervously than the first offense. I could feel the rush of air come flying across my face as she whacked his knuckles with the nearly broken ruler. I will never forget that day and am positive poor Flick will not either.

The appearance of second grade was a bit more welcoming. Fortunately, the only direction to go in the morale department when leaving the misery of Sister Mary Dominic's classroom was up. There was more color, in general, and bulletin board displayed letters and numbers. My teacher, Miss Clooney, was a pleasant teacher who had such a love for Limburger cheese that she kept some in her car until lunch time. She would send a boy classmate out to get it and no matter who it was that did the fetching, they would return with the most contorted, grimaced face and have cheese in their hand. As if the car-warmed Limburger was not enough, she was the largest woman I had ever known. When you walked behind her to lunch, you could watch her dress sway back and forth. Only once did I get the chance, along with many other classmates, to deliver notes to the seventh-grade teacher from Miss Clooney. They must have been in love because they got married soon after I left second grade. We must have been quite the cupids.

You got to go upstairs in third grade of the original St. Philip school building. We were fortunate this time to get a nun as a teacher, more of her legs were showing and she had a smile and a twinkle in her eye when she spoke to the class. It was a fun year, especially during fire drills. My best friend at the time, Beth Lizarn, provided a very comedic spectacle one day for us all. As we were put into lines at the end of the day, we would lean against the wall waiting for the signal to go down to our buses. It just so happened the fire alarm lever was in this vicinity and as a result Beth activated the alarm with her shoulder. There generally were no fire drills at the end of the day. So much concern erupted with the teachers running here and there trying to figure out where the fire was. The boiler room was directly beneath us. Of course we tried to tell our teachers, hysterical by this time, what had happened. It took several minutes for the mystery to be solved. Rest assured there was no more leaning on the wall after this event.

Math became harder for me. I just could not grasp fractions and multiplication took much practice. Needing help at home with my arithmetic, I asked Dad for help. He grew impatient with me and called me names to reinforce my ignorance of the homework. I felt the strong hold of his alcoholism and something else that angered him, which was more frequent than I care to remember. I learned to distance myself until I knew he was very inebriated. I would use this tactic very often and especially if there was anything important to tell him. I wondered what it was like for other kids, because by this time my parents gave me a baby sister, Martha Jean. She was tiny and had the reddest hair when she was brought out into the sunlight. I was already six years older than she.

There were roots, lots of them reaching out like the ribs of an umbrella. This was a haven for building houses on the big kids' playground at school. There was never enough time to construct the perfect house which we would scrape out in the ground as if we were a chicken in the barn yard. Ridges of gravel would serve as make-believe walls. Endless were the many rooms which could be built under the tall maple and catalpa trees. Catalpa trees produced long, skinny pods that we would try to light and smoke when we were older. Recess was never long enough for our building plans and we would have to continue the next day after lunch. There was not nearly enough hand-washing going on either. I am sure most of us kids were naturally inoculated by the time we were in fifth grade by all the germs we picked up from our play.

After four grades in the original old building we graduated and were placed in the new addition to the school. Gone were the days of the big playground and lots of recess time. Recess was now spent with girls playing tetherball, volleyball, walking, or talking. The boys had their games too, namely playing baseball or basketball up near the large maples and cemetery. I loved inside recess. The girls would play records. I brought some forty-fives from home and the result was a group of girls singing out a melody *"You Belong to Me."* The footstool in the room became my stage and I would happily belt out this song over and over mind you until someone– probably a boy- would say *"Shut it off!"*

Fifth grade was interesting as we kids had our first but not last male school teacher. Other than that, nothing else really stood out. After teaching a while he took a delivery job somewhere in town. I cannot say that I blame him, trying to teach a bunch of squirming, mostly immature pre-teens.

Sixth grade was fun and busy. My friend Beth, nicknamed Lizard, would keep the discussion lively in the bathroom. Thank God we never got caught trying to ballet walk on the toes of our shoes or squealing while Beth would act out her lizard impression. My first junior-high kiss was in a relatively clandestine location that was the boiler room. It was dark and musty. I can still smell the oily mops that hung above our lovelorn heads. The kiss was sloppy and overrated. Given, there was not much to compare it to, and I would not care to try again until I was in high school. Perhaps the boiler room was not the most romantic of places anyway. My first kiss was actually less romantic, if you can believe it. A boy named

Jerry sat behind me in the third row of wooden desks. He always tugged on my brown ponytail or braids. One day after his many attempts to aggravate me, I told him to stop. His reaction was to plant a kiss right onto my lips. Embarrassed, I told my teacher. Jerry was seated at another desk and thankfully the one-sided tryst ended there. Years later at a class reunion, Jerry planted one on me for old times' sake. He must have wised up though because this one was on the cheek.

May Crowning was a big deal. The eighth graders would pick a queen of their classmates and she would place flowers at Mary's feet during a song-filled Mass provided by all eighth graders. Then the fun would begin. Tournaments on all of our playground competitions would put us to the test. The highlight of the day was when we were handed a sack with our choice of hamburger or hot dog, a random bag of chips, and a delicious Slo Poke candy on a stick. They finally figured how to keep our mouths busy and quiet. Other than this, grade six was pretty uneventful. We had a nun again, Sister Calmalita. Oh those names! I always joking that they drew names from a hat and you had to take it with the name Mary in front of it, of course.

By seventh grade I now loved to draw or paint just about anything. In my younger grade school days, I would draw multi-storied classrooms filled with nice rows of children and always the presence of a Sister Mary Somebody drawn somewhere in the room *without* a ruler. Perhaps that is why I sometimes dreamed of being a teacher. One particular memory involved a tightly-ran art contest between a male counterpart and myself. We both had much talent. I picked a sketch of a man I think was on the back of a matchbook cover. I can not recall what he drew but I felt mine was better. Much to my dismay, he took first and I followed with second place.

It was no surprise that nearly every nun we had as a teacher had quit the convent. My class had a reputation beyond all others as the *"nun-wreckers"*. I am not sure but maybe it was just the sign of the times that they left the cloistered life. Without exception, we had the meanest boys that ever walked through those seventh-grade doors at St. Philip. One day before Sister Mary Hildegard sat down, the scheming boys placed at least a half a dozen thumbtacks, pointy end up, on her cushioned chair. Much to our horror when she sat down there came no reaction from her in the slightest. We figured at least a peep would come out of her- but nothing happened. The rest of the class was in sheer panic and refused to be tattle tales. This was not the last time they tried to be so dangerously squirrely either. We still had the old wooden desks with the fold-up seats. One bright boy decided to give one of his chums a quick stab in the butt through the crack in the seat during math class with a nice, pointy compass. There was a yell of pain and embarrassment. I can still remember hearing that boy's yelps from the library that doubled as our first-aid station and sick bed. He let out a scream as the hydrogen peroxide met his not so precious, compass-driven behind. No one ever fessed up to it, so the whole class got punished having to write something many times over. What a use for a compass!

It hardly seemed possible that we were finally the big kids once eighth grade started up for our final year at St. Philip. I remember thinking how nice school was because it was absent of any alcoholism. Then came our old, dirty bus driver. His quick hand seemed to go higher and higher up under our skirts. Our only retort was a huge slam of our books on the bus driver's shoulder or head- whichever was the easiest target. By today's standards this obviously would have never taken place, much less lasted as long as it did. Our guardian angels must have been with us, protecting us from his reckless driving all those years.

At home the alcohol was in the form of beer that was readily stocked in a small refrigerator at the foot of our basement steps. Quite frequently my siblings and I were runners to get Dad a cold one. I do not recall him being gone much, to a job that is. His job was watching every move you made. Rarely were they to his liking. One did not sit and watch television or hang around the house. A friend's house or the woods or a long bike ride was a refuge. Something seemed very wrong about all of this and I did not share much about it with my friends. He always seemed to be home on the couch. Depression had taken hold of him.

There was a plaid, almost life-size baby carriage. I was so proud of it and would take my baby dolls for long sunny walks up and down that long driveway. One day I thought up the most original idea and fun was quick to come from it. I took my baby sister Marty for a ride. She was plucked up from the sand box, her plump legs just barely fit. She smiled and giggled and wiggled a lot. Then, to my horror the fine carriage collapsed on to her arms and pinched them tightly. She let out a scream so loud it scared me into a complete panic. I could not release the metal sides that had now clamped down on her arms. I screamed at the thought of my baby sister losing her arms. Mom came running and managed to free her, scolding me at the same time. To this day she kids me about the day I almost chopped off her arms. There was neither blood nor side effects for she uses her arms freely now delivering mail to hundreds daily as a rural route carrier.

I loved my baby sister. She likewise loved me and many of my things. I proudly had a ruby ring, ruby being my birthstone, that Grandma and Grandpa Koressel gave me for my birthday. Marty liked it well enough that she wore it and lost it in the acreage of Posey County, never to be seen again. For years I would kid about her losing my ring. Several years ago she surprised me with a replacement ring. I forgive you sister. Your love has meant more to me than any ring.

When not at school, I dove into the mysteries of our big house with a three-year old Mike. From the house a brick sidewalk led down to a chicken house, with part of the water pump and outhouse to see along the way. Next to the white house that we lived in sat a one-story, two-doored, old and brown wooden house. We both were told to stay out of there; something like monsters were supposedly in there was used as a scare tactic. It worked. We never looked in that place or even touched it. I remember my distant cousin Bobby as we shared a laugh when I told him how scared I had been to go near that place as a child. The outhouse was frequently used as it was our bathroom. The big opening on the seat always scared me and I quickly did my business in a hurry before I thought I might fall in.

To contrast, the boxwoods always smelled good, just like boxwoods do. To this day, they remind me of old farmhouse living. There were the white, prolific August lilies that surrounded the foundation of the house. I shall never forget their sweet perfume that was nearly intoxicating us as it permeated the open country windows. I loved the smells of this old house. Mike and I tore up that old sidewalk with bumpy rides on our trike and a metal police car studded with small, red plastic buttons. One day a red button came up missing on my shirt and I accused my brother of stealing it and putting it on his police car. We shared everything, including fights as was the case that time. We had two slim-line telephones that Grandma Koressel picked up at the five-and-dime store and would play for what seemed like forever calling each other back and forth to chat about who knows what. We had a brown and white collie dog named King. When we had our squabbles Mom would have to take us inside to spank us because the dog would turn on her at the first sight of a raised hand against us kids. One time I mouthed off to Mom about something and she told me if I did not like it she would let me run the house and she would go away. It was winter time and much to my horror she did not answer me when I later called out her name. As I looked out the window down the road, she was there in her fur coat walking away from the house down Carlton School Road. My heart froze! What would I do now? Just then she appeared from out of nowhere and hugged me and consoled my crying. It seems King had taken a jaunt down the road without Mom. What a relief, them both being back home.

Living in an old farm house was gloriously breezy and cool in the summer, and breezier and colder in the winter. We had to keep a coal-burning stove stoked up in the living room that literally became one of the only rooms we could live in besides the kitchen. I remember carrying out the ashes and sitting next to the stove for warmth. Many times the hand pump in the kitchen froze, which meant no running water for the house. It also meant cold trips to the outhouse that were especially arduous when the snow was deep.

Mom bought a white porcelain chamber pot with red trim for our indoor use during the blustery wintertime. I remember one cold night my brother and I were tucked in a bunk bed set behind a wooden, three-panel screen. You could clearly see through the slots in it if you got close enough. Mom thought we were asleep in our living room bed next to the coal stove. Out she came with that chamber pot and perched herself upon it after turning the television to Dr. Killdare. What a memory and one that my mom would wish I would soon forget! We survived the winter in that old house while Dad found property not far away to on Grebe Road. Mom and Dad planned to build a house there. We would be staying a while longer in the old farm place. I still have happy childhood memories of the place where Mom shared hard work and the memories of no indoor plumbing, cold nights, hot days, and frozen water pumps. Most of her friends lived in modern homes with all the modern conveniences.

I continued my love for school and managed to get home before suppertime or before the sun set- whichever came first. Dad, Mom, Mike, and I moved into a trailer at the building site of our new home. I cannot recall much about the details of the building except there were the comings and goings of Dad's brothers and cousins that came to help with the building plans. Living in the trailer was cramped compared to our last home but unique with all its cubby-holed cabinets for storage, a bed, and even with windows to look out. Soon Mom was expecting again with my brother Christopher Allen. By this time, I was six years old and did not have a care in the world except adventures outside the trailer. Dad built a large sand box under a budding dogwood tree that acted as a canopy. Mike and I would play for countless hours in that sandy enchantment. It was especially nice to sink your feet in deep and feel its coolness. We played hard and fought even harder. I am still not sure what the altercation was about, but it resulted in a true brother and sister fight. We chose our weapons- bricks! Neither one of us could throw worth a darn, so there were no scars to show for it, but we both got in trouble just the same.

Dad dug a well to furnish us with cool-tasting sweet water. I could never really drink the chlorinated city water after that; the taste was too foreign. Grandma and Grandpa Koressel had sold the shotgun house and moved into the newly built home. We kids spent lots of time there too during the construction of our new house, which was at Box 215, Route 2, Grebe Road. My brother Chris spent most of his toddler days in a playpen that most likely contributed to his bowlegged walk. Mom blames it too on the well water that went into his bottles; not sure why that made a difference. For some reason I recall a time when the water did not come from the well as it should have. Somehow the mice had gotten into the water line, and poor Dad had to take much time to remedy that predicament.

A moderate size barn was soon erected near the house to store necessary things in it. It was pretty much off-limits so Mike and I resorted to playing cars and trucks in the dirt with hand-etched roads. We used bricks for houses and spent countless hours building towns and country roads under the shade of a cluster of sassafras trees.

As years went by, so did the alcohol consumption by Dad and more demands were put on Mike and me from our drill sergeant. He was always proud of the half-acre garden he put out each spring. We could hardly ever keep up with all the weeding and watering and hoeing. There was no play until after the garden met his inspection. Carol would come to visit on her new bike and just sit and watch us work. On a few occasions, she got her hands dirty if we were trying to go swimming or planning a long bike ride in which our company was wanted. There were no other neighbor kids our age nearby so she was stuck with me for a playing partner.

The tumble and bumble of the words bind my head before the sound of birds this morning. The joy and rhythm of my pen are absent. I stutter in expression. There is nothing there just a dark, unflinching, and dull depression. Nothing and everything make me cry. The slightest action takes a gargantuan amount of energy and even more mindful, focused attempts to accomplish. I warned you of this reader. This is my world of goals interrupted. My story will resume on another day, but not this one.

༄

My eighth-grade year went quickly after the Fall Festival. To my surprise, I was voted to represent my school and classmates in the Westside Nut Club Fall Festival Queen Contest. There was subdued excitement at home. At this time things were peaceful as long as the beer was flowing and Dad had the permanent fixture of his green, square plastic ashtray. It was constantly full of cigarette butts on our kitchen table. Around all of this my mom happily made me a long dress out of burnt orange fabric. The style matched that of the other grade school contestants from the westside. There would be a photo session while wearing a crown and an interview by some of the *Nut Clubbers*. I had not had much practice with small talk or fun-teasing in my family like some of the other girls experienced by having older siblings and family very interested and encouraging. I think this was a turning point for me when it came right down to the fact that I lacked self-esteem and social polishing. My photo turned out to be a sheepish-looking, almost scared lamb of sorts with the crown cocked on my head. I hardly felt like a queen. Next came the interview. The questions may have been random. Some contestants were asked what they wanted to be when they got older. Who thinks about that at our age?

My question came up. *"Please give directions to St. Philip from here."* I just shuddered in panic. I may have even wanted to swear. Simply put, I should have said *"Hit Highway 62 west and follow the signs to St. Philip."* Instead I mumbled a series of lefts and rights and stop signs and curves and oh what a mess the answer soon became. It is just as well I was not asked *"Where do you want to be someday?"* My answer would have been *"somewhere besides here."* I felt so humiliated and foolish for being there. It would take me at least thirty years before I could truly feel sure about myself. It was fun riding in a convertible in the parade and waving to my classmates from the stage. The winner won by saying she was going to be a lawyer someday. Looking back now, I should have answered, *"I'll be a survivor someday."*

I have purposely waited until now in my writing to share an event that happened during my third-grade year. When you look at most school children, it is hard to see that they are different from others in their class, especially if they have become as keen at hiding their home environment as I had. From all outward appearances they go with the flow. Today is different as there is more help for troubled children and their families. Part of this is due to the fact that known family histories play a huge part in diagnosis. We did not know what it was so how could we ask or receive help?

I spoke to my father's mother, Bennie May, years before she died. We would have sweet grandmother and granddaughter talks, but she also shared stories and feelings about the dark side of the family. At that time, she gave me permission to tell the story, the good with the bad. My dad has also granted permission to share this story. Rarely is just one family member affected. There is a trickling down impression that molds a person forever by those particular life events. I believe that on one's age and experience determines how well you may or may not survive the ordeal.

Grandma tells me it was not her idea. As a matter of fact she spoke highly against it. The nuns had arranged a plan for six of my cousins to stay with our family. Divorce and alcoholism had ravaged the bonds of matrimony for my aunt and uncle. It was told that *if our family* would not take them in they would be sent off to St. Henry's Orphanage. My grandmother was not only wise, but had experienced the misfortune of an illness that was oppressive during her entire married life. The taking in of children reminded her of the calamity it could cause. She loved all of her grandchildren, but a handed down gene would cause terrible suffering and misery. She knew it all too well.

My dad had worked for a life insurance company and had earned the top sales status for in his local office during my third-grade year. He was working and not lying on the couch. The running for beer continued as well as the heavy cigarette smoking. When my parents learned of the nieces and nephews plight it was decided rather quickly they would not be turned out into the cold, but taken in to live with us four kids and my parents. This would cause our household to grow from four to ten children. I do not remember a family discussion about this particular event because one did not take place. My cousins came in ages ranging from two to eleven. We had three bedrooms and shared bunk beds and other beds whenever possible. I do remember the St. Vincent de Paul Society bringing us grocery sacks of food from time to time. Thank God for them. I did not know what happened to Dad's work, but he seemed to be around home more often and it took everything Mom could do to keep us fed, clean, and clothed. Not much time allowed for individual attention or endearing moments amidst the gang of kids. We shared the dinner table with my cousins by running two long, handmade wooden benches next to the table. I always sat next to my cousin of the same age, Susan.

My dad filled the house with books on preventative health. Readings from them suggested the intake of cod liver oil to ward off many ailments. It was decided that each and every one of us would have a full teaspoon every morning. I did not, and still to this day, believe in corporal punishment but would have welcomed a swat instead of a reluctant gulp of cod liver oil. It never failed; Susan would start gagging the minute the brown bottle and its spoon hit the breakfast table. We usually had a bowl of oatmeal and rarely did we miss any meals, especially breakfast. As it came Susan's turn to take her dosage, she spat the cod liver oil into her steaming bowl of oatmeal. My dad angrily made her eat all of the spoiled breakfast.

There were many instances of harsh punishments doled out for all of us, especially the older kids. My dad had been a Marine, so many of our drills were reminiscent and full of what a drill sergeant would execute to get results from his subordinates. I do not always remember the cause of the offenses but keenly remember their punishments. It did not take much now to set off my dad. You can imagine the opportunities that took place among boys' ages spanning from eight to twelve years. They were playful at best, but arguments sometimes erupted. Dad was quick with the belt or most often used what was called the *dew drop run*.

Forsaken was what we children were. There never was a time of learning discussions about life or what it may have brought us. We could only depend on militant commands and would do better to respond similarly with our actions. I remember sadly the punishment my older male cousins received one rainy summer day. They were ordered to *"hit the dew drop running!"* The shape of our circle drive in front of the house resembled that of a dew drop and it became our frequent training ground. No matter the age or reason we found ourselves there running and, of all things, singing as we went about it. On this particular day the three oldest were ordered to strip down to their underwear as to not cause more laundry for Mom by getting their clothes wet from the downpour. They ran for at least a half hour in the pouring rain as we all watched in silence. There was no laughing or snickering between us dry kids. We knew better that the hand of wrath might soon be upon us for little or no reason at all. We all took our turns running and running. Dad would sit and watch with a beer in one hand and a cigarette in the other, just waiting for a screw up or loose word.

When Dad would leave we would sing songs. One in particular that was popular on the radio at the time included the lyrics *"first gear alright, second gear hold on tight, third gear faster, faster, faster"* and then we would run faster to the cadence of the beat of our running, bare feet upon the soft, cinder driveway. Rarely did we get many visitors, except for the father of those six orphans, another uncle or cousins to my dad. They knew the fridge downstairs was always stocked with cold longneck bottles of beer. We kids would almost be tickled to death for we knew it would free us up from any harsh treatment. We often were used as entertainment as the drinking progressed. The older kids would be positioned into one long soldier-like row. This particular game was to put our arms out at shoulders length and see who could outlast the other at holding that position. At first it was fun, but it soon became painful. You could not let a sibling or cousin outlast you and at the same time you could not be out done by the drunken party. Then it became serious and no longer fun as he returned to his harsh comments of *"What a loser..."* or *"I am tired of looking at your damn faces. Get the hell out of here."*

We would all take off to the four corners of our five-acre woods never to catch a glimpse of him until he was passed out on the couch asleep long after the company and, more importantly, the beer ran out. These events seemed like an eternity, but my cousins only lived with us for a year. The time may have been short but the horrific memories remain for a long time thereafter. A cousin of Dad's arrived frequently, especially on weekends with his wife, who also drank, and their two young children. Also in the mix was a younger drinking uncle that arrived as well.

The ten of us were minding our own business, quietly and away from the ensuing drinking melee. As the day passed everything went smoothly until we all were ordered up to form in line and face up the driveway. What now? We had never done this drill before. The commands of *"left, right, left"* came slurring from my deeply intoxicated father's mouth. This seemed harmless and maybe fun for a while until we headed to the top of our winding driveway. We marched to the laughter of our three drill sergeants, all of whom had been Marines. This was becoming humiliating and tense with every jeer they could muster. And then it happened. Someone saw us. A couple stopped and asked of all things where Dam 48 was. I was so angry I felt like breaking rank but dared not out of fear of what would happen to me. I am sure the same feelings were felt by my siblings and cousins. We were a pitiful sight with our barefootedness and ragtag clothes marching to the Marine cadence song when these poor misfortunates stopped us. We definitely got *the look* from them. Lord knows what they thought as they drove away, likely looking in the rearview mirror saying, *"Those people are nuts."* We finally disembarked when we reached the haven of our yard and once again slipped far away from any P.T. may have taken place.

It was a double-edged sword, getting company. It would be a break in the norm but it would more than likely become unusual. For either self-satisfaction or just pure boredom Dad would have us stack bricks, lots of them, hundreds of them, in various locations on the property only to restack them in another location. We never could figure out the rhyme or reason for this other than he always had to have absolute control over us.

My mother was present, always there until she escaped by getting a job at a local K-Mart after the cousins left. I am sure she was much relieved by the opportunity it gave her to escape, socialize, and bring in some minute, but at least routine, income compared to the shoddy reliance on Dad's work. Things were tight so often that my mother's parents would help out with groceries or things us kids needed for school, nothing frivolous, maybe a pair of shoes. My dad grew fierce and acknowledged his displeasure of their caring actions. So much was done without much fanfare or without his knowledge. Mom did much canning and cooking when the cousins stayed and even after they were finally taken to St. Henry's Orphanage to live.

Despite all this, I am still able to remember some positive memories from my cousins' stay. We did not have many toys so we relied on building cabins in the woods and digging tunnels in the ground of ravines around the house and singing and dancing. One of my cousins, Bob, had a severe phobia of cooties. The funny thing is he was probably the most unkempt cousin of all, but according to him everyone *else* had cooties. His dad could play the piano and was our entertainment which was made possible because Mom had a piano in the house. He would whip out the *Boogie Woogie* and to our delight he would add the tinkling of the keys to his version the *Bumble Bee Boogie Woogie*. He drank and played and we danced to his tunes- barefooted of course. When Bob's dad was not around to bring us to life with music, Bob would do the *"Boom Bah Bah."* He would twist himself at the waist front and back while singing *"boom bah bah, boom bah bah ah boom bah bah bah."* We would laugh so hard we would almost cry. We survived all those crazy days with simple pleasures and I guess today is why I enjoy the little things and fun-loving events.

৯

Mother tolerated more than she ever should have, but one summer's day she had had enough. Dad had returned home, drunk as usual. She had been canning all day on a defunct stove with only one working burner. There was no money to buy a new stove. She witnessed Dad's attempts of trying to park the car one night while he was drunk. The parking space at the roundest end of the dew drop was not sufficient for him to park the car. He kept backing the car into an innocent gum tree. As Mom watched she grew angrier at his attempts. Finally, she told herself *"If he hits that tree one more time I am going to town and get me a new stove."* Of course, he hit the tree another time and Mom went to town the next day to Sears and bought a double oven, four-burner working stove on the credit card. God knows she deserved it.

Piles of beer cans began filling the ravines one hundred yards away from our house. If one were to dig up those dumps today, I would have witness to my misery growing up. Dad's self-medicating through alcohol went on into my high school years and his behavior became more bizarre, unlike the unusual silliness and expected drunken behavior. As a result, Dad at some point soon after became a loyal member of Alcoholics Anonymous. Of course my siblings, Mom, and I were expected to participate as well. We were dragged to St. Clement's and other places for A.A. activities. I remember being the oldest at Alateen. It was nothing but a glorified babysitting service for younger kids and I was in charge. There was not much for us on coping skills learned, or anything else for that matter.

Dad would hit rock bottom after days of Bible reading. For some people who experience mania, one of the counterparts can be religious hyperactivity. When you add this to the fact that Dad was not getting much sleep at all, the following can happen. The Bible now took a prominent place next to the ashtray on the kitchen table. He babbled on and on during the day about this scripture and that scripture. Sometimes he would literally get in your face with the chatter. I cannot measure how long this went on because by now I had a boyfriend, a true friend who was also a means of getting away. He had given me his high school ring that I proudly wore wrapped with various colors of angora yarn so it would fit my finger. I remember waiting to receive the rainbow of yarn choices to come in the mail that would match my outfits. It took me even longer to tell Dad I had a steady boyfriend, but I knew how and when to quickly tell him any news. It was usual to take drives with Dad. He would pack the cooler with beer, drive the Corvair to the river bottoms, and say *"Get us back home."* He would drink his beer while I drove usually before I even had a license to drive. What was worse, an underage driver or a drunk driver? I enjoyed the freedom it gave me and I loved punching the buttons on the dash. Finally I had gathered up enough courage to tell Dad the news. I told him and then waited for a reaction. It never came, he just drunkenly asked *"Is that so?"* There was never another word spoken of it. That day driving, I learned Kings Road was one long horseshoe that started and ended at Old Henderson. I had basically driven in a circle many miles long, as would be the cyclic nature of my life at the time, not really getting anywhere.

By this time I was a sophomore in high school. There was no one to tell about the episodes my dad was having. When I attempted to tell friends, they would dispel any of my accusations. It had become unbearable. During an open confessional at school I drew enough courage to sit down with one of my school priests. I thought I would ask for help and confess how guilty I felt in doing so. All I could do was cry and get up from where I sat. No one approached me after that or asked what was wrong. A counselor at school told me my grades were not what they should be and I was definitely not college material. I had not given any thought to college. I came to school and used it as a survival mechanism. The counselor did not and could not understand my situation. What a great help he was... So, I told no one. Of course, Tim, just then my boyfriend, saw and heard bits and pieces of what was happening at home. I was lucky to have him as a friend and someone I could share my darkest hours with. I met him by chance, but I believe now that God put him there for me.

It was midway through my sophomore year of high school that I met a bubbly, blonde-haired, blue-eyed, popular girl by the name of Laura. We went to dances together. I spent the night at her house many weekends. I noticed she received calls from different boys. On one particular occasion there was a CYO (Catholic Youth Organization) dance. I accepted the invitation. Her family headed up the refreshments that evening. We were selling soft drinks through a window of the kitchen that adjoined the dance area when something happened. Two young men poked their heads simultaneously through the window and asked, *"Where's Laura?"* She gasped and hid herself from their view. *"Oh, no! What am I going to do? Both Tims have shown up!"* Quickly she thought and said, *"Michelle, take one of them off my hands! Which one do you want?"* Surprised, I looked their way and surveyed their faces. One was shorter than the other with a baby face and a huge smile. The second had a head full of wavy black hair, a pleasant smile, and a prominent nose. Promptly I answered, *"I'll take the one with the big nose!"* Before I knew it I entered the dance floor and introduced myself to Tim Krack. He did not know what had happened to Laura. He never so much as asked about her again. We danced the rest of the night together. We attended the same high school where I learned he was two years older than me. We began walking each other to class.

Our first date was April 22, 1973. I asked him out in the Hilltop Inn parking lot in a carload of teenagers. We dated for five years until we married in October 1978. I want to thank Laura for letting me make the right choice. After all, I picked the right Tim!

During our five years of dating we worked hot summers at Wes Lake. Tim worked as a lifeguard and I took money at the gate and worked the kitchen. After work we would have John Denver sing-outs with fellow employees who had guitars. We had bonfires, ones so large it brought German Township firemen out in their pajamas. It was a wonderful life, those marvelous summer days. But I always had to go *home*. I often wondered what it was like for my siblings who were less fortunate to not travel away from the ever-declining mental health of my dad. Any chance I had to be gone I took it. My boyfriend's family quickly understood my home life. They were immensely supportive in letting me stay whenever I needed.

IV

A Fierce Task

⮾

Tim's uncle had a car for sale for five hundred dollars. I had earned and saved enough cash from my summer job that I bought it from him. I was so proud, and by now I was somehow graduating from high school. A teacher at school inspired me by telling me I would make an exceptional nurse, so I signed up for Licensed Practical Nurse class through North High School's vocational program. Not long after I had purchased my like-new Dodge, it would be taken for the ride of its life during a blizzard out west. My dad, who had a great love of the Indians, wolves, and the American West in general, had reached the height of his mania. One cold day he loaded my car, which operated the best out of our broken down fleet. At least he had sense enough to pack the car like he was going on a long camping trip. Later we would learn how far away his wanderlust would take him. My mother feared the worst for not long before my dad's excursion he had been seen by our family doctor as having manic-depressive illness, which is now called bipolar disorder. It was a new diagnosis at the time, but ran long and deep in the genes of many families. Ours was no exception. Where had Dad gone and for how long? What would happen to him? Who would help him? We could only worry and think the worst.

The whole year of nursing school had been so very difficult. Studying was a fierce task. When I would try to study, I would start to underline a key word in my books to learn. Before I knew it, I had underlined and highlighted the word and its meaning so many times it bled through to the page behind it. Some nights I just slept out in the car to catch some sleep before I returned to the classroom. Dad's behavior now robbed my world of any sanity or peace anyway, so why return home? At times, this stress would break through and affect my appearance. My picture with the class depicted a weary girl with rings under my eyes and hair not as flattering as it could have been. I remember forgetting the day was for a picture. Like many of the days I

was unprepared and exhausted before I even arrived at school. I wanted to quit but I had the strong support of Tim and his family and I had a determination to succeed no matter what. It was a difficult time and honestly a miracle that I passed with some of the grades.

It was nearing graduation time when Dad had struck out on his journey. Mom and I lay sleeping, or at least trying to, when the phone rang in the middle of the night. It was a jailer calling from somewhere in Minnesota. Our hearts raced and an awful pit formed in our stomachs. What had he done to get there? The jailer thought he was drunk when he was arrested and brought to the jail, but the time had worn away and he still appeared to be drunk. His behavior was odd and bizarre, so Mom explained his diagnosis in a shaky voice. The jailer would intervene and find some psychiatric help for Dad. As Mom hung up the phone the anger in me took hold as I asked Mom while holding her in a strong embrace, *"Why do you not divorce him Mom?"* I said in a sad, tearful groan. Days later he called sounding slightly more coherent than when we heard him before he left. He said he had made friends with some Indians and would stay with them for a while. How long had he thought about staying gone? When would he return?

We soon believed there was no clear thinking on his part and the whim of his ailing mind would cause him to wander to wherever. We were at the mercy of his illness. We could only pray for this, it went on for weeks. I would later learn of his Indian friends as they came to visit Dad at home from their western homes which were their cars, bars and jails. As I entered the house two

American Indians sat at the kitchen table with Dad. A smoke cloud had formed around their heads and the kitchen. They said hello and asked me *"Do you want to smoke the peace pipe?"* Barely could I believe my eyes and ears. Surely this had to be an illusion, a bizarre dream. No, this was the life of a bipolar family in its *ordinary* daily life, at least one without any treatment. I was unable to be scared, there was no recall of any emotion. I just said *"no thank you"* and quickly went to my room. I quite frankly did not know what to do or whom to call. They finally left never to be seen again. A year later Dad would learn one was found dead in a snowdrift in the Dakotas and the other succumbed to alcohol poisoning in jail. He loved the Indians but loved the alcohol more.

While I was at school Dad somehow was finally where he needed to be, in a psychiatric hospital. He was a typical, classic bipolar patient. He had let this illness take over him for so long that it took a lot of medication to bring him under control. He did not want to be in the hospital and he let Mom know it. Anytime she would be near him she became his nemesis. He would blow up and curse her and make the visit to him a disaster. It would reinforce the decision to keep him there longer. After a while he would rally and come down from his manic high and could return home only to fall into a deep depression and the world of self-medicating by drinking lots of beer. Dad was hospitalized many times with each event taxing any energy or finances the family had. It was straight out of a Frankenstein movie. Dad had refused to take his medicine during a stay at Welborn Hospital. His alternative was to take the medicine or be admitted to the state hospital for thirty days. He would not be let out on a good behavior; he would be committed for thirty days, period. A short time lapsed for him to change his mind and take the meds and soon enough he took residence at the state hospital. Mom and I went to visit him. It was easy to visit him there. The moon was full that night and had a werewolf or vampire jumped out at us, I would not have been surprised. Being there was surreal. There was nothing we could do but visit. I recall the tension and the attempt at small talk which escalated once again into Dad yelling at Mom over some financial concern. The thing about Dad was he always knew enough about everything. So any discussion would lead to his winning, or so he thought of any topic you might bring up. I truly hated how smart he thought he was while at the same time how ignorant he was about his own illness. Years had passed and with Dad on a regimen of lithium and alcohol he finally seemed to be more approachable and tolerant.

Tim was very much aware of my family history, being my long-time boyfriend. By no means was he walking into this marriage blindly. Our wedding had been quite storybook. We dated five years before we got married and he knew there was a genetic link connecting me to the bipolar history in our family. We had three children eighteen months apart. I loved being a mother and put some of my nursing skills into action taking care of my family. My world was a happy one. I was in control of it. We had our fourth child, a boy five years after our last daughter. We now had two boys and two girls. Many friends and family, to their astonishment, said we should have stopped having a family when we had the first son and daughter. Tim and I always talked of having a family. My parents had four children, his had five. We loved kids and each other so the result was no surprise. We lived a normal life of baby diapers, baby illnesses, bills, groceries, cleaning and more cleaning.

I still love being there for my children. They were my life and we could not have been happier. The oldest three children were in school. Their ages were eleven, nine, and seven respectfully. The youngest was now two. I had just celebrated my thirty-first birthday. I was happy and busy with my family. My oldest son's birthday was two weeks following mine in July. I had boundless energy and felt unstoppable in my long daily routine of keeping my family on the move. I noticed I would get up at three or four in the morning and just go at it all day long and have difficulty going to bed at ten in the evening.

This pattern of sleep continued until I was getting a narrower window of it. Finally, I was not sleeping at all. I was keeping up with the kids until one day I could not. I found myself walking aimlessly around the house with a pile of things in my hands and arms trying to find a place to put them. I felt confused, agitated, and had no idea what was going on around me. Then again I would resume some form of normalcy. This bizarre feeling lasted for almost five days without any sleep at all. By this time Tim was bewildered by my behavior and knew he was in over his head as to what to do with me. He began to talk to my parents and they came to the conclusion that I had been struck with the same carnage my dad had suffered. It looked more and more like the manic depressive illness. Forgetting to eat, to sleep, comb my hair, or even bathe was the norm. I would cry for no apparent reason then run off to try and accomplish some domestic task. Little did I know that many of my external stressors would contribute to manic episodes.

It started with the beginning of the year in 1989 with my youngest son being burned after he somehow flipped hot turkey juice from a roaster pan in the oven while I was tending it. His treatment demanded my every waking moment and vigilant eye at night. This lasted for weeks. He had painful experiences with the countless whirlpools and bandage wrapping and rewrapping. It was the saddest and most painful thing a mother could endure. As he progressed with his treatment it was discovered that we had a large infestation of termites and eradicating the pests also eradicated our bank account. I received a call one day; Mom was on the other end of the line. She said *"I can't do this anymore. Your dad is sick and needs to be hospitalized. I am going to work."* She asked, *"Can you help?"* It was not going to be a normal day. By this time I had no recollection as to what normal was. I proceeded to call his psychiatrist and tell him the details. Dad was refusing treatment with his meds. He was talking to the television set. He was talking about some gun a family member had sold him and he would use it on anyone who came near.

There is something I have learned and have been taught. When a bipolar person threatens himself or others, it is time to get help. The doctor told me I needed two signatures, one from him and one from the police department. I numbly drove to the downtown area where I needed to go for the signatures. Familiar landmarks were no help to me. I became lost many times trying to reach my destinations. Upon gathering the correct signatures and hiding myself into the furniture at the police station, I realized the doctor had signed on the wrong line of the necessary document. I had to find my way back to his office to get what I had set out for. The day seemed to last forever. I was concerned about Dad's strength which I had witnessed before during his manic state.

Two officers came to me at the police station. It was too funny, the shortest police officer I had ever seen along with one of the tallest. I had to laugh. This was the help I would get to wrestle my dad to the hospital for treatment? I told them of past experiences and I would feel better for their safety and Dad's if they would get more officers to help. It was agreed two units would be sent. I had come to do what needed to be done and now I had to wait. Where would I spend the next few hours and how soon would I know that he had been secured by the police? I called Mom at work and told her the situation had been taken care of. She insisted on being at Dad's side. I insisted she go to my house and be with my kids. I would tell her when Dad was in a safe place. I drove to the Zeidler's on the westside and bought Mom a bouquet of flowers. Feeling guilty for how I had talked to her on the phone made this easy. Not wanting to aggravate the securing of Dad by the policemen, I had to see that they had got him without me being noticed. I did not want to complicate things more.

The two police cars passed the florist's windows. There was a gas station several blocks from my parent's home, so I decided to park there and watch. All I had to do was wait and pray he would go peacefully with them. Maybe it was minutes or even an hour. I do not recall the time. It seemed like an eternity. All of a sudden I saw the two police cars with Dad sitting still in the backseat of the second car. Thank God. I prayed under my breath. I finally could breathe again. I hurried home and told Mom the news, we both cried as I handed her the flowers. We knew things would be better that night. We knew where Dad was, he was safe and so was everyone else. It was bad enough getting Dad where he needed to be. He had threatened to use a gun. On whom I did not know, but there was a gun somewhere in the house or at least Mom said so, except it was not where it usually was. Did he have it conveniently at his side, tucked under a couch cushion or hidden in his truck to join the other camp contents he had packed for another road trip? He had talked of leaving again. We had every right to call for help. We thought the worst was over. Certain things would take place at the hospital and it terrified Mom and me. Dad was admitted upon arrival at Welborn again.

It was several days before Mom and I attempted to see Dad. We were requested to appear for a psychiatric hearing. It is the patient's right to have one. We felt that we were warranted in seeking treatment for him. We arrived at the hospital at the dreaded hour of his hearing not knowing how we would find him or how he would react to us and especially me for putting him there. The room was cramped with people from the staff. The doctor, nurse, psychiatrist, and legal representative were there. The only room left to stand was at the foot of his bed. Mom and I stood quivering, tightly holding each other's hands. Our eyes met Dad's. He reacted with a nonchalant, slight grin. He was trying to eat a full orange like an apple while his hands and legs were shackled to the bed with thick leather straps. We choked down our tears as the questions were hurled at us, which began after a statement about Dad's condition. *"Why do you think Thomas needs to be here?"* asked a man in a white coat. Was it not obvious?

He had to be restrained and no doubt medicated or he would not have been as calm as he was then. He was ranting and raving and threatening to shoot someone. We now were on trial, or so it seemed. I drew a deep breath and answered *"He is sick. He threatened to shoot someone. He had his truck packed to leave in this condition to once again visit the Indians out west."* There was a long pause. Another official retorted with, *"He said there was no gun at all. Can you prove he had a gun?"* My brain went numb. I could not answer. All of a sudden I blurted out, *"Would you second guess a man who possesses a gun and threatens to use it in a pressured, manic state- knowing he's bipolar?"* There were nods of heads and the room fell silent. Dad by now had orange juice and parts of the orange dribbling down his face with the remainder still in his clenched hand. He smiled at us and gave a nod. I fell into a deep sleep that night exhausted from the day and sickened by the thought that we were questioned at all. But remember the patient has rights too and he was given that right to a justifiable hearing. I was afraid what Dad would say to me or if he would even speak to me once I saw him again upon his return home. He would later say *"You saved my life."* I later cried a sense of relief knowing I had done the right thing. Little did I know it was just the courage I would need to survive more of life's many curveballs.

That same summer, Tim and I planned a trip to Garden of the Gods. The kids were excited and happy to get away with their parents and climb on the rocks in southern Illinois. We started out as a family would with a full picnic basket packed and a full tank of gas in the car. As a child, I had always wanted to see the old slave house that offered paid tours of the historical place. Dad would drive us to the Garden up the long road to the winding way that led to the multi-storied, old frame house and sit there at the sign that told of how much it costs and its operating hours. We would sit for a few moments and then turn around and leave. That is how it was with him. It was like the proverbial apple dangled in front of you just out of reach. It was probably more like we never had the money. Either way, it was tormenting. I decided this trip we would stop and see this place before it no longer existed. My husband complained he had a headache and he would nap with our baby, Andy, in the car while the kids and I would take the tour. We entered the musty smelling, wooden-frame building and were greeted by what seemed like a seedy character of a man. He took our money and rattled a brief history of the place, and told us we were free to look the place over. The house was typical of its period: four large rooms, a barely furnished downstairs, and a small back door that led into a smaller hallway to the kitchen. This was the slaves' entry and exit to the working kitchen. We climbed up the long creaky stairs to an open dorm room that held at least twenty or so wooden stalls. There was a worn out newspaper that had been grossly laminated and displayed. It told how one black man was used as a stud and had fathered over a hundred children all conceived in this room. I grew sick of the thought and was glad the kids showed no interest in the reading. I could only imagine what life would have been like for these people. I said a prayer asking for God's forgiveness on this sight. The children were growing restless so we toured the outside buildings only to find old farm implements and a shackled, old half-fallen house. I was saddened that I had paid into this misfortunate piece of historical real estate only to have the suffering of its tenants presented as a sideshow. It humbled me though seeing these birthing stalls or whatever you wanted to call them. It represented ignorance and haughty ownership practices. I was relieved to leave this sad place. Years later I learned that there were no more tours and forever gone were the many tears shed there.

Upon returning to the car I found my husband still fast asleep after two hours of our tour. The baby had been stirring and had not wakened Tim in the slightest. I sensed something was wrong. As I gently shook him awake, he once again complained of a new and thundering headache. He insisted we drive to the Garden and visit the glacier-made towers of sandstone. We had been driving all this way, so I reluctantly went along with his notion. We found a parking place and the children rolled out of the car with great anticipation. We followed the trail and I noticed Tim was falling behind the rest of us and was having trouble keeping his balance as he walked. I approached him and asked what was wrong. Once again he said *"Terrible headache. The sun's hurting my eyes."* I could not see him climbing the rocks that teetered on deep ravines and valleys. The now scrambling bunch of kids had to be rallied. I explained to them that their daddy was very sick and we would need to go home. I was very sorry that we would have to come back another day. I do not recall them giving me so much of a whimper. Their dad was never sick and they must have understood the worry in my voice. Tim handed me the keys and said *"You drive home."* I do not think he could bear the thought of it. It was a long enough drive home but now the drive seemed to drag on and on. The familiar landmarks could not pass quickly enough. He slept the entire way home. I felt the urgency to get him to a doctor. There had to be something terribly wrong. After arriving home it was too late to call a doctor's office and Tim assured me he would be okay until morning. I regretfully went along with him. The next morning I called the doctor that saw him late in the afternoon.

Tim's headache had worsened. He complained now of his neck hurting and he had difficulty touching his chin to his chest without discomfort. I imagined a diagnosis but held back my fear slightly knowing the doctor would finally get to the bottom of this. Dr. Toon diagnosed Tim immediately, after several questions and once more checking Tim's inability to touch his chin to his chest. He said in a nervous manner *"He has meningitis. I want you to go to the emergency room. You will be directly admitted and will be sent straight up to a room."* By now, Tim needed my arm to steady his gait as he stumbled to the car. A temporary relief due to an accurate diagnosis was quickly replaced with an overwhelming wave of fear. We finally knew what was wrong but what would happen next?

Shortly after Tim was admitted he began projectile vomiting and a slight fever had risen to 103 degrees. He responded only slightly to me and his surroundings, he did this through the day and into the evening. The doctor ordered a lumbar puncture and I insisted on staying with him during the procedure. I explained I was a nurse and could be of some assistance. Tim's older brother Paul offered to spend the night. He had been a respiratory therapist, so I felt some relief in his presence. I had to return to our bewildered children who had been kept by Mom and Dad during my absence. After a restless night I returned quickly the next morning. The nurse came in and sat down a pan of water with a washcloth and soap and told Tim *"Here's your bathing supplies. It's time to give yourself a bath."* My mouth dropped open in shock. The man could hardly hold his head up and needed help to the bathroom. It was obvious that I would not leave his side, so I could diligently watch out for his welfare. I felt hopeless and helpless as the projectile vomiting covered his bed and he groaned to the new and unbearable throbbing of his head. Dr. Toon came in and said *"There isn't much hope for him. I've never seen anyone sick like this with meningitis and live."* The spinal fluid from the tap was clear with small, white particles floating in the vial. Dr. Toon reiterated,

"He probably won't make it through the night." I became sickened, utterly distraught. I had to do something.

It was as if a light bulb had turned on in my head. My dad had worked on my feet, as he called it, before with a technique called reflexology. It was our only hope. I fumbled around Tim's bedside table and pulled out the bottle of lotion and began massaging his feet. He did not react to my touch but I continued to massage all parts of his feet that correlated with his spine. The majority of all nerves end in points in the hands and feet. My steady strokes continued until all the lotion was gone. I did not care how long it took, but felt satisfied in my efforts and in knowing that I had cared for him with my own two hands. How many Hail Marys and Our Fathers I prayed I do not know, but they were many. I kept my vigil with Tim and his brother Paul who came late in the evening to spend the night. My mind was so disturbed I could barely find my way to Pennsylvania Street that led nearly straight to my home.

Early the next morning the phone rang. It was Paul. He was ecstatic! He said, *"It's unbelievable. Tim just sat up in bed and asked 'What's for breakfast?'"* The vomiting had stopped and his fever was much more manageable. I could not get to him fast enough. He spent several more days in the hospital. The masks we had to wear were discontinued and Tim was on his way to recovery. He suffered double vision. The doctor said, *"It should go away in six weeks. He could have various abnormalities and side effects from this, maybe his hearing or heart could be affected. We just do not know."* I was happy to have him back and hoped there would be no complications. His vision-related issues would hopefully subside when the doctor said they would.

V

Cry for Help

❧

Constant stress had become the norm for me by now. Several days after Tim came home, firemen came and stayed at his side while I grocery shopped or ran errands. One would bring me a gallon of much needed milk; one cut our grass. His fellow firemen were like family to us, but there was no telling when or if he would return to his fire department job with the city of Evansville.

I woke one night during Tim's recovery with chest pains like I had never experienced before. My body felt like a heavy, lead ball. I could barely move. I woke Tim in a panic and told him I was scared and thought I was having a heart attack. He said *"I'll drive you to the hospital."* It was not the time for humor, but I said *"For God's sake, you're seeing two of everything. You can't take me."* It was decided I would call 9-1-1 for an ambulance. My body was so fatigued and overworked. The emergency room released me by saying *"Your potassium is low. Go home and eat some bananas."* Did I look like a monkey? I felt awful and yet foolish that all I needed were bananas to fix my ailing body. My sleep was all but gone and I could feel myself being pulled down into a deep, dark, and depressive abyss.

Days later I became infuriated and flung applesauce at an even more infuriated and confused Tim. By now I was calling him the devil then pleading with him as if I was confessing to Jesus all of my sins. Three times he said, *"Michelle, you're scaring the kids."* By the third time I realized somewhere in my brain that something was terribly wrong and I must have scared the kids somehow. What had I done? My yelling and cursing had sent them to another part of the house. I was able to calm down only slightly when I heard the train whistle its menacing scream. The devil had come to get me and all the lost souls I thought. In days prior I had all-night tea parties with my kids. I played on the playground climbing up and over the round jungle gym at the Tekoppel playground without any hands holding on. I was invincible. I could do anything.

The last straw for Tim is when I said, *"Let's return to the days of Adam and Eve and take our clothes off."* I danced around the house and near the door when Tim grabbed me fearing I would walk outside. I screamed and somehow lunged out the door and into the sunlight. I felt freedom I had never felt before. For some reason I ran to a neighbor's wooden gate and let myself in. Tim was close behind me as the gate closed; I started to take off my clothes and danced on their lawn furniture. *"Michelle!"* Tim yelled. *"Michelle, put your clothes back on."* I only danced more and spoke of the freedom I had. From deep inside a struggling brain came a cry for help. *"Please call an ambulance. I need help,"* I screamed. I screamed it again. Tim somehow convinced me to put my clothes on and corralled me into going back home. He quickly called my parents and 9-1-1. Shortly thereafter my parents arrived. Dad stood in the kitchen looking at me and the state of agitation that I was in. I was a mirror to him and how the many times he had danced around the house, babbling some religious prophecy and acting like a crazy person. I looked at him sternly and screamed *"What are you looking at? Take off your glasses so I can see your eyes."* I stood in the kitchen and became defender of the very spot I stood. I filled a glass of water and threw it on Dad, baptizing him again. He warned Tim of the water; I threw more in his direction and missed. I felt cornered and that something was strategically closing in on me.

A policeman and two ambulance attendants whom I did not recognize filled the kitchen along with my husband and parents. I was told *"You need to go to the hospital."* This only angered me for the flag-waving *help me* voice was overpowered by a fierce conscious that would fight for freedom. I would not go peacefully. As I was confronted by this rescuing mob, I flung my hand and broke the glass out of my hundred-year-old china cabinet. I was subdued and taken to the hard kitchen floor. It took five people to hold me down. I did not know where my kids were at the time. I screamed their names for help, a help that did not come. I grabbed the glasses off the nose of one of my rescuers and flung them across the room and they crashed into the front door of the stove. *"Be careful,"* someone yelled, *"she's going for your glasses."* I once again grabbed some glasses, this time the police officer's, and flung them across the room. I was strapped tightly to a backboard and taken out quietly to the alley for a waiting ambulance. I later learned this positioning of the ambulance was done so as to make my transport somewhat discreet. There was already a police car in front of the house and the neighbors had witnessed my sun dance of sorts in their backyard.

Earlier that day I watched the sun rise and stared into it and watched it conform into a butterfly flapping its wings. Friends had stopped by and I felt a religious purpose to their arrival like they were my disciples. I saw a man walk up the street with a shotgun along his side. All of these hallucinations were real and especially vivid. I would not stop there. As I was locked onto the gurney in the ambulance a pretty attendant sat at my side. As we started to move, I told her *"Please open the doors and let me free."* She could only smile at me. *"I promise we'll awake on a sandy tropical beach,"* I said. She only smiled more. By now the ride had become bumpy and I started to take my frustrations out on the driver. He knew my husband from his fire department work. I yelled at him saying in a loud, nasty tone, *"What the hell are you doing? You don't know how to drive this thing?"* After a few more miles, I lit in to Tim pretty good with the same accusations. He had of course accompanied me to the hospital. I am sure it rattled him a bit, knowing how I used to be and what I had become.

Years later, the driver would embrace me and tell me how happy he was to see me well. Not today though. Things had escalated past the boiling point. I wanted out of this ambulance at any cost. I did not care if the doors would have spontaneously opened and I would be hurled into the following traffic. My mind raced from denial to anger then to pleading for my release. My mind raced faster than the ambulance could ever hope to drive and get rid of me. I kept going back to the previous thoughts of the devil, of Jesus, and was angry being paralyzed from movement due to the restraints. The flash of the corridor's overhead lights leading from Welborn's emergency room to the psychiatric ward only further stimulated my brain. The gaiety that I displayed I am sure only amused the hospital staff. I would learn each of their names and would call out in a flirtatious slur at them each time they entered the room to complete the tasks set before them. They all wore bright blue jumpsuits or shirts. This threw me back to the memory of Mary represented by blue. For some uncanny reason the color comforted me only because of my deep-seated belief in Mary. It would keep me calm until the medications could go to work. All of a sudden I felt a deep, yet sharp pain in my right hip. It was as if a pencil was being jammed into a concrete block. My muscles were so tense it would not allow the needle gentle passage through its intended target. For many days after my hospitalization, my main complaint would be the pain that remained from the injection site. I fell into a deep sleep, a sleep I had not had in months.

My attending doctor, Dr. Karlton, would later tell me I was the first patient that gave him some difficulty in diagnosing between bipolar disorder and schizophrenia. Once he found out the family history of bipolar disorder, he was convinced that that was my diagnosis. I slowly awoke, opening one eye then the next. I felt a pinned down sensation. My body ached all over as if I had the flu. Before me was just a wall. It appeared to have a brown carpet covering the entire expanse from end to end. Where was I? I now looked to my wrists and felt and saw that I was shackled with thick brown strips of leather. I so wanted to move and relieve the stiffness and soreness that fatigued my body so. The ringing of hallucinations, rapid firing of religious ideas, and heavy fear had finally ceased. A calmness and deep relief came over me. The sweet aroma of flowers reinvigorated my sense of smell. I closed my eyes and enjoyed its presence. A few minutes passed and then I heard someone approaching. The same calming blue shirt donned by the staff was on Tim, at first glance, who was wearing his blue uniform shirt. I knew who he was and was happy yet sluggish with my *"Hello."* He asked me, *"Do you know where you are?"* I said no. He continued, *"You are at Welborn in the Psychiatric Unit."* I replied, *"Really?"* in a subdued, surprised voice. He said, *"You're here because you have what your dad has. You are bipolar."* The news was not as upsetting as it was a relief to answer all the behaviors and exhaustion I had experienced. He added *"You have to take medicine. Are you willing to take medicine?"* I answered with a resounding *"Yes."* I could instantly see the relief in Tim as he leaned over to kiss me. A nurse came in after Tim left the room to give me my first dose of medications to calm my brain.

Tim was dressed for his fire department job, so he had to leave me to get back to work. A male nurse now set me free of the heavy restraints. I could barely move. I felt like I had been in a crushing car accident. The pain was unbearable. Slowly, I raised myself from the bed and steadied myself. It felt as though I was taking my first baby steps. Clad in a hospital gown with no strings, only snaps, I walked from my room to a larger common area now well-lit and piercing to my recently-slumbering eyes. The nurses' station was glass and I saw a young man in the same room as myself. As I examined the room I saw a large blackboard and large letters scrawled on it indicating that it was July twenty-ninth. *"July twenty-ninth,"* I repeated to my exhausted brain. Today was my oldest son's birthday! *"Oh no,"* I thought to myself. Where had I been and how could I get to him and at least wish him a Happy Birthday? A sudden sadness filled my heart for we always celebrated birthdays as a family and with great fanfare. I felt so defeated and had to reach my son. I asked the nurse if I could call home and deliver my message to him, the only thing I had to give him as a gift. My mother answered the phone *"Hello."* I said, *"It's me."* *"Hi, how are you?"* she said. *"I am not really sure; they're starting me on my* medication. *Tim was here and I just noticed today was Matt's birthday. I called to wish him a Happy Birthday."* She responded *"Remember, he was getting ready for a scouting camp when you went to the hospital?"* I had forgotten. I had not helped him prepare for the trip and learned that at the last minute she had to scurry to purchase some of his camping supplies. I said, *"I am sorry Mom for all that you had to do." "It's alright honey,"* she said. *"I'll be okay,"* I said knowing I would be where I was for days by recalling Dad's hospitalizations. I hung up the phone and sighed, saddened by the thought of what I now had to face and what I had to do from here on out: take my meds and do what I was told to do so I could get out of this place and find my family again.

Just as I turned around after getting off the phone, the young man that had shared the room with me now approached. He said, *"I need some cigarettes. How about I give you a back rub in exchange for a cigarette?"* I thought I was hallucinating again. All at once, a male nurse approached before I could stammer out a *"no"* to this guy. He demanded that the impetuous man leave me alone. I fumbled over myself back to my room and fell fast asleep. I slept a lot those first few days in the locked section of the ward on the third floor. I soon found out that as your recovery progressed so did the level of floors you were on. Eventually reaching the first floor and being released. I gave no trouble to my caretakers, religiously took my medications, and steered clear of the obnoxiously addicted cigarette guy. All too soon was I able to leave the unit for a walk outside. It was a refreshing change to what happened just days before. On the second floor I drew close friends from the people who were there, only to see them for a moment; they moved either up or down the floor depending on their stage of recovery. Chuck was a middle-aged man and was crying. Everyone rallied around him and offered warm support. As I grew more accustomed to the other patients, I learned that he soon would be taken to shock therapy. I offered my support of *"You'll be okay."* I had not the faintest idea what the result of his treatment would be. Actually I believe I was telling myself *"You'll be okay."*

The sun shone brightly and warmly on my face. The small group of ward attendees followed our escort, like ducklings huddling close to their mother, for a walk in the park. The homes and yards were beautiful on this wondrous July day and I could taste and feel freedom in the air as we walked and talked. How good it felt to be out. Within five days, I had made it to the first floor. I was ready to leave this place and return home. I was not for sure how the kids would react. Matt was still on his camping trip and I pondered on how all this affected he and our daughters, Amy and Carrie. The last time they had heard or seen me I was ranting and raving and probably scaring them to death. It would take a while for them to see I was okay and getting help from my medications and the doctors. I would explain to them, *"Mom was sick and is doing better now."* I am not sure they really understood but I tried to continue my motherly way of doing things for them. It was important to me being there for them and especially not to be locked up in a mental institution. There was no missing of birthdays for a long time to come. I had to return a visit to my psych doctor every week until finally the visits would extend to every two weeks, then every month, and then extend to every six months. The six-month interim was the longest spread of time that was tolerated between visits.

I felt I was doing rather well compared to that day in July of 1989. Months went by without a hitch. I enjoyed nearly eight years of wellness with both myself and my family. I thrived on a schedule, which was a focal point for time. It revolved around three kids' middle-school lives and a very busy toddler. There were basketball, baseball, volleyball games, and multiple overnight vacations that took place not far from home. I promised to write a book on weekend vacations with family, within a hundred mile radius of home because we became quite accomplished at it. There were experiments in the kitchen from science to cooking. There were numerous pets from dogs to bunnies to fish. Sorry Amy for cooking all your mollies and their babies while cleaning the fish tank! We were a family, with the usual reprimands, I love yous, hugs, and kisses. We were a happy and fulfilled family, hectic as it may have seemed.

&

Medications worked well in my recovery for nearly twenty-five years until I started showing serious side effects. But one day, out of the blue, in the late summer of 1994 it hit me and I became terribly depressed. I cried at any time and for any reason. It had become increasingly hard to keep up with the hubbub of my family's circus and their demands. What was wrong and what had caused it? Summer was the busiest season for our family. I felt like going a hundred miles an hour and then suddenly crashing into a wall. These heavy feelings stayed with me for days and never lifted. It was time to call Dr. Karlton. Due to my increased activity, the longer days of summer, and my increasing difficulty with sleeping, my mania changed. Then the depression surfaced. I was hospitalized once again, not for the depression but because of the treatment. I now know that antidepressants for my bipolar treatment cause mania. Why had I ended up at St. Clement's psych ward? This time I recognized the path my mind was moving along. The Jesus, the Mary, the devil train, the *baptizing* of anyone who attempted to come near me were all present. It was not fair to be hospitalized; I had taken all of my meds. What could have gone wrong? I soon learned that summer was my cautionary time. It triggers my illness due to the longer sun lit days which created longer lasting activities and kept me up late at night. The antidepressants did not help. This was my first time at St. Clement's. I was processed at the front desk of the ward. Everyone seemed polite but business-like. *"What's your name?"* a nurse asked me. *"Michelle Krack,"* I answered while nervously looking the place over.

The room was sunny. There were chairs placed around a television. There was a wall complete with thick reading materials and finally a table near a set of double doors that led out to a garden patio. How refreshing I thought! All of a sudden my mapping of the room was broken by the nurse continuing her questions. *"Do you have allergies,"* she said. *"Yes,"* I said *"to sulfa drugs."* I once had a rash after taking them. I was shown to my room and given a handful of papers; I seemed confused as to what to do with them. Tim was not there to explain their importance to me, nor could I focus on their contents. Later I would learn there were schedules for meal and therapy time. Along with the *Call Before You Fall* brochure. I did not quite understand that one due to the fact that I was completely mobile. Before I knew it someone called out, *"Michelle, it's time to eat."* I could feel the medications they gave me taking effect while entering the dining room. I felt more groggy than hungry. The food was not bad as I recall. I would have five more days to learn the menu and selected my meals by circling various food options. It was frustrating to focus on this task. If you did not circle a necessary item for your meal, you quite literally did not get it. Luckily there was extra coffee and condiments in the unit as well as a refrigerator stocked full of milk, soft drinks, and snacks. It was kept locked at all times except for designated meals and snack times. There was always a nurse attendant to hand out the provisions.

It was time for group therapy by playing games. The attendant chose Wheel of Fortune. I disliked this game on the tube for all the noise it produced and just the way the game was played. The unit's version only made it worse and we, the player-patients, would only prolong the playing time. A cardboard wheel was used and the *fun* began. You have to remember most of us were sedated and desired more than anything to go back and be left alone. It was pure drudgery to stay awake while hours seemed to pass between each answer. The attendant only spoke with a drawn out cheerful supportive incantation. *"That is good Michelle. "Who's next?"* she would coo. I could not decide what was more irritating, her overemphasized affirmation or the game itself. The game seemed redundant and for the life of me I could not understand the intended therapeutic reasons for it. I would have rather stayed in my room, listening to a soothing radio station of gentle rock, or drawing, or painting a picture. Not long after my arrival, I quickly learned the names of my cohorts. Some were in different levels of consciousness. Some slurred. Some were poor. Some were angry. I merely wanted to do what I needed to do to get out of this place.

There were half-hour breaks between meals and therapy sessions. Another favorite phrase of the teeming-with-energy staff member leading a bootlegged version of Wheel of Fortune was *"Go on."* It was typical how the therapy sessions dragged on and on. We would be asked by a shrill, high-pitched therapist in a slow affirmative tone *"Michelle, what is your goal today?"* *"Finish my menu plan, take my meds, and go home,"* I answered in a sedated manner. Each person was asked this as we went around the room. Remember most of us were heavily sedated and the responses were sometimes serious, but one that sticks in my mind was *"Tie my shoes."* For heaven's sake! Was he serious? I think he was serious. I asked for tapes and a player to listen to *Child Discipline Approaches.* I felt disenchanted as to what my children would think of me when I returned home new and improved. Discipline and its application would be hard at best, especially coming from a sick mom. I was thankful I did not have to become restrained and was able to participate in my treatment under my own recognizance. The days became a drum of routine and boredom. I was allowed a radio from home but it had to be kept at the nurses' station until I had *free* time. I was allowed to take it to my room and play it quietly.

Tim brought my colored pencils and paper from home. The unit did not have art supplies. Art materials were my very existence! It was the greatest therapy for me and yet it was not offered. I did it on my own. I colored bold letters on paper of each person's name in my unit and brightly colored them and would then watch happily as the recipient received their artful name. It was self-expression that made me happy. Dr. Fish, as I would call him, would visit each day. Each day he would interchange his attire with a flashy, Hawaiian shirt or a multi-colored green, mosaic fish shirt. I thought he could afford a change in scenery when it came to his ensemble. It was irritating to see him in these crumpled shirts that were outdated and totally frumpy. I had guessed he wore them to see your reaction. If you were irritated by them and commented, he knew you were alert to your environment and closer to going home. If you were belligerent about their existence you had a couple more days. I am convinced that is why he wore the shirts, but maybe he just had a quirky taste in fashion. Who knew? In a deep voice he would ask *"How are you today, Michelle?"* I would answer *"Better than yesterday."* There was not much dialogue and with a nod of his head he would say as he turned away to the nurses' station, *"Keep up the good work."* And then you could hear him ask the next patient the same thing. Sometimes they would retaliate for being there and he would respond with *"Let's see what happens tomorrow."*

I would soon return home. Déjà vu all over again with the kids, starting over with even more meds. I was still on antidepressants. I visited yet another series of the demons in my head, only taking the storyboard in my brain further. I became the chosen one. I would refuse to go this time. Receiving messages from the television, undercover agents, secondary flashes from the television set, or extras in shows only fed my psyche. I did not sleep. The mania was fast at work. I had worked so hard to stay out of the hospital. I had entombed myself in the basement on the couch. I told Tim, *"I won't go. I would rather die than go back to the hospital!"* He eventually called 9-1-1. I could hear the sound of footsteps above my head moving around the kitchen. *"Damn,"* I said, *"he's probably brought the whole militia!"* Shortly thereafter a woman police officer descended the basement steps. She was cautious but pleasant. *"Hello"* she said, dressed in dark blue. *"Hello"* I said back to her. She started her trained scenario of wanting to help me and told me who she was. *"Would you go with me for help?"* I suddenly recall the experience of being zip-tied wrestled to the floor, breaking the China cabinet glass. Although at the time you have no control, I could always retain every last detail to what was going on at the time. Hesitantly, I told her I would. We walked up the stairs quietly. I said nothing. I looked at Tim sternly as if to say *"You've won this time."*

In a matter of seconds I was put on a gurney in my living room and whisked outside to the ambulance that was waiting. The neighbors all stood watching. For a brief second, a flash of reality set in; what would the neighbors think? The next thought was that I simply did not care. This time I did not ask to be let go to an island paradise. I kept my silence, for the previous session had proven it was in my best interest. Will, the EMT at my side, was a classmate of mine and a good friend of Tim's from the fire department. He refrained from the usual chatter those guys had. He took my vitals. Tim softly said, *"She's bipolar."* Nothing much was said after that during my quiet ride to the hospital. Will was sadly hanging his head and Tim sat next to him holding my hand. I could feel a need to cry well up inside of me. When would this hell stop? The car ride would have been much cheaper but could I have even gotten in the car? Probably not. It usually took police officers, family, and an ambulance crew to subdue me. This time there would be no fight. My mind raced but I kept sealed lips. Secrets were my own. It was the same routine at the hospital.

I was put in a room with another, now sleeping woman. Quietly the meds were given to me. The red glow of the night camera fell upon me through the darkness of the room. In my mind, the camera was now emitting a ray of some sort that made my legs tingle and become alive with movement. Sleep did not come. I tossed and turned. There seemed to be no reason for restraint. I became obsessed with the rays that hammered against my legs and then it happened. My roommate began to snore, loudly. She began a rhythmic, loud snore. Something had tripped my anger button. *"I may as well have stayed home!"* I yelled. Before I knew it I had wrestled my mattress into the toilet-shower room. The mattress fit perfectly in the shower stall! During overnights in hotels with my husband, also an avid snorer, I would sneak cushions off the furniture and into the bathtub where I would go to curl up to sleep. It would infuriate Tim when I did this.

The heavy bathroom door clicked behind me. At last. Some peace and quiet. I was ready to lay down when the bathroom door bolted open and there stood the whole nightshift staff. *"You can't sleep in here!"* said the nurse in a surprised but comical tone. I am sure I am the first that had pulled this prank on them. I began to loudly say *"I want a private room now. She snores."* The staff began a mad scramble. It was comical to say the least, but I held my ground as they wrestled the mattress back to the bed. One grabbed my personal items from the bedside stand and off I was to finally sleep in a private room. I slept well and offered no further complaint. The next day I would meet my former roommate during therapy. The group sat around in a circle like they had many times before. She sat with her chin on her chest. I guess she also had not been able to get much sleep. When she finally raised her head I saw fresh stitches that were neatly sewn from one side of her neck to the other. She looked like something from a horror flick. I felt remorse for her, a sadness that caused me to stare at her. Our eyes met and she quickly shifted hers away from mine without a word.

Even through all of the turmoil that I had experienced, I failed to understand how someone could do such a thing. Thank God I never had the urge to hurt myself intentionally during my mania. Suddenly my thought was broken by all the too familiar, whiny voice of the therapist, *"What brings you here Michelle?"* she asked. For a brief moment I had no real idea. *"I tried to purchase a five-hundred dollar stuffed horse by the name of Spirit. It was the original prop for a Disney movie."* She smiled back at me and went to the next person to my left and continued around the room.

VI

Spirit- the 500 Dollar Horse, Crazy Barry's, & A Crayola- Created Paradise

I had just run a meeting for the senior class at my son Andy's high school. It was for Project Graduation. We were all at the west side Hacienda. I was not drinking anything but tea. Ironically, we were planning the annual drug and alcohol-free party for the twelfth-grade class that would be held at their school's baccalaureate ceremony. Many parents ordered drinks with their meal. A slight feeling of uneasiness came over me but I continued with the meeting. The theme was a western one. Many of the props had been made and would fill the gym and transform it to a majestic cowboy arena. I became obsessed about getting this horse I had seen for five hundred dollars cash– no refunds, at a going-out-of-business furniture store. I had talked Tim into going into Crazy Barry's store where *my* horse was. I made a scene there begging him for a whole set of living room furniture. The salesperson could not have been happier and Tim cringed at the idea. He finally found his way to the door, fully knowing I was on the cusp of yet another breakdown. The horse was the last thing I saw as we left.

The meeting continued; I pressured the group by *saying "We have plenty of room for storage and it can be used again for another school event."* Someone chanted half-inebriated by this time, *"Go ahead. You're in charge; you have good judgment."* Little did they know how bad my judgment had actually become. There was plenty of money in the decorations fund to reimburse me. I set out to the Fireman's Credit Union to retrieve the money from our meager savings account. I thought I would get the reimbursement later. My oldest son Matt happened to be working there.

I asked for five-hundred dollars out of my not even nine-hundred dollar savings account. I began to rattle on about the kids' planned party and what I was about to purchase. I caught the credit union employees by surprise. It was not unusual for me to be creating or planning something but this was *a lot* over the top. Little did I know that Matt quickly called his father and told him of my intended spending spree. Arriving at the store with five crisp, one hundred dollar bills in hand, I began to enter Crazy Barry's. I felt justified in this purchase. Hey, it was for the kids after all! It had hit me again. As I entered the store a woman brushed by me and I quickly changed my mind, returning to my car. I decided I needed a haircut and new clothes.

By now my cell was ringing and Tim was talking, nearly frantic on the other end. I could hear him holding his breath. Calmly he said *"Honey, where are you?"* It became a game of cat and mouse. I was having too much fun and he was not going to ruin it! *"Somewhere on the west-side,"* I uttered. I was not lying but I am sure he was relieved to know I had not purchased the horse. He was sitting in Crazy Barry's parking lot hoping to steer me clear of my insane purchase. There was a long line at Gloria's Hair Salon so I patiently waited then wrote my name down on the next line of the waiting list. I told them *"I'll be next door, shopping."* The girl nodded and off I went to Fashion Days. I still had five hundred dollars in my hand. The phone rang again. I could sense an urgency in Tim's voice, *"Where are you now?"* he asked. *"I am still on the west side getting a haircut,"* I replied. *"Stay there,"* he said, *"I'll take you to lunch."* He knew exactly where I was. I had frequented this salon before. My gig was up. When he arrived I had already decided, after trying on a dozen outfits, to purchase two hundred and fifty dollars worth. As the clothes stacked up on the counter, he tried to intervene and the sales clerk just chided him teasingly that I was almost done. While shopping, I said *"You'll have to wait your turn buster."* Tim stepped off to the side and nervously waited as the clerk put my stack of clothes in the bag. We walked outside and he said, *"Where would you like to go to lunch?"* I mentioned a Hardee's location on the west side and he proceeded to drive my butt to St. Clement's. I got my wish for once. There would be no ambulance ride, just a quick drive in the car. There I was again. Same place. Same questions. Same shirts.

The next day, the round-robin style questioning had reached the lady with the recently cut neck. *"What brings you here Lydia?"* the therapist chirped. There was no reply. There was no emotion from this woman. What was her story anyway? It must be some dark place for her to resort to such a morbid and horrific action. By now the therapist was growing tired of the prodding. *"Are you afraid of the bills? What do you plan to do?"* I became edgy like the rest of the bunch. I could see them rolling their eyes as the last few minutes ticked away for this session to end. Everyone shifted in their seats and looked at Lydia for her to answer. She said nothing. Silence. The therapist continued to question her with other seemingly useless banter. The group was starting to moan and groan by now. I could not help it. I blurted out *"Why don't you leave her alone!"* The crowd applauded. The now irate therapist looked me straight in the eye while pointing her finger at me, raised her voice and said *"You're bipolar!"* *"No kidding,"* I muttered under my breath. *"I want to see you in my office immediately!"* She stomped ahead of me and plopped herself in her desk chair. *"Don't ever interrupt me when I am counseling someone,"* she said in a demanding tone. I sat for a moment and said calmly. *"You know..... I am an LPN and I could easily go back to school and come back and take your job!"* The room fell silent and she said not another word other than asking me to find the door. She busied herself at her computer. I think afterward we understood one another.

This place made me question my sanity even more. You knew when the door locked behind you there was no turning back, at least temporarily. A part of your life would be put on hold or rather taken away from you never to be given back. I felt lost and betrayed once more by my own thoughts. When would this ever stop? I then promised myself I would write about it someday. Maybe it could help others, or at least be therapeutic in the process. I tend to get my multiple visits to St. Clement's Hospital mixed up but I do have notes and dates from some of my visits.

I have had a total of seven hospitalizations in thirty years. Only one would be out of town, the rest local. It never interfered with my work, except once with my eight-year job as a cafeteria worker at New Hope High School. My hospitalizations were usually over the summer months and did not interfere with any part of my part-time jobs. It was a stealth illness. No one saw it coming except my family. Sometimes. There were no visits, cards, or flowers from my friends or co-workers. They never saw it coming. I was *never missing* in their eyes. I always thought I would get more support if I had broken my arm or leg or came down with cancer. Mental illness just did not fit the bill for the attention other illnesses often received.

I grew weary of this stay. The routine was significantly more monotonous than before. I could only count the days and hope the medicine I took would relieve my symptoms well enough so I could go home and start my life all over again. I am sure these sections would be longer if I asked my family how they felt each time I went into a manic state and was put up in the slammer, as I would sometimes call it. Even to them it is too hurtful and embarrassing to ask. I can only imagine their frustration, confusion, and the deep sighs they took when grappling each episode. At one time, I sat down to attempt to write my story, only to be frustrated by the many aspects of my illness. It was overwhelming to consider myself the guinea pig in determining the appropriate regimen of medications. For the hell of it, I would fill a Christmas popcorn tin with all the discontinued meds I had received over their twenty-three year reign. Still, it did not account for all the pills I had ingested, all the futile attempts to make me better. I would cry wondering how many dollars were spent on doctors and hospitalizations. I surmised that we could have bought a new house and cars with all the finances that my illness required. A shameless feeling would overtake me and then anger would creep in. I gave up many writing attempts in countless notebooks, at least six, where I had started my story. This time it is for keeps.

I recently attended a women's seminar and spoke to a widowed lady sitting next to me. We had small talk before the session began. Before long the conversation went to our occupations. *"Nothing,"* I first thought to myself and then with great pride I said, *"I am writing."* She said, *"My name is Jenny."* She then asked *"How long have you wanted to write?"* I answered, *"fifteen to twenty years."* She smiled and said, with a twinkle in her eye, *"You are ready!"* I thanked her for her affirmation. Here I was talking to a total stranger about my dream, a dream I knew would someday become a reality. I could not help but have a little fun with this lady. She said it like it was. That comfort allowed me to take the conversation a step closer to my true identity. I asked her, *"Let me show you something."* She only smiled. I wrote the name, *Michelle May Krack*, upon a piece of paper found in our guest folder. I turned the paper to her and asked her to read it as it was written. She let out a small laugh. I said, *"This is my first, maiden, and married name together."* She laughed again and the feeling was mutual. *"Why,"* she said, *"you have your pen name too."* I agreed and felt I already had a reason for being there and meeting this special lady. I would continue writing and tell my story.

Her name was Jo. She called a few months ago, out of the blue. She had a deep, southern twang to her voice. She lived in southern Illinois. She would say things like *"honey"* and *"I declare,"* epitomizing a southern belle. I knew and loved her as a *slammer* friend. Her smile was always ear-to-ear and she had blondish hair that was shoulder length. When our eyes met, a true bond of friendship was made, like soul sisters. Her giggle would burst into a joyous, hearty laugh. We had to be careful, for our fun may be mistaken for hysterical mania or misbehavior at best. At times, the ward seemed to keep track of our emotions. There was occasional laughter but none like what we were about to experience.

For the life of me, I could never figure out how a wall of thick fiction and non-fiction books could do any good in a place like this. In fact, the volumes lined an entire wall of the television sitting room. I never saw anyone approach it or peruse the many titles. Who in their altered, sick mind would even care to look at a book, much less read one, during their stay? I could only imagine the reasons they were put there – some intellectual thought it was proper. I would ask the staff, *"Where are the books about my illness or psychiatric books that we could all relate to?"* You know like the *Idiots Guide to Bipolar Disorder*, or *How to Keep Your Wits by Merve the Manic*. All I know is that I could not relate to *Moby Dick* or other such books at this time. The next best thing was to arrange the hundreds of magazines by their date, which quickly became futile. I did my best by putting them in nice stacks and throwing away the cardboard cards that always fell out of the flimsy pages. When that was accomplished, I would meander over to the game area. It looked as if a cyclone had wreaked havoc on the cabinet, which seemed to correlate with the current condition of my brain. There were parts mixed in with wrong games. There were too many checkers, at least five game boards worth. I felt challenged to make order out of this mess. It gave me something to do and above all, control over just a shred of my existence at St. Clement's.

I had a few minutes before Dr. Barbery would arrive to see me on his daily visit. He alternated with Dr. Fish. I dumped all the checkers out, a huge mix of red and black discs. There were only two boards to play on and enough checkers to throw away three times over. As I gathered up the needed amounts for each board, there sat Jo. She had come for a good laugh and cellmate company. We talked. *"How was lunch?"* I would ask. *"Okay,"* she said with a twang. *"What are you doing anyhow?"* she asked. *"Oh, I am bored and thought I would get a discount on my housing bill here if I helped organize the games!"* *"Oh"* she said with a giggle. I know we would have fun as the nurses and attendants peered out from their station.

"We'd better keep it quiet" she said. *"They might force us to take more medication."* I could not agree more.

There were old stubs of crayon that I held carefully in my hand and after asking for a piece of paper, scrawled her name on the blank sheet: Jo in large black letters. I continued to color them in with a few select colors that matched her bright and cheerful personality. The border of purple now showed twirls of green leaves and pollywogs encompassing boldly-petalled flowers with round centers. Those too were colored in with the sparse choice of colors to express my appreciation of our friendship, which was also bright and cheery. She wanted to exchange the gesture and saw a clear box containing thin, watercolor markers. She was pleased to find these delightful artistic tools that would show how much she cared; she loved the artful exchange. She took the lids off one-by-one to find that only two colors out of twelve had any life in them. It was a disappointment.

As we sat I noticed a small opening to the garden doors at the bottom adjoining gaskets. The outdoor concrete containers had been filled with flowers and some small tomato plants. We had begged to be let out in this garden paradise only to be told no. An expression of, *"You are a level two. You have to be a level one before you can go out."* We were never told why and it just added to the control they had over us. I told Jo, *"How about we make a rainbow out in the beautiful paradise we can't visit?"* Our hands ached for the touch of a plant or soil that held it in place in the oversized pots. We could smell traces of the delicate flowers. The smeary, dirty double-door windows only added to our dilemma of trying to view the garden. She looked at me as if I had missed my last round of medication and had really lost it. I said, *"See that hole at the bottom of the door?"* *"Yes,"* she said bewildered. *"Well we're going to take these ancient dried up markers and shoot them out the hole and make a rainbow on the other side."* *"You do not mean it!"* she crackled. *"Watch me"* I said. She became my lookout post and I became the rainbow-maker.

One by one I flicked the skinny markers into a design starting with yellow and making my way along the entire spectrum of the rainbow. They shot out and lined up next to one another. There were two left, purple and blue. I kept watch while Jo delivered the purple marker. We were so pleased with our creation, bringing ourselves one step closer to our Crayola-created paradise! So close, but so far away from our reach! By now we could not control our pure delight and what resulted was a purge of laughter loud enough to turn most heads. We kept giggling while the nursing staff looked our way. They soon became disinterested as to what was so funny and continued to do whatever it was they were doing. By this time Tom, who had been watching television, got up and meandered over to our table. *"What are you girls doing over here?"* He asked not knowing of our accomplishment. *"Look,"* I said. *"We made a rainbow on the patio!"* He dragged himself to the door like a slug under deep sedation. *"What the ...."* he said in surprise. *"Magic,"* I said. He looked at me with a drugged grimace. *"No really, tell me how you did it?"* I had one marker left, a blue one. I looked at Jo and she smiled and nodded back at me while I held up the last thin marker. *"Now Tom,"* I said, *"we'll tell you the secret but first you try to figure it out ok?"* I handed him the marker and he tried to push the marker through the top and midsection of the door. We laughed quietly until it hurt so bad we almost started to cry. We had better watch guard or they would for sure take this man and his marker and sedate him more for trying to escape. The situation became hysterical as we tried and we kept a watchful eye for him. Finally he gave up trying and I showed him the small exit in the door through which he flung the marker so hard it extended two feet beyond our current rainbow. We all three laughed at our endeavors, and laughed aloud each time we passed each other at meal time or in the hall. It was our secret until the level ones got to go out to the patio with one of the nursing assistants. *"How in the world did these get out here?"* you could hear her say in a surprised voice. We laughed even more. Best trick ever pulled off, at least in any mental ward I would be in. Classic!

Jo had called me years later after she found a note in a purse with my name and phone number on it. She said she always smiled and thought of me when she saw a rainbow anywhere and a warm feeling would come over her at the sight of sunflowers that matched her name that I had drawn for her while at the mental ward. She began to tell me *"My husband was killed by a drunk driver. It broke his neck. I could not force myself go to the funeral home."* She had two boys, ages five and three. *"I could not believe he was gone. I know I am a survivor but it was hard to deal with. I became depressed and started losing ground I guess. They said I was 'at risk.' So I was sent to St. Clement's for help. That is when I met you. I remember you talking about writing. I am telling you now, you have to write your story. You just have to."* Her voice rang out into my head once again, reaffirming what I knew was true and was becoming more and more of a reality. This reality being all the insane events that led up to my full life of having bipolar disorder and the days in between. I am thankful Jo was there and she reminded me of an event that she remembers vividly.

I had been in the hospital about three days. I was very confident, about as much or more as a sick, bipolar patient could be. It was time for me to make my visit with Dr. Barbery. I kept my calm and my wits about me. He said *"Michelle, how are things going? How are you doing today?"* I took a breath and said, *"I am doing so well I think you should let me go home. I am taking my medicine and attending therapy. I have things to do at home and my kids miss me."* Without looking up at me he wrote a few notes. He did not look at me. There was always a *look* about my dad that Mom and I always recognized when he started to become sick and in this case the apple did not fall far from the tree. Within the hour I was packing up and heading for home. It was not a day and a half and I found myself returned to the caring hands of St. Clement's psych ward. I had refused to take my meds at home, quit sleeping, and had verbally accosted my poor husband over my hospital stay. There was some creative notion that I had that was not received well from Tim. He knew I had to return to the hospital after I refused to stop buying purple paint to paint the yellow kitchen that looked perfectly fine a month ago.

Jo remembers me stepping on to the unit, she exclaimed, *"Returned, our angel!"* As she approached me and gave me a hug I had a white sheet wrapped around my head for whatever reason. The others that were in on the rainbow escapade were now applauding my return in the hallway. How humiliating! I thought, *"And how many more days did I face staying in this place?"* Jo and I continued to organize the art, puzzles, and other scant drawing materials for several days. It was time for her to leave and reluctantly I said *"Goodbye and keep in touch."* She called me several times while I stayed in the unit. *"Hang in there,"* she said with her soothing, southern twang. *"I will,"* I said. We would not talk to each other until that surprise call that came out of the blue. She suggested we were the *Rock of Ages* and I watched the lava lamp make globs of one melting one atop another until the fifth layer landed two small lava bumps together side by side. There we were in the like of the bumbling flow of lava not knowing what turn or formation our lives would make next. I could only smile at her voice from down the phone line and thank God for her call that day and her loving support.

Still to this day I take art supplies every few months or so for the artistic and not-so-artistic mental health patients of St. Clement's. I remember how much a hefty supply of paper and art materials helped my brain in reasserting reality. Such is a driven force in me to create and make others smile. That is such an integral part of my sanity. There is a lot to say when you include others in your recovery. This was my way to relieve any tension and anxiety I might have. This last time I was hospitalized I left a peace lily behind, and played *Amazing Grace* on my flute for those who wanted to hear it. I would be called a week later to be asked if I wanted my plant back. I reluctantly entered the locked doors at St. Clement's and saw the large plant my sister had brought me all fallen over in its large pot. It was like the souls and minds of those that filled the ward. No matter what help was given, there would be no hope for some. It is just the way it was. Some days were good and some not for many patients. I was thankful for a loving and supportive family. They would nurture me like I would nurture the plant back to health. There was only so much a nursing staff and doctors could do for me. It was only in your mind that you agree to a plan and stick to it by taking your meds and going with the flow. I knew all too well how this system worked and I knew the game plan to keep me well enough to be a productive person in my own right. I continued on the regimen of medicine which no longer included antidepressants.

I later learned that my recent hospitalizations would not include antidepressants like Dr. Karlton had prescribed, so I got better under the hospital doctors' care. When returning to Dr. Karlton he would literally get in my face and say *"When are you going to start acting normal?"* Luckily I always had Tim go with me to any of my psychiatric office visits. This day I looked at Tim after the doctor's comment as if to say *"Get me the hell out of here before I explode."* My lips were pursed and I imagined steam shooting from the top of my head. I never went back to him. I felt my wellness was a combination of doctor and patient working together. Now, he blamed me for all the hospitalizations and did not look to his inability to prescribe the correct medicines to me. I was furious and felt not only rejected but misled. I thought of all the unnecessary mayhem, confusion, bills, and outright insanity of it all. I was totally angry at the whole mess of things. It was time to find a different doctor in the small pool of psychiatrists in our area. For now, I would be seen by my family doctor who knew my situation.

VII

An Integral Part of Me

I had many jobs by this time in my life. Up until now I have failed to mention them. I guess the illness itself became such an integral part of me and it seemed to have stifled my productivity at times. So, I am quite blessed for all the work experience that I have had. Without question the most important was being a mom.

Before Andy was born, I pretty much stayed home with the kids. We had a babysitter named Karen who lived across the street. She was eleven and very mature for her age. Karen loved to play with my children, then ages six, four, and two and would come over frequently and ask to play with my family. It was always a resounding *"yes"*. One day I began to realize that a large part of my husband's time was being spent at the volunteer fire department. He worked at K-mart then and when at home he would make fire and emergency rescue runs with the department in the rural area. Expenses to us were gas and use of our car, not to mention the interrupted meals and social events of our family. I had had enough. *"Why do you have to leave us so much? You leave at the worst times,"* I bellyached. He soon took on more responsibility as a trainer and even scuba diver for the Bartel County Fire Department. I became anxious and downright jealous of his activities. I began to ponder joining myself. They needed more daytime help, especially when most of their members were at work.

During the summer months Karen would be available so I could attend training in the evening. Since her parents lived right across the street, it was agreed that she would be able to help me out with my new venture. The old adage *"If you can't beat 'em, join 'em"* rang true.

Training was difficult for me at first. I usually caught on quickly but had some reservations about driving these vehicles. Never let your husband teach you how to drive a standard shift, tanker fire truck or at least have some patience if you do. Old No. 4 from Station 2 was my challenge. We headed down Hogue Road to Red Bank Road that was filled with steep grades. The drive was uneventful compared to the 1966, manual transmission Chevy that my Aunt Nettie taught me to drive on. I can also remember Nettie letting me drive her Jeep until I got it right, many years ago. We approached the steep grade that resulted in me flooding the massive engine right in the middle of the hill. *"No,"* he said impatiently. I said, *"What do you mean?"* He became furious with me and nearly took over my seat in the truck. By then traffic was building behind me and with each attempt the truck began to roll a little further back each time. A good reason to stay five-hundred feet behind a fire truck was now quite apparent. I started the huge red monster slowly and let out the break, quickly put on the gas, and clutched into gear. At last the truck began to creep up the hill. Needless to say, my days of driving any fire truck ended before it really ever started. The other trucks were automatic, but they usually had regular drivers that showed up day and night.

During this time my illness was kept at bay. I still felt a sense of uneasiness and self-doubt was always a battle for me. I felt I could not always perform like the rest of the crew. I gave it my all. At this time women were joining the ranks. There were four married couples that volunteered their time, some more than others. Tim and I were now a team. I usually stayed home in the evenings when the radio alarm would go off in the night. "Bartel station 1...." it rang out, *"a structure fire at Johnson Lane and Broadway."* Tim would jolt out of bed and leave me to rescue some unknown, misfortunate family. I began to realize how important his volunteer work was. It was now in my blood too. After several years I decided to extend my services as a second-class firefighter and try to conquer some of my anxiety and broaden my horizons a bit. I signed up for an EMT class. My LPN class from 1977 would surely aid my understanding and passing of this course. I gained experience and improved my technique for helping in automobile accidents, heart attacks, and even consoling those at times of death in some cases.

One summer night, a call came out that a car had flipped over and someone was trapped on Upper Mt. Vernon Road. It was still early in the evening. I called Karen and she eagerly ran over as Tim and I got into the car and put our blue, flashing light out. By now the fire trucks were making their way to the scene. Tim had become very astute at using the Jaws-of-Life and I knew I could be of some medical assistance. We arrived to flashing lights and a t-top sports car laying upside down in a deep ditch. The driver was a tall man and word quickly spread among the rescuers that he was an athlete from the local university. He was trapped inside and Tim knew just what to do.

Someone had to get inside to check the patient's condition. Windows were accessible from the sides and I was small enough to crawl inside. The inside of the car was cramped as I crawled closer to the young man. I could hear the Jaw's generator start up and knew I had to secure the head and spine of this badly injured man. He was mumbling something about his girlfriend and had alcohol on his breath. He was not moving. I placed a cervical collar carefully around his neck while trying not to move him anymore than necessary. As I surveyed his injuries, he said he could not move his legs. Minutes passed as the Jaws made their way through the heavy framework of the car. I placed a turnout coat over the victim's face and body to protect him from the debris that now fell upon us from the rescuers attempts to free him. It was difficult to put him on a backboard because of his height. He was positioned with his head stabilized and we were most careful. *"One. Two. Three!"* the fireman would call out as the moaning young man was pulled from the wreckage.

I would have a chance to meet him years later when Andy was so badly burned. Don had a series of whirlpool baths that he needed for circulation for his tall, paralyzed frame. *"Hello,"* he said in a deep voice while Andy played in his whirlpool bath. *"I've met you before,"* I said caringly. He looked at me in a puzzled way as he combed my face for a sign of familiarity. I began, *"I was the one who crawled in your car with you the night of your wreck."* He sat up in his wheelchair and said appreciatively, *"thank you."* The next time I had heard about him he had passed away. I was saddened by his choice to drink that night and the wreck that resulted. He was exactly my age.

I continued rolling hose, helping extinguish fires, and taking vitals at wrecks and on heart attack runs. I learned a lot about people, especially during their most dire need for help. It felt good to be of assistance in these times. It was about this time that my bipolar reared its ugly head again. I discontinued my volunteer fire career which included teaching fire prevention to small children. Once again stability was reached that lasted for several years. For nearly thirty years, I have kept up my LPN license as a backup for a possible nursing job in the future hope of someday using it again. As it would turn out, I would have use for it. A caretaker was needed for an elderly neighbor that was wheelchair-bound. She needed assistance in daily care to some degree and needed help with light housework and shopping. We enjoyed each other's company for several years until her passing.

I then took on cleaning of several other homes of friends that knew my family. If I was having a sick day from depression or was being hospitalized, my jobs were always there for me when I was back to myself. I enjoyed the freedom of my hours. The joy of knowing I could help pay the bills to some degree helped. Through one of my cleaning jobs I learned of another that paid well and needed people who were not afraid to work hard. I thought maybe this would be a great opportunity for me. My mother and aunt had the job of being rural route carriers for the post office. I took a test or two and was quickly hired by the U.S. government. The rural route I delivered to served over four hundred families.

It would take weeks to learn the layout of the homes and where their respective mail went. I would go in to work at 5:30 a.m. and would come home at 5:30 p.m. until I learned the order of the routes. My days became shorter as I could go home around three or so. I enjoyed the challenge of each new day. The seasons changed, I even carried mail while I was plump and pregnant with my fourth child, Andy. The mail would rest on my belly as I sorted through it before placing it in the mailbox perched along the country roads. I usually worked only one or two days a week. Hardly much time to give up breastfeeding my newborn, I would pack a cooler and during my lunch break on Howards Lane I would release my aching breasts and retain mother's milk for baby. Placing the milk in the cooler made for an inexpensive way for me to feed my young one and still remain a multi-tasking mail carrier. The days were extremely hot in the summer and cold in the winter. Even the worst weather forecasts did not provide a break in my work. I worked eight years and had no Saturdays off. My mail route days were largely free of illness. I was able to function very well under the yoke of some anxiety and mood swings that had not gotten too out of control. Days passed as bundles of mail piled high in my back seat were worked down to nothing- only to repeat the drum of names and addresses the following day. I prided myself on being able to sit on the right side of my 1977 blue Nova and drive with my left hand and foot. There was not much training for this part of the job, so I would practice in the New Hope parking lot until I got the feel for it.

One year there was a particularly bad ice storm. The chains on my car came off and I was fighting a losing battle. Luckily two men and a truck came along and dug me out on a blind curve. They threw my shovel into the back seat of my mail-filled car and told me to go back to the post office. The roads were treacherous. I was the first to arrive back at the station and was told I was about to be fired for not delivering the mail. At this point I did not care. *"It isn't worth losing my life out there,"* I retorted. Within minutes the other five rural carriers returned prematurely without finishing their appointed rounds. It was the worst ice storm ever. I kept my job and worked summers that were so hot my head would pound under the metal roof of my car. I would take towels and dip them in ice cold water in my cooler and relieve my heat-parched head and neck. It was one of the hardest jobs I had, but one of the most rewarding. A number of the patrons on the route were like family. Their tractors pulled you out of the deep snow if you slid off the road. They offered cold water or warned you of the wasp nest in their mailbox. One family gave me a bottle of wine and a smoked chicken for Christmas. It was a good job. I hated to leave it.

Tim joined the fire department with the city of Evansville. We had since moved from Karen's neighborhood; she had grown up and had started a family of her own. Babysitters were hard to find at 5:30 a.m. Tim worked twenty-four hour shifts and usually was not home until 7 a.m. Reluctantly, I gave up my postal carrier position to once again stay home with my family. I would eventually take a job at a chiropractor's office and learn how to assist him while he did spinal manipulations. It was sort of like a dance in the room as you had to move from side to side of the chiropractor table. By this time my meds were continuing to be effective in stabilizing my mood and things were going well for me. One day however, the chiropractor suggested a cleanse diet and I was not sure it was a good idea with the slow acting release of my medication. He said, *"If you take the supplement at opposite times of the day as your medication, it will surely not alter it."* I trusted his judgment because he was a well-respected chiropractor in the area. I started the regimen of supplements. Within a week I started to lose sleep and became easily irritated.

I could not remember what color of work smock correlated with the days of the week. I told Dr. Letterman one day, *"Your white coat is filthy. Take it home and clean it."* It was usually hung at the back of his chair for weeks at a time; it was indeed dirty but I had overstepped my bounds. Dr. Letterman's associate called me into his office, *"Michelle,"* he said sternly, *"some people are just not cut out for this job."* He needed my assistance from time to time and was not in any mood to teach me or walk me through his steps that were quite different from Dr. Letterman's. I was let off with this warning of sorts, but my head was spinning. I was putting people in the wrong room and unable to fill out the proper medical and insurance forms needed to complete my job.

My probationary time had passed and I had earned a permanent position. I knew this because one morning when I arrived, my new crisp white coat that I had earned along with an assistant's pin hung in the break room. Not a word of congratulations had been mentioned, a fairly odd way to say you got the job. I thought I was losing my mind as everything came in a whirlwind of confusion. There was definitely a lack of communication at this place so, I left the office in a hurry and never returned my uniforms or provided any form of explanation as to why I left. I went to my psych doctor who told me that Dr. Letterman's suggested cleanse had indeed interrupted my maintenance level of medications and the supplement had all but erased its levels in my brain. I felt ashamed not to have known better and felt gullible due to this chiropractor who told me later he wanted to learn more about the brain. I later learned he had a psychiatrist in his office that treated mental cases of people whom the chiropractor could not help. I was a guinea pig again and had all the reason not to give this *professional* my reason for leaving. He called me several days later not asking me how I felt but said, *"My office has spent much money on training you. When do you plan to come back?"* I was horrified at the thought. I believe in basic chiropractic and reflexology treatment, but this experience had pushed me over the edge. I told him, *"No, I won't be returning."* There was no response and so ended that job.

My main job now was driving kids here and there for various practices. I had volunteered at the grade school to assist a dear friend, Terry, with coaching track and cross-country. In charge of forty kids, we quickly organized fun as well as workout plans for the bustling 5th, 6th, 7[th,] and 8th graders. *Kick the Can* was popular as well as running the block that encompassed the school grounds. Our friendship grew and to this day we are the best of friends. We worked hard and made it fun, not only for us, but for the team.

During one of our cross-country practices at the heavily-wooded nearby university we noticed one of our runners had not returned. Terry and I carefully retraced their steps along the routine workout path. All of a sudden we heard laughter and banging of metal in the distance. As we crept up onto a bluff we could see our boys' team constructing a cabin in the woods. This whole time we thought they were practicing their running. I grabbed my whistle from around my neck and blew a long hard shrill echo from its chamber. The heads of the boys lifted quickly and they darted every which way. They had been caught red-handed. I yelled, *"Get down here immediately."* They had crossed a creek to make their way up to the bluff where the make shift cabin stood of old boards and planks. We laughed quietly to ourselves as the boys bounced off each other and scattered like broken pool balls. I hollered *"I do not care if you have to swim the creek to get over here. Do it now!"* The creek was only two feet deep and by this time they were practically walking on water.

Terry and I expected our kids to work hard and we had respect for them. We had children of our own and we knew that fun and expectations were the tools to getting these kids to perform at their best, and they did. We shared their pride in finishing a race or event. They knew we cared about them and we coaches for each other. We had paved the path. Some of our young talent would reach Nationals for the first time at our high school. A mother could not have been prouder. I enjoyed having children around and the liveliness they brought to my life. As my children grew, I followed them as an assistant coach at their high school in track and cross-country. The head coaches were namely male and they needed the presence of a female for the girl's team. I became the first-aid mom and helped the team wherever I could.

My involvement with high school students did not end there. I was involved with helping design and make sets for proms, dances, and the annual party called Project Graduation. I began to get a reputation for my creativity and enjoyed every minute of it. It was especially gratifying to see the look on the high schoolers' faces when you knew you had provided an enchanting place for their festivities.

❧

The word was they were hiring in the cafeteria of New Hope. I applied and started the job immediately. Of course, it paid less than other jobs but only required half days, part time and would allow me to pay into Social Security. I felt safe in this job knowing the stress or my superiors would not ask me to do something I felt was outside my comfort zone. I would work there for eight years. After five years I had a conversation with the psychology teacher, Mr. Green, and had revealed my history of bipolar disorder. He said he had a family member that also had the illness. We talked a while longer and he invited me into his class to talk more about it. We agreed it would be more interesting to the students if it did not come straight from their textbooks. I introduced myself by writing my name on the board, *"Michelle May Krack."* I asked a student to read it aloud. There were reluctant chuckles in the class. I told them as psychology students they may have to be a friend to someone with a mental illness someday. My name was a way for me to find humor in my illness. Some people were not as fortunate as I, and had horrific consequences as a result. The worst results included loss of a marriage, spouse, all their savings, or even their life. Humor helped me manage very difficult times and then I told the story of how I first became ill with bipolar disorder. I began, *"Imagine being a child of a mentally-ill mother. Seemingly, everything appears normal until significant events start to change her."*

In my case, events started changing month-by-month. I quit doing my usual housekeeping and chores that kept the family going. This had never happened to me before. We lived by the train tracks and with the passing of each train I became terribly fearful and in my mind I actually pictured the devil riding the train and lassoing lost souls. The sound of the train made me shutter and relive the horrible images over and over each time the train passed through. Today the kids do not recall many details of those days before I was hospitalized.

This illness is treatable and part of my treatment is being an advocate for those suffering from bipolar disorder. There was usually a flood of hands going up after the class was able to ask questions. *"How do your kids feel about you now?"* I replied, *"It was hard for them when I was sick, but they know as long as I take my medicine I do well every day."* Another hand went up slowly. "My mom is bipolar. She scared us *when she got sick. She's been to the hospital several times."* I assured her the best thing was to keep trying the medicines and to let the family help each other. I would tell them to be a friend to someone with mental illness.

The local coroner, Maggie Sawyer, saw me at a fundraiser. She said, *"Michelle, tell me you're not bipolar!"* I had gone to high school with her and shared my story with her. She continued about her daughter, *"Sandy shared your story with me. She's in college now. Believe it or not her roommate became ill and was diagnosed bipolar. Your story helped her recognize the symptoms. She got the girl help. You know usually the people I see are not alive but have died because of their bipolar illness."* I explained, *"I take my medicine and watch for signs of the illness. My family is diligent about recognizing the symptoms."* I told Maggie I was happy to hear that the story helped her daughter and that she had done the right thing. She nodded and said, *"It's hard to believe it all. Thank you for telling your story."* I only wish similar words had gotten to the many victims' families or friends before they took their lives or possibly harmed others.

During my talk to the high schoolers I tell them to not be afraid. I then ask how many of them plan to go to college. A large show of hands goes up. *"Please remember this story of Sandy. If no one helps you like the R.A., go to someone who will listen- a teacher or counselor. You can be a great friend and may very well help save their life by getting them to the help they need."*

I have become a member of NAMI, the National Alliance on Mental Illness. Several years ago I took a class and trained to be a presenter for a twelve week family-to-family class. The program was started by a Wisconsin grassroots group of families that had loved ones with mental illnesses. The director of this program is

Dr. Joyce Burland. The sessions were filled with revealing facts of how families struggled with a mentally-ill family member. Tools and training in interactive sessions made the caring for a person with mental illness much easier. A large factor was simply listening and understanding. There were advocates that stood by your side. I helped present Dr. Burland's program twice and continued my advocacy through supporting NAMI and telling my story to educate others.

VIII

Setback

༔

Another setback came. I could hear a small voice inside me saying, *"Do not go"* and then, *"turn back."* I drove steadily down the highway ignoring the intuitive signals that were plucking at my brain. I had planned an outing of morel mushroom hunting in the unfamiliar woods of a friend of the family, northeast of the city. My youngest son Andy was at my side. After we arrived I gave strict instructions for Andy to stay with me. Of course that lasted about five minutes. My son was off four-wheeling with encouragement from the property owner. I made my way down into the wooded area full of oak trees and thick blankets of leaves on the ground. I rummaged around, peering over banks of what I thought would be the perfect place for the succulent fungi to grow. I wore jeans and a t-shirt, and felt comfortable until I came across a dead mole. I quickly turned in to another direction. About fifty steps away lay a dead rabbit. How peculiar I thought to see two small, dead animals in the same area. I soon realized the trip had been for not and slowly made my way up the hill still looking for that one mushroom to put into my paper bag. It was hard to get Andy's attention. He finally came to me after much coaxing. We went in the house and visited for a while.

It was almost lunchtime and the romp in the woods had brought on an appetite. It was decided Andy and I would treat ourselves to a sandwich at a nearby Subway. On the way into the door, I noticed a brown tick climbing on my arm. I flicked it off outside and did not think much of it. We ordered our food and sat down. Much to my surprise as I opened the paper of my sandwich, two more ticks appeared and one had dropped onto my sandwich. I quickly removed them and headed for the bathroom. I had never seen anything like it. I had not sprayed myself with any bug spray. It was early spring and I could not see the need. On closer inspection in the bathroom I saw another tick climbing on my neck. I flicked all three into the toilet growing uneasy of the presence of all these ticks. We hurriedly ate our lunches. I was eager to get home and shower. Upon inspection I found one more brown tick and an odd circle that appeared above my ankle. Very small deer ticks had encircled my lower left leg at exactly where my sock top had ended. I tried to brush them off in the shower. I found no other ticks and felt clean and rid of the blood-sucking varmints. I kept my busy schedule with ball practices and chauffeuring runs.

About a week went by and an outing was planned to an Amish restaurant and store. I looked forward to the outing with my mother and kids. We ate the wonderful meal and started to browse around the shop. All of a sudden a dull headache pounded my brain and the fluorescent lights seemed to blur. The now enjoyable trip caused me to now grow increasingly anxious. I felt nervous and lost interest in anything that surrounded me. A heavy feeling came over me. I could barely move. It was like my arms and legs were in quicksand. What had come over me? I thought I was getting sick with the bipolar again. No. This was different. I became so tired I asked if we could leave. Everyone was having so much fun reading slogan pillows and smelling candles. Their laughter became a dull drone of sound to me. I had no idea what was going on but whatever it was it had a brute grip on me. The days that followed revealed that I slept far too often. I began to ache all over especially in my back. Tylenol and Ibuprofen did not give me any relief. After four or five days I knew this could not be the flu, as the symptoms were stronger than ever. I lost interest in everything around me and felt only comfort sleeping on the couch with a heating pad and staring into a barely audible television. Tim and I went to the doctor after an appointment was made. By now I needed assistance to walk any distance. The walk from the car to the office waiting room was exhausting. I could not imagine what had struck me down. What had I done differently? While we waited for my turn to see the doctor, I realized several weeks had passed since I took that walk in the woods. I remembered seeing the small, dead animals. I had to wonder if there was some connection. Had the small deer ticks that surrounded my ankle caused this?

We were quickly taken back to a small room where we waited to see Dr. Anderson. He entered the room and asked, *"What brings you here today?"* I explained the terrible discomfort and tiredness I had been having, a loss of appetite and aching all over my body, especially my back. I said, *"Almost two weeks ago, I was in a woods and became covered in ticks. Small tan-colored ones were embedded on my leg, and large brown ones were in my hair. I started feeling bad about a week later."* *"Did you have a round bullseye rash?"* he asked. *"No,"* I replied. *"We'll do some blood work and see what's going on as well as a panel for Rocky Mountain Spotted Fever and Lyme,"* he said affirmatively. I felt so weak I could not hold up my head. I prayed we could get to the bottom of this. I wanted my body and my life back. The test would take a week to come in. They had to be sent away to a lab out of town. I kept to my routine of sleep and more sleep. The aching was unbearable. The doctor started me on Septra, a very strong antibiotic.

One day I had to drive Andy to ball practice at Golfmoor Park. It was only five minutes from home. I remember praying again, this time that I could stay awake long enough to get him there and back. We set out in the car. I almost fell asleep twice while driving. After arriving I sat my lawn chair next to a concession stand being built. There was a row of five blocks already in place. I leaned the side of my head against the blocks while sitting in the lawn chair. Falling fast asleep, I did not wake until Andy shook me awake to be taken home. *"Mom, Mom wake up! It's time to go home,"* he said with a pressured voice. This thing had a real hold on me, and I was sicker than ever before.

For energy, I decided to make a trip to my favorite health food store and purchase some All-in-One powder. It did boost my energy ever so slightly and it was something that could not really hurt me. Finally the test results came back negative for Rocky Mountain Spotted Fever and also negative for Lyme. The doctor said there were no active cases of Lyme in the area. I begged to differ. He also said the test could be inconclusive depending on the cycle of the arachnid in the body. It was decided to take another test of my blood. I had insisted upon the ticks had something to do with my condition. My house and motherly duties became difficult; I became entombed upon the couch. I had never seen or heard of someone hurting or sleeping so much. Weeks later the tests revealed a positive on the Lyme disease. The Septra was continued but fell short and seemed to not help my condition much. If only I had not gone to that woods. Thank God Andy drove off to go four-wheeling or it could have been both of us on that couch. Why did I not wear any insect repellent? I would learn later that had I tucked my jeans in my socks, the deer ticks could not have directly attached themselves to me. Do not be fooled. I had no bullseye ring anywhere, but I was indeed infected by the spirochete.

A friend of the family, Mark, had also been affected by Lyme disease. He had suffered for eight years and had shown signs of improvement. I would call him to find out what he had done to gain his health back after suffering for so long. I hoped my recovery would not be anywhere near that lengthy. I had known him since I was a young girl in grade school. Our families shared many fun times together with annual burgoo making, scouting adventures, and family-centered weekend picnics. After seeking mental health help, I could now concentrate on the physical aspects of this dreaded illness. Mark told me, *"I have tried a treatment that the doctors don't use anymore."* I was curious and anxious to hear more of what he had to say. *"It's called colloidal silver. It's a natural antibiotic, a precursor to penicillin. I even make my own."* I asked him how it worked. He said, *"First, the history explains more about how it works and what it helps heal. There is a booklet by a man named Al Fleming."* There is the disclaimer about the fact you should also work with your doctor on healing,"* he said. I had worked with my doctor for several months and the progress had come to a standstill. I did not feel much better; my aches had just slightly improved. I wanted my total life back and was willing to try anything to get it. Mark continued, *"Colloidal silver was manufactured in the late 1800s and early 1900s and used as an antibiotic. It was used for various illnesses. Before refrigeration, a silver dollar was placed in a jug of milk to keep it from spoiling. From then until now, silver nitrate was put in to babys' eyes to prevent gonorrheal infection. Silverdene is used to fight infection in burns."* This made good sense to me and I asked for further information. *"It's very effective in destroying pathogens and microbials such as Lyme disease and many others. It destroys enzymes that supply pathogens with oxygen. The pathogens suffer and die."* I asked *"How soon does this work and how do you know it's working?"* He said, *"The silver helps the immune system. It takes a while for you to notice improvement, maybe a month or so. You know it's working because you will experience what is called Herxheimer's reaction, which is a side effect of the killing off of the Lymes. You will feel like you have the flu, you may have diarrhea and headaches. There are more details in the Al Fleming book on what to do when this occurs. I have had it happen to me many times over and feel better each time as the Herxheimer resides."* *"Where do I get this,"* I asked. *"There is a local health food store that carries it."*

He gave me its name, wished me luck, and told me to keep him posted on my recovery. I made a phone call and mustered up enough energy to drive to the place and purchase my first bottle of colloidal silver. I was prepared to start the treatment and prayed that this would finally give me the relief I so desperately needed. I could not sleep at night or even much during the day. I was desperate for a cure. I started the regimen of colloidal silver for three weeks along with my doctor's supply of Septra. I began to notice a difference along with the Herxheimer effect, a good thing. I felt slightly more energetic. I surely did not feel up to taking on the whole world, but I could begin to stand at the sink and do dishes or prepare a small meal for my family. I could feel a sense of control over this struggle with Lyme.

After several months of taking the silver, I had returned to the doctor's office. The nurse commented on my noticeable improvement of energy. Just weeks before, I had asked for a chair to sit in while I shopped at a local health food store. I did not even have enough energy to stand for the fifteen minutes it took to gather my supplies. The doctor had been seeing me frequently. I began to say, *"Dr. Anderson, I want you to know I've been taking colloidal silver along with the Septra."* He listened but did not react or acknowledge my excited exclamation of how I was feeling better. He only listened to my chest and made notes on my chart. I once again mentioned the silver, *"Have you heard of such a thing,"* I asked. He said, *"You seem to be better. I'll see you in a few weeks."* I realized it was not the usual accepted treatment for Lyme. Only months prior I was told Lyme did not exist in this area before my test results revealed that it did. I was not going to make a believer out of my doctor, but I could feel the difference and would continue. After all, he did not tell me to stop doing what I was doing.

I finally felt a sense of dominance over this hellish condition. Mark had mentioned something about *blue blood* while I was first talking to him. I called him back to tell him of my improvement. *"Hello,"* he said with enthusiasm, *"How are you doing?"* *"Much better,"* I said. *"Thank you for sharing this with me. It's been a miracle. I meant to ask you more about the 'blue blood' you mentioned before."* *"Oh that,"* he said. *"Well, if you take too much of the silver it turns your skin a blue color permanently."* I answered, *"You're kidding!"* *"It began with royalty or well to do folks that had access to the silver, as it worked its marvelous action the folks would take more than necessary– you know – like 'more is better.' They soon learned they had blue skin, hence the name 'blue blood.' I never knew that is where the term came from originally."* *"Wow,"* I said. *"You know as desperate as I felt I did not think I would care what color I might turn out as long as I felt better."* *"I am glad you're doing better Michelle! I keep making it and taking it myself."* I thanked him again.

It was a long year and a half but I continued the silver for that length of time until I no longer kept feeling the symptoms of

Lyme and regained all of my energy back. I had heard of a firefighter in Florida over the internet that was suffering from Lyme. We had just gotten a computer at the time and I decided to share my story with this desperate man as to what I had done to help my Lyme condition. I rallied with a long letter to him on the computer and just as I had finished the letter it was lost. I became angry and swore I would never use the computer again for correspondence. My deepest regret is that I never sent the information to the suffering fireman. I was still dealing with the remainder of the illness and self-pity had taken its toll on me that day. I am still sorry for not contacting the ailing man. Thankful to God and a dear friend, I could now get on with my life.

IX

A Well-Oiled Machine

❦

It was 1999 and the family began to work like a well-oiled machine. I no longer depended on my kids to take me places. I could now drive myself and perform my usual household duties. I could not be any more thankful. As I look at the pictures from then, I had gained so much weight, at least eighty pounds from the ordeal. This was evident when there was a party for my daughter Amy. She had just graduated from high school and had enlisted in the Air Force. The celebration was a joint high school graduation and farewell party. I looked huge in the pictures taken that day. I had mixed feelings of her joining the Air Force. Of course there was a full sense of pride, but the mother inside me knew I would miss her dearly and worry. To this day she has lived at least a two to three day drive from home. The miles are many but as I would tell her during basic training and the first year of Air Force, *"Just look up honey,"* I would say on a moon lit night, *"We share the same moon."* It seemed to soothe the loneliness the miles distantly placed between us.

My husband, mother, and I were able to travel to San Antonio for Amy's graduation from basic training at Lackland Air Force Base. She nervously showed us around. At one time, we asked to drive down a small road. She blurted out, *"Do not go there. I'll get into trouble."* We teased her that we would and she was clearly upset with our suggestion. We recalled not being able to use the water fountain in her barracks. It had taken all morning for it to reveal its perfect shine. It was a sign of the discipline and work for her fellow airmen had experienced together. I knew she was no longer ours, but a significant part of a greater entity of proud soldiers. She said, *"Mom, I am group leader now."* I smiled as she continued, *"Mom you wouldn't believe it. There were some that came here that did not even know how to tie their shoes."* I thought it an exaggeration, but learned quickly that it was indeed a fact. She had become a leader, and I was proud to know her dad and I raised an independent and knowledgeable young lady that had gained respect from her officers. Before we left Amy, a bus of new arrivals had pulled up. Amy exclaimed in a tenacious manner, *"The 'rainbows' have arrived."* We understood that she once was a rainbow and now looked upon this group as new arrivals that were green beneath *their* collars. She had earned her title of airman and had just started her career in the Air Force.

Back home I decided to find some work to help with the bills and enjoy a job that would not be full-time. While grocery shopping one day I noticed a local grocer that was seeking a part-time florist. I loved working with flowers and people. This would be the perfect job, I thought. It was not far from home, just blocks away. I felt a sense of pride and optimism inside. Finally something that I was good at had come my way. I could not wait to discuss it with Tim. It was now the fall of 2000 and my eldest son, Matt had graduated from college. My daughter Carrie was a junior in high school and Andy was a seventh grader. Things were busy but everyone had become self-sufficient to a certain degree. They knew how to open the fridge, turn on the stove, and start the washing machine. I began to feel a sense of freedom. I enjoyed a time when my illness would not interfere with a position change, or new job itself. I quickly learned the prices and styles of arrangements that were sold in the floral department of Heiber's Grocery Store. I saw people I knew that lived in the surrounding west-side area. It was very pleasing to add my creativity to the department. It felt right and I loved every minute of it. I worked at Heiber's through the fall of 2000 and enjoyed the Christmas hustle and bustle. There were so many poinsettias and special Christmas orders. It took all three of us, JoAnne, Bobby, and I to keep up with all the orders. Valentine's Day was even busier. There were many a man that came to our floral counter with wide eyes and forlorn as to what solution they would need to fulfill this day reserved for lovers. We prided ourselves in helping every loyal husband, boyfriend, or sweetheart pick out the perfect combination. It was especially nice to combine sweets or treats in special baskets along with flowers, balloons, or stuffed animals. It seemed like a dream to me. I was definitely in my element.

I had thoughts of going back into nursing, but the dread of recurring manic or depressive episodes, or at least the threat of them, would sabotage my efforts. The longer I stayed away from my nursing career the more comforting it felt. But, there was always a small dig in my soul and heart that was a calling to the profession I had first started. The encouragement of a dear high school teacher, Donald Sheridan, was inspiring too. Despite the fact I was not an excellent student, he managed to see a side of me that led him to believe, as he would say, *"Michelle, you'd make the perfect nurse."* He mentioned his wife was a nurse and he could recognize special people who would serve well in this profession. He caught me by surprise. I had never made plans beyond high school. There were no dreams, plans, or expectations. I had many talents but had not formed anything solid. For now, a bud of my creativity through floral design filled the void. It was a safe place to be when you have a bipolar illness.

The summer months passed as did the hours of watering and caring for flowers inside and outside the grocery store. I became known to the customers. The job was starting to feel comfortable and rewarding. School had started back up again- the routine of readying (now two) back-to-schoolers had been welcomed. Summer nights were longer than I liked and mornings came quickly, especially when I had to report early to Heiber's. I was happy to know another summer had passed and my medications had worked well for me. The environs had not rattled the beast that seemed to always be within, lurking.

My Family Scrapbook

My parents on their wedding day in 1957. Tom & Mary May

My parents & me on my baptismal day at Sacred Heart Church.

Top: 5 months old, 1958

Bottom: 2 years old, 1960

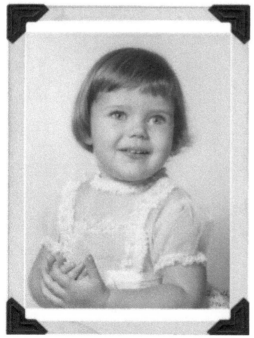

Smile for the camera!
Kindergarten

Top: Our rental farmhouse on Carson School Road

Bottom: Learning to play the flute, 5th grade

Fall Festival Queen Contest
St. Philip School
8th grade

1976
Receiving the
Student Council
Citizenship
Award

1978
Brother Mike in
Eagle Scout
uniform & me
in my Licensed
Practical Nurse
uniform

Tim & me on our wedding day
October 14, 1978
St. Philip Church
Mt. Vernon, IN

Four Generations L to R: Me, Great-Grandma Mary Morris, Grandmother Lucille Koressel, Mother Mary May

Me with my Great-Grandma Morris Little Sisters of the Poor Christmas 1978

Top: Tim & me fishing, Summer 1979, pregnant with Matt

Bottom: picture taken at Post Office. Rural Carrier Relief, Route 8, 410 families served in the 1980s

Top: A League of Their Own extras at Garvin Park fountain. L to R: Carrie Krack, Tracey Ramsbey, Amy Krack & Me; I am seen in the movie in this outfit, 1992

Bottom: Mother Daughter Dinner of Evansville Fire Department Auxiliary
L to R: mother Mary May, Me, granddaughter Kassidy, & sister Marty May ; Kassidy's mother, Amy, is deployed.

1990s
As a busy mom with four children & a
husband, I took time to get this picture.

Amy &
Kassidy with
San Damiano
cross at
church in
Surprise, AZ
2001

My 50th
birthday.
Kassidy is seven.
I would soon be
admitted to the
hospital.
2008

Top: *Five Generations at Grandma's House*
Dad, Kassidy, Grandma Bennie May, Amy, & Me

Bottom: *2002 Family Photo,*
Kassidy, Amy, Matt, Tim, Me, Andy & Carrie

Top: Tim and I, August 2018

Pictured with our children, daughter-in-law, sons-in-law, & grandchildren.

X

One Hour at a Time

It was a September morning like any other. Tim was in the shower and had gone downstairs to fetch a clean set of clothes for his sales job. He had just finished his twenty-four-hour shift at the fire station. As I entered the kitchen from the basement my eye caught the image of a plane crashing into a tall building on the television screen. I stopped and turned up the news. At first I thought it was a preview of a must-see action movie being advertised. It looked horrible. I quickly learned it was a commercial airliner that had flown into one of the World Trade Center towers in New York City. I immediately thought of the firefighters and what they would have to do to extinguish the flames and try to rescue any survivors. I called to Tim, *"Come here, you have to see what's happened in New York!"* As I waited impatiently for him to join me, my eyes stayed glued to the nightmare that was being revealed. As he joined my side, I witnessed the second plane crash into the second tower. My husband now caught the second act of terrorism.

The phone began to ring from different firemen from his shift. *"Did you see what just happened?"* Similar to any tragic event, the response and actions of one isolated group of firefighters affects firemen and their families throughout the entire country. There was utter astonishment thinking of what the actions of the New York Fire Department would be on this fateful day. The local companies put themselves in the boots of their comrades. It did not take long for news of first-hand accounts to reveal that firemen's family members closely related to us were some of the rescuers to this horrific scene. We held our breaths and numbly tried to manage our day like it should have been. Our lives and the lives of our fellow Americans were changed forever.

My next thought was of my daughter Amy. She was based at Luke Air Force Base in Phoenix and lived in nearby Surprise. How had this terrible event touched her and the many airmen at her base? We finally reached each other by cell-phone that day long after the Pentagon had been attacked as well as a plane downed in a rural field in Pennsylvania. She was in just as much shock as we were. On our phone call she said, *"It's taking several hours to enter the base as to what used to take five minutes. They are checking each and every car for the possibility of concealed bombs. Mom, they're using mirrors to look under each and every car. It's unbelievable."* I had to ask how her daughter, seven-month old Kassidy, and husband, Aaron, were doing. *"I can't talk right now Mom,"* she said, *"I'll call you later."* I had heard her voice and knew she was okay for now. Freedom, oh sweet freedom. What liberties I have in writing and living in this country. These terrorist acts were meant to harm and tear at the very heart of what it means to be American and be free. They would soon find out that they were mistaken and had in fact accomplished quite the opposite. September 11th, 2001 will never be forgotten.

Days passed as we and others glued ourselves to our televisions watching and listening to the countless, terrifying reports of the attack on our nation. A numbness replaced our peace of mind as we tumbled through our daily lives. My intuition led me to believe that Amy was entering a zone beyond her military duties. A mother knows by the sound of her child's voice when something is wrong. A week had passed and there was no news from Amy. We had tried to reach her but to no avail.

On September 18th the phone rang and Amy was crying. She could not be consoled. It was difficult to understand her, *"Mom,"* she sobbed, *"I want my baby back!"* I tried to comfort her. Confused

I asked her, *"What happened?"* Her sobbing had only increased. She replied between deep breaths, *"Aaron and I have separated. I agreed to let him take Kassidy to his family in New Mexico. Mom, I miss her so much. I want her back with me,"* she shuddered. The information clouded my brain, asking myself why would he do something like that? They had worked separate shifts so they did not need a babysitter. So now, the broken marriage also broke their sharing of watching Kassidy. Twelve-hour shifts complicated the overall picture. I began to understand the dilemma. Feeling helpless I answered, *"What should I do? What can I do?"* She began to cry again, *"Mom, I need you. I need a babysitter. There's no one here that can help me. Can you get Kassidy in New Mexico and bring her here to Arizona?"* My heart sank. My ears could not believe what I had just heard. It kept resonating in my brain. *"Can you Mom?"* she pleaded. Without a doubt, I of course wanted to help her and reunite her and Kassidy. I trembled and said, *"First I need to talk this over with your dad."* *"Oh please Mom,"* she began to cry again. My heart was already breaking. I understood the love of my children and her pain became my pain. *"The planes aren't flying Amy. I can't get to you fast enough. The car I have wouldn't make the trip. I do not know what to do!"* I had to let her go and make some kind of a plan.

I did not have time to cry although a deep sadness wrapped around me. Dialing Tim at work, the numbers jumbled in my head. I had dialed the wrong number. *"I am sorry,"* I said to the unknown person on the other end. Tim answered the phone with his usual, calming voice. While my voice was shaking, I tried to convey Amy's story the best that I could. A brief pause came over the phone. *"We would need to rent a car,"* he said. *"How long would you stay? I am worried about you making the trip alone,"* he said.

Thinking of my parents and how helpful they have always been I told Tim I would call them for some suggestions. My mom had a newer car. Would it be possible to borrow her car just long enough to make the trip to get Kassidy and drive back home? I could only ask. Tim said, *"Call me back after you talk to your mom."* Much calmer now, I phoned my mom and relayed the story once again. *"Oh my gosh,"* Mom replied. *"When did all this happen?"* I said, "*I think the separation was a long time coming.*" They had only been married for a little over a year. "*What should I do?*" asking Mom in an overly concerned response. "*You could borrow my Subaru,*" she said. I had hoped she would say that, but it seemed like a large imposition. "*We have the van or could use your car to get around town while you're gone.*"

By now the minutes that Amy had waited for my response seemed like days to her. For me, the day seemed like it was in slow motion. Mom insisted on me driving her car and said, "*It's sad what has happened to Amy, but I know you girls will figure it out.*" I had been well now for several years and life was pretty stable. My sleep was good and daily life was as normal as it could be. I felt assured in making the trip. I would of course take all my medicines with me, a month's supply just in case. After more discussion and slight pleading with Tim, it was agreed that I would make the trip to Saline, New Mexico to pick up Kassidy and then to Surprise, Arizona. I felt relief and I knew things would be better.

Returning Amy's desperate call I said, "*Honey, I can make the trip, but first I have to tell them at work of my leaving for emergency purposes. It will take me a day to get things packed up and ready. I will use Grandma and Grandpa's car for the trip. You need to call Granny and Grandpa and let them know how appreciative and thankful you are.*" "*I will. I will,*" she said. My dream job at Heiber's came to an end as I explained the situation to the store manager. "*Jim,*" I said, "*I have to leave immediately for a family emergency.*" He understood.

Now I had to pack and start my long drive to New Mexico. I gathered the road atlas along with emergency provisions for myself in the car. I double-checked my supply of medications, and made sure they were packed with my summer clothes. The next day I was packed and ready to leave. I gave Tim a long kiss and told him, "*I'll call you on my cell any time I stop so you know where I am. I love you.*" He had carefully mapped out the shortest distance to my New Mexico destination. There was no time for AAA.

Mom and Dad were more than gracious to loan me their car. They also offered me several hundred dollars for the trip. I was lucky to have a dependable car and luckier to have such great parents. I called Amy and told her, *"I am on my way and I will see you in three to four days."* She had made arrangements with Aaron's family. They knew I was coming. Hopefully they would be willing to let me take Kassidy back to Amy. There was not much to be known of his family for we had only met a few of them at Amy and Aaron's wedding. After saying goodbyes to everyone I drove west of town toward Cynthiana Road that would connect me to I-64. My journey had begun. I could not help but notice the numerous American flags that seemed to be in places I had never noticed before on this drive through the countryside, with its rural fields and farms. I felt anxious yet secure in making this journey. I felt content knowing I would soon see my granddaughter and daughter together again.

The trip would be bearable if there was music to serenade me along the way. It kept me awake. A local station of rock soothed my weary mind and as I lost the station, I turned to the stash of CDs that were resting in the passenger seat. I popped in a patriotic instrumental and listened as, at a distance down the westward highway, I could see a huge American flag draped over the highway from the above overpass. There was a crew working on the north side of the highway near the flag. A sense of pride swelled up in me and I gave a honk as I approached the symbol of our country. The workers waved back in response.

I kept the usual speed as to not chance a ticket that would delay my trip. To stay awake I paid attention to the license plates of the cars that seemed to pass me at greater speeds than the speed limit. Once I started doing this I noticed cars filled with three or four businessmen brandishing New York license plates. Two or three times I saw this. The planes were not flying. I could only imagine what the premium of getting a rental car in New York might have been. It was one of the few modes of transportation for these business folks trying to get back home. I wondered what their destination was. Colorado? Oklahoma City? California? I wished them well and said a short prayer for their safe voyage home, wherever that may be.

I had hoped to reach Tulsa my first day. The hours had passed quickly as I voyaged through all the towns along I-64 to St. Louis, then 44 to Springfield, Missouri. I made a stop at a McDonalds and called Tim to tell him where I was and that everything was alright. *"Hi hun,"* I said. *"What are you doing?"* *"Thinking of you and wondering where you are. Is everything okay?"* he asked. *"Yes,"* I replied. We exchanged I love yous and the voyage restarted. It was going to be getting dark soon and Tulsa was on the horizon. I passed through Tulsa and stopped to sleep in a small town of Sapulpa. The attendant was pleasant and said there was one room left in the small hotel near the desk and lobby. I was growing tired and somewhat hungry. I asked where there would be a place to eat. She said, *"There's a good steak restaurant down the hill."*

It was pleasing to know I did not have to get back in the car, so I walked down the hill after checking into my room. I felt lonely and ached for someone to talk to, tell my plight to, to share my weary thoughts with. I had to keep a strong faith for my family. Staying well and having control of the situation was my main goal. The place was packed, a good sign I had picked the right spot. Eventually I was shown to a table. All around I could hear conversations and bits and pieces of the 9/11 attacks. There were some conversations about family. Some spoke in Spanish. After a while the voices just sounded like noise to me. I had to eat and felt I had to get out of this place. Only eating half of what I ordered I returned to my room. Hoping for a good night's rest, I began to toss and turn. Every conversation in the lobby was audible and the loud banging and dumping of the ice machine was just outside my door. Finally falling asleep to exhaustion at around ten, I awoke fully at three in the morning and then again at four. Sleep would not come, so I dressed and decided to drive once more. The morning was quiet and calming to my weary head. As I checked out, the night attendant wished me well on my travels. *"Have a safe trip."* *Noticing my ID and seeing that I was from Indiana,* she stated, *"I see you're far from home."* *"Yes,"* I stated hesitantly. I felt compelled to tell her why. There was no one else around so I told her, *"Because of 9/11 my family was separated and I am traveling to New Mexico then to Arizona to reunite my granddaughter to my daughter."* She very caringly said, *"Be careful honey. I wish you well on your trip. God bless."* I said thanks and headed for my car in the darkness of the early Oklahoma morning.

It was nice having the road to myself. There was a peacefulness about it and it gave me time to think. As I saw signs that announced the upcoming town of Oklahoma City, a flashback came to me, of the Oklahoma City bombing that had taken place in 1997 and my family's visit to the memorial. There were many unfilled chairs and reflective ponds of water in the heart of downtown. I began to wonder when the terrorism would stop. Would bridges and modes of transportation be their next target? I prayed, *"Dear Lord, save us from evil and grant us your peace. Amen."* Without thinking, I accidently drove up an Oklahoma City exit ramp as if something was steering me in that direction. I stopped and realized what I had done. There were no cars in the darkness behind me, so I backed down the ramp and continued my way on I-40. I needed to focus on my driving and not let my mind wander. I was thankful for a safe car and once again, had a talk with God. *"Thank you for this reliable vehicle and thank you for keeping me safe."* There would be many talks with God on this trip. Asking him why all this could happen, how our lives were turned upside down knowing there would likely be no answer. The time would be taken one day, one hour at a time. We had to be thankful for that and for each other.

As the morning came, I called Tim and told him where I was- between Oklahoma City and Albuquerque. He said, *"Did you sleep last night?"* I told him about the noisy sleeping conditions. I could sense a feeling of concern in his voice. Assuredly I calmed his fears and promised a better night's sleep tonight.

I had never driven this far southwest before, so the scenery was new to me. There seemed to be more American flags than ever before proudly displayed from many homes and businesses. A definite welcoming sign for the unification the country was feeling.

By the time I had reached Albuquerque, Amy had called and said Kassidy was no longer in Las Cruces but closer to me in Copper City, New Mexico. I was relieved to hear the news. I now had to stop and map out the way to Copper City. It lay west of I-40, south of Albuquerque, halfway to Las Cruces. There were no directions from Amy as to the best way to get there, so I chose what appeared to be the shortest means of highway to connect me to this sleepy little town nestled in the mountains. As I drove, I saw a sign for a town called Truth or Consequences. I drove through it before I knew it! Wonder what the story was to this little town on the map... Driving and driving took me further into the desert plains. Occasionally I saw a makeshift shelter for roadside sales of Indian blankets, baskets, and jewelry. I wanted to stop but was too much in a hurry and fearful that I would encounter some misfortune if I did stop. So I chose to continue down the highway.

The vastness of the desert was intriguing and it contained its own beauty. The plains gave way to rockier terrain as I headed south to the Elephant Butte Mountain area. A small highway sign pointed west to Copper City. By my calculations I would be there by nightfall if no unforeseen obstacles would arise. After just a few miles, I noticed a large panoramic view of what became mountainous terrain. I could see the road winding up at its feet. Before I knew it I was driving switchbacks. Back and forth, back and forth, I climbed the mountain. The Subaru handled well. I went slowly enough so I could drive with just one hand, as I took the gently curves on the mountainside. As I came to the peak of the mountain top, I looked out after slowing the car to almost a stop. There it was. I had seen it in my mind many times in the song, *"Oh beautiful for spacious skies, for amber waves of grain. For purple mountain's majesty...."* I could see, as far as I could see, beautiful purple hues of mountain peaks. It took my breath away. I had only wanted to take a picture but saw that it was too dangerous to linger long on this narrow, winding road. I slowly traversed the downhill side of the mountain that took another hour to descend. I would never forget the beautiful and majestic mountains.

At the foot of the mountain were small wooden homes with wooden fences and gates in the yards and sandy driveways. Trying to see the colorful details of the homes I tried not to stare but took in the presence of a part of the country I had never seen before. The rains had come and a sweetness filled the car. I could only wonder where it had come from while I enjoyed the aroma. It smelled of sweet pine and honeysuckle. The sun was hanging low in the sky, just along the pines. I had finally reached the town of Copper City. I called Amy and asked her for directions to Kassidy's grandparents' home. Al and Maria were awaiting my arrival. I had never met them before and was anxious to do so, but even more so to see Kassidy. I had to curb my anxiety once again and keep at the task of finding their home in this new town. I passed a new Wal-Mart Amy had mentioned. I found my way to the town square as Amy had described, but made a wrong turn. I pulled the car to the curb in the park and asked a young couple pushing a stroller, *"Can you show me how to get to Miller Street?"* They pointed over my shoulder and said, *"It's right behind you."* They continued on their way and spoke Spanish as they disappeared around the corner. I knew I was in the right place and in just a few minutes I would arrive.

I traveled up the steep hill and saw a stucco house with a wraparound porch and heavy brown, carved wooden porch posts. Two hand-carved bears greeted me as I rounded the corner of the house. The sandy driveway led to the back of the house. It was a beautiful view of the surrounding mountains. As I opened the car door I could see a small garden patch and a small walk up to the back door. As I stood on the porch and began to knock, I noticed a large screen perched on two chairs. Upon the screen were loads of red, yellow, and orange peppers laying out to dry. The house gave me a sense of warmth. Lost in the beauty of my surroundings, the door flew open. There stood a small Hispanic woman. She said in broken English, *"Are you Michelle?"* I said, *"Yes"* and asked, *"Are you Maria?"* *"Yes,"* she said with a large smile. She quickly invited me into her home. And there sitting on the living room floor was Kassidy. *"We are so glad to meet you. How did you ever find our house?"* she asked. I could not believe myself that I had found my way, but I felt as if God had a lot to do with it. Besides, I had talked to him most of the way here! Maria offered me a glass of tea as I began to pick Kassidy up and give her hugs and kisses.

"Thank you for letting me come to get Kassidy," I said gratefully. Maria had started making supper before my arrival. The roasted chicken smelled delicious and I entered the small kitchen. The house had stood for many years and lent a feeling of home in its walls. She began to prepare guacamole for me to taste with warm chips. She said, *"Do you like guacamole?"* I said yes while lowering Kassidy onto my knee. She said while showing me, *"you leave the pit in so the guacamole doesn't turn brown."* I smiled at her and enjoyed her sweet voice. She said, *"I speak better Spanish than I do English."* I assured her, *"You speak English just fine."* We both smiled.

Shortly after, Al returned home from his job at the copper mines. He introduced himself, *"Hello, I am Al, Aaron's father."* *"Glad to meet you,"* I said with a warm handshake. Once again I thanked them for their hospitality. After a delicious meal we sat at the lace-covered dining room table. Al confessed, *"You know, one time Amy sat exactly in the chair you are in. I told her it was best not to marry Aaron. I am sorry for all that has happened."* I could only smile and agree.

He was a large-shouldered man with hardworking and rustic hands, yet had a soft voice. We talked about our families, our children especially, and how our lives had unfolded up until now. We laughed when I asked him about the Elephant "Butt" Mountain Range. Obviously I was not familiar with the terrain or its mapping. I found out there was a highway north of Copper City that would have me bypass the mountains. But what a beautiful sight it was. It grew late and he said he had to get up early to work at the Copper Mines. So I said, *"Good night."* Maria had made me a place to sleep on a daybed inside an addition to the stucco living room. It was comfortable and I felt at peace knowing my journey would soon be over. It must have been five in the morning when I awoke. It was still dark outside and I could see light under Al and Maria's bedroom door. He must be getting ready for work. Try as I might to go back to sleep, I just could not. I lay quietly as he let himself out the front door to his car. I imagined what the rest of the trip would be like. Would the baby be good for me? Maybe she would sleep a lot. I prayed again for help and assurance.

I began my climb from the Copper City valley after saying my sad goodbye to Maria. I thought to myself, *"When would I see her again?"* As I drove I noticed a sign that read, *"Entering the Continental Divide."* It was hard to believe I had reached such an interesting place. I slowed the car down as the sign approached "Sight of the Continental Divide." The Great Divide was the place where a line separates areas draining to opposite sides of the continent. It separates the westward and eastward flowing water. Pondering for a moment, I slowly accelerated the car and continued down the snaking road as far as the eye could see. Settled in for a long five hours of driving ahead of me, I noticed occasional dots of the Saguaro cactus with its thick arm-like appendages stretching out into the desert sun. What caught my eye to the right shoulder was a large at least ten-foot-tall cactus with a large bird on its upper limb. Once again, I slowed down, noticing that no cars were behind me. The bird sat stately on its perch. I had recognized this bird before. It was far from any tree. It seemed out of place, out in this hot, arid desert. On further discovery, I saw what appeared to be a large, eagle-type bird. It wore a white headdress and had a thick gold beak. I stopped the car and gave a keen study of this beautiful bird. Its symbol to me on this trip was so meaningful. I thought at first I was hallucinating, but it was as real as the thick, tall-standing cactus. I thought deeply about how this beautiful bird was a symbol of our country. With our great country so grief-stricken, it was hard for its citizens to keep their heads up like this fine specimen. It gave me great courage and I thanked God for its presence and drove away, slowly embarking once again on my journey. The vivid picture has always remained fresh in my mind.

I thought back on my previous days of driving and how I had traversed a large part of the country. My mind drifted as I drove. There were no contrails to be seen in any direction in this vast, open sky. I imagined how the grounding of the planes had interrupted so many lives. A small prayer was offered for the return and luxury of flying. There were no radio stations to be found except for one faintly mentioning baseball. It seemed insignificant at the time to be discussing baseball for whatever few stations I did receive were revolving around the tragedy of 9/11. I slipped into another time and place while the white lines of the highway sped by my navy blue Subaru.

୧

I was taken back in memory to 1991. It was a good year. The kids were in school and I was enjoying a *normal* time of my life. There was talk of a movie being made in town. Its name was *A League of Their Own*. I had not given it much thought. There were pleads over the TV and radio for extras to dress in the 1940s period. I decided to give it a try. The first filming of the movie was in Huntingburg, Indiana. I spoke to my mom about going. She thought it would be a fun excursion. Maybe, taking my eldest son, Matt- thirteen at the time- out of school would be a learning experience for him. We rounded up the necessary historical attire to wear and headed for Huntingburg. We soon learned we were not needed in the ballpark where the filming was taking place. So there we stood with nothing to do. We took pictures and headed home. Within a few weeks there was a need for more extras, even children were called this time. Would it not be ideal to take my two daughters Amy, age eleven, and Carrie, age nine, out of school to let them experience the movie set too? I felt sure that this time we would get to enter the ballpark.

We were greeted with hundreds of others at trailers that were designated for makeup and costumes. I had also brought a friend's daughter along, Tracey, who was Carrie's age. Her mother was watching my youngest at the time. The four of us followed the line and were given vouchers in exchange for our clothes. We looked like we had just stepped out of the WWII era. The girls had bobby socks with cutely-printed dresses. Their hair was done up in high braids. Amy wore her hair long with a rosette made from her hair. The girls would not change their hairstyle for days afterward. I was dressed in a blue, knee-length skirt with a coral blouse and matching hat of the same color. We were given tickets for a free lunch, hot dog, popcorn, and soda. The popcorn boxes and soda cups were vintage in design and were used during the filming.

In makeup there were no shortcuts. Lines were even applied to the back of the ladies legs to emulate the lined, seamed stockings of the time. An eyebrow pencil was used from above the back of the knee to the back of the ankle. The only prop I brought with me was a white hankerchief. Women of this time always carried a hanky! We were all herded to the stands and sat patiently as more of the filming crew sat up their equipment on the baseball field. A sense of excitement filled the stadium. There were cardboard busts of male and female extras that dotted the stands and we sat in and around them. It drew a few good laughs. The girls were especially excited over their new clothes and hairstyles, and the fact that they were out of school. We shared refreshments as the movie crew started placing people down in front and behind home plate. All of a sudden a person with a rolodex of Polaroid pictures waved towards the crowd near me. It was unclear as to what the instructions were. There was pointing and a gesture to come down. There was confusion as to whom they were directing to come down from the masses. Finally it was clear they wanted me! I told the girls *"Do not move from here and stay together. I'll be right down there,"* gesturing toward the bleacher seats behind the front corner stands. *"Hurry,"* the woman said, clad in blue jeans and a t-shirt.

As I approached the area I discovered the aisles were blocked. *"Climb over the seats and sit right here,"* said another person dressed in every day attire. I followed their abrupt orders. There were not many *"please"* and *"thank yous"* at this point. I could sense the urgency of their requests. It was not long before Penny Marshall was standing right in front of me behind the seat that came between the extras and the baseball field. She said, *"There are times we want you to cheer, but with no sound. There will be times when we want the sound and cheering."* I was mimicking how to cheer in a timeless, exaggerated manner. She looked directly at me and said, *"This isn't the silent movies. Just act and cheer naturally like you're at the ball game."* I took her direction and sat back in my seat with the rest of the crowd. By now, the lighting umbrellas were being placed upon us and we were instructed to cheer loudly and excitedly with no sound. We stood up and clapped and cheered silently. It was difficult at first but fun, as you got into it. I waved my hanky as if to cheer the team on as I cupped my hands and let out a loud soundless cheer.

This lasted about half an hour to an hour. Occasionally I looked up into the crowd. I could barely see the girls and knew by now they were probably growing restless. I had much to share with them about the experience that had just taken place. As the afternoon wound down, so did the need for the chosen crowd to remain in their assigned parts. We returned our costumes after taking some pictures with a Racine team ball player and a group shot of us near the fountain at the entrance to Garvin Park, near the Bosse Field Stadium. The stadium had been transformed to the movie sets depiction of WWII era All-American Girls Baseball League playing field. We enjoyed our fellow Evansville west-siders that showed up in costume the day of the World Series shoot. A friend of mine, Janet, had her parents arrived on the scene looking rather, what I would call, frumpy. From that day forward, any time I would see them out and about I would address them as Mr. and Mrs. Frump.

It was fun to watch the movie stars featured in the movie. Geena Davis, Rosie O'Donnell, and Tom Hanks kept the crowds entertained between shoots and Madonna, who gestured to the crowds, would later state that Evansville was like visiting Prague. We did not really care what she said about us anyway. We were having the time of our lives. The crowds were large and there was definitely a good show of community support. It would be months before the regular extras and plain extras, like me, would learn if we had been snipped and fallen to the producer's floor. I later learned that I had made the cut, hanky and all, in the first row left of screen. This took place during the World Series scene. I always kind of thought about my hanky possibly being an SOS for mental illness, waving alone in the massive crowd.

For miles I had followed the seamless landscape of large rocks and boulders and sandy land as far as the eye could see. I had to leave the beauty of what had been and become more aware of my surroundings. What innocent and happy times I remembered. Look at the state of things now. To stay awake, I would continue to count the occupants in cars and pickups and note where the license plates indicated they came from. I had placed, carefully in the back window of the car, two decals, one being the school New Hope and the other a fire department patch belonging to Tim. I felt this could be of assistance if I had gotten into any trouble. The fire department family extended throughout the country and they would recognize me as one of their own. I also wore a Maltese cross on a golden chain for the same reason. Before I had left home, I placed a medium-size flag to show my solidarity to my country on the dash above the back seat. Passing semi-trucks would give a short blast when I would pass them as they too would share their union of our spirited nation's feelings. Playing the plate game, I continued to keep my mind alert and from drawing the stories from my traveled mind. My sweet granddaughter Kassidy had stayed asleep during these hours of travels. I only had to stop once, at a truck stop, between Albuquerque and the Arizona border. It was time for a Kassidy's diaper change and I needed to try to get something to eat. I purchased a hamburger that tasted like a huge chunk of cardboard. The soft drink went down smoothly. I had not eaten much since leaving Al and Maria's. The baby took a bottle and fell fast asleep. Thank God the car's humming tires cradled her into a deep slumber while I counted the miles to my destination in Surprise, Arizona.

There was still little to no traffic on the highway. At last, I saw and approached a white tractor-trailer and glad for someone else for this lonesome highway. Maybe I would get the usual, a toot of recognition, as I passed. There were no identifying marks on the trailer. The plates were simply black and white. Most of the trucks I passed were from Arizona or Texas. Creeping along the side of the truck, I noticed no name or company on its door. I thought it sort of strange. After returning to the right lane of the highway and looking and checking my mirrors, I caught the glimpse of the male truck driver. He had a terrified look on his face.

Unlike all the others that usually brandished a smile or blasted gesture from their horns, the man wore a white turban upon his head. I had never seen a face like his on anyone else before. It was not so much a frightening look, now that I caught a really close look at him. But it was an indifferent, menacing look. I shuddered to think who he was and what he was hauling. There was no way of identifying the white truck and I felt helpless in a car by myself with a baby. There was no good way to call somebody to report this sighting on my cell-phone. Would it do any good anyway? I sped away, not knowing what to do. I could not have felt any lonelier or afraid at that very minute. Longing to arrive in Phoenix and then Surprise, I decided to call Amy. She had worked late into the evening. My mind was in shock over the truck driver. Was he someone I should report? I denied for now what I had seen and continued my conversation with Amy. She gave me directions past the landmarks in Phoenix, past Luke Air Force Base and finally to her home in Surprise. By now, I was only two hours away. I knew relaxing and embracing my daughter finally would be my next stop. I thanked the dear Lord for cell-phones. I could not have made the trip without it and the saving grace of God that led me through the lonely times along the way.

Amy said she would meet me outside her house. She was a sight for sore eyes. She quickly ran to the back door of the car and screeched a shout of joy as she snatched Kassidy up from her car seat. I almost cry now thinking of this reunion. We quickly entered her home where we sat and talked while she fed Kassidy. The baby and I had traveled so far. It was now time to take a deep breath and finally have some peace of mind. There was still an uneasy feeling about the truck driver I had seen several hours earlier. I explained to Amy the look in the driver's face and the fact that there were no distinct markings on the truck. It was too late for me to get the license number as I passed the truck. Although I had remembered the first few numbers as 705 and could not recall the rest. I told her maybe I should call someone. The truck had been headed for Phoenix. Reporting it would probably not do any good at this point, but at least it would ease my mind. Reporting calls like this did not happen every day. But what was normal nowadays? I continued rehashing the experience over and over in my mind as I looked up the number for the police who directed me to the number of the F.B.I. A deep voice answered *"Federal Bureau of Investigation."* I took a breath and explained the story to the man at the other end of the line. *"I know it's probably too late by now, but I was unable to make the call at the time,"* I said. *"In what direction was he traveling ma'am,"* he inquired. *"West. West on I-40 toward Phoenix."* *"There's not much we can do now,"* he said. *"But thank you for your call. You did the right thing."* I hung up and felt some relief, but still wondered what the man's destination was.

For several days and nights I took care of Kassidy: her feedings, naps, and diaper changes. There was not much else to do. I would turn to the TV while Amy continued her twelve-hour shifts. When she returned to her home, she was pretty much exhausted and slept most of the time. I called Tim and Mom about every day to tell them how things were. A week passed and Dad was asking, *"How much longer are you going to stay?"* *"I am not for sure, Dad. We need to find a babysitter to take my place so Kassidy can stay here with Amy. I am working on it."*

Amy's house was barely decorated, but I began to notice how much red was in the scant décor. A large picture of her husband, Kassidy, and she adorned the wall above the couch. There was a garland of ivy and red flowers above her kitchen cabinets and a note board by the phone trimmed with a red floral design. She had blue Ball canning jars to store dry food items in on the counters. The dining room was furnished with a table, chairs, and the baby's highchair. Kassidy's many colorful toys dotted the floors when she was awake. She had begun to crawl and play with them. The room where I slept contained an air mattress and was an office with a desk, chair, and Amy's computer. All of Aaron's hunting posters and a wolf calendar adorned the walls. Aaron had not been heard of for the first few days after I had arrived. He was no longer staying at the house. Amy had a large bedroom that still contained Aaron's personal effects and she had no idea when or if he would return. There was a feeling of uneasiness about the two.

Discussing the reasons for him leaving was not disclosed. Just a small comment from Amy, *"He's with his high-school sweetheart."* Amy and Aaron had met not but a few years prior. They both had worked in the kitchen together on the base. The next thing they we knew Amy told us she was expecting and there would be a summer wedding in 2000. With reservations about the wedding, Tim and I made the trip to Phoenix and attended at the justice of the peace in a court building. Friends and some of the two families were present. I was disappointed there was not more of a larger church wedding, so the whole family could attend. This is what Amy wanted. I brought a bridesmaid's bouquet from my wedding. It covered the tradition of something borrowed, something blue. Usually a mother has a sense of family. Both Amy and Aaron were young and had not really shared the same viewpoints of husband and wife, much less a mother and father. Amy was a good mother to Kassidy. Aaron was more concerned about vehicles and had expectations like that of a young, teenage boy. There was hope they would have a future, especially for Kassidy's sake. Within a year that promise was proven wrong. I did not want to get in the middle of any squabbles and felt the urgency to find a sitter for Kassidy. Another side of me was in no hurry to leave. One afternoon after feeding Kassidy and putting her down for a nap, Aaron came bouncing through the front door of the living room, unannounced. He surprised me with his visit. I was happy that we were into a routine of meal and nap time with the baby. He said loudly, *"Where's Kassidy? I want to play with her!"* I firmly but calmly said, *"She's taking a nap. Let sleeping babies lie."* He would not hear of it. He started for the baby's bedroom door. A little louder I said, *"You do not live here anymore and I am telling you to let her sleep."* He stopped dead in his tracks and turned to me without uttering a single word. He calmly sat at the kitchen table. I returned to the sink and continued to dry the dishes I had washed by hand. Hoping to ignore him and carefully deciding what to tell him next. From the corner of my eye I saw him take a bowie knife from under his pant leg. Immediately I thought, do not panic. Do not say a word. He continued to raise the knife up and down and run its sharp blade between his fingertips, repeatedly. The silence was broken not words but by him putting the knife back in its sheath. He got up and left the house without saying anything. Trembling I called Tim, *"I can't believe what just happened here,"* I told him while fighting back tears.

Tim could not believe what I had told him. In a protective tone he said, *"If he so much as touches you, Amy, or Kassidy, I will find a way to come out there and kick his ass."* I thought to myself it would be too late for Tim to do anything if Aaron decided to hurt us. Tim added, *"I do not care if the planes aren't flying, I will get to you as soon as I can!"* To settle things down I asked, *"How are the kids? Tell them I miss them."* I assured him I would be careful but firm with Aaron. I would call the police and there were other people I could call at the air base if things got out of hand. Explaining the day's events to Amy was upsetting. By now she was, again, fed up with Aaron's behavior. I soon realized why their relationship had come to be so negative.

Amy continued her twelve-hour shifts and I began to have trouble sleeping at night. The overly active dog would knock his metal food dishes together during the night. The hamster Amy had inherited from a friend had a metallic squeal and grind to its wheel and it ran through the entire night. I could feel myself losing ground. Aaron called several days after his last visit. *"Good morning,"* he said in an elevated happy mood. There was a long pause on my end of the phone. I started, *"Excuse me young man. The next time you visit here, you had better call first."* *"Yes ma'am,"* He replied. *"You had better not lay a hand on me, Amy, or Kassidy. Do you understand?"* *"Yes ma'am,"* he said reverently. *"I might add if you hurt any of us for any reason you will have my husband to deal with."* Once again, he answered, *"Yes ma'am."*

His military training in regards to authority figures must have kicked in. *"We are packing your items that are in the house. Amy will call you when we're finished boxing up your stuff. You'll be able to pick them up in the garage."* *"Yes ma'am,"* he said softly. We were finished with our conversation and I put the phone down. A sense of relief came over me. I did not look forward to a visit from him again, knife or no knife.

Amy and I went yard-saling as she finally got a Saturday off of work. I think she remembered all the fun we had yard-saling when she was younger. We did not know the area that well, but mapped out the sales by following the signs. Amy's house was in much need of some decorating and Kassidy needed some larger clothes, so we set off on our rummage adventure. We drove a mile or so away and came upon an old, two-story wooden house with a dilapidated garage and chickens running around a jimmy-rigged fence with gates for fencing. All the sale items were on blankets near the sandy shoulder of the road. The sun was hot for September so we left the air conditioning on in the car to keep Kassidy cool as we quickly looked over the merchandise. At once my eye caught a set of beautifully hand-painted, oil still-life paintings. The rich tones of browns, reds, and yellows portrayed the apples and pitchers remarkably well. They were signed by Zori. The family did not have any information as to where the paintings originated. I snatched them up and gave five dollars for the framed art work. We quickly returned to the cool comfort of the car. I had forgotten how hot the desert is even for the fall season. We traveled a short distance down the main thoroughfare and turned into a nice suburb of newer, two-story homes. This sale was spread upon the concrete driveway and there were many items to look over. Amy saw a sash that could be used above her large window of her living room. The price was right so it was ours. We rummaged through a tall stack of children's clothes and found some cute outfits for Kassidy. We even picked up a like-new Disney VCR tape of The Emperor's New Groove. We had managed to fill the trunk for less than twenty dollars. It was a good day for us shoppers.

Amy and I were pretty frugal and kept most of our dining to home. We ate out only a few times during my stay with her. We both had limited budgets. The only time I used the credit card was for gas and a stop at a health food store. I had developed a nagging sore throat and knew if I could get some Mediterranean oil of oregano in me, the symptoms would be relieved. We found a store not far from Surprise and inquired as to the location of the oregano. The sales clerk quickly showed us the oil; it was the exact same brand I had used at home. Nearby I noticed a book on how to better your health by use of oregano oil. I used the credit card for this too, along with the outstanding box of blackstrap molasses licorice I purchased. We had an eventful day and that evening came rather quickly. We were all tired and rested well for the night.

The next day was Sunday. After feeding Kassidy, we set off for Amy's Catholic parish, St. Damiano. It was about a ten minute drive to the new church. There was a one-story brick church with an adjoining social hall and offices. We arrived early and were greeted with friendly parishioners. I was used to larger churches back home with side altars and stained-glass windows. Amy told me the parish was planning for a larger church. So much of the growth in the area was putting a pinch on many neighborhood services like the post office and schools. The growing parish community was no exception. As we sat and waited for Mass to start I looked up to the altar. There were no adornments except for the single large San Damiano Cross that hung upon the tan-painted concrete block wall. I would later learn the story of the San Damiano cross. It is a Romanesque crucifix that St. Francis of Assisi was praying before when he received the commission from the Lord to rebuild the church. The iconic cross intrigued me by its many images of other saints and people related to the Christ's crucifixion. The church needed no other decoration or spiritual reminder that you were in the presence of God and his people. I had noticed stacks of holy cards depicting the San Damiano Cross as we entered the church. I dropped a few dollars in the small collection box near the cards. I took eight of the cards and put them in my purse. Sometime during the mass, I thanked God for all his blessings. Christmas would be fast approaching. I asked how I could prepare a simple gift to my family. The trip to Amy's and the length of my stay would hinder my usual preparation of homemade gifts for the family. I thought the cards could be put in frames and given as a special gift for my children, parents, and grandmother. I was happy to share my God-given talent and set out to make the unique Christmas gifts.

After a week or so, Amy, Kassidy, and I enjoyed another Saturday of rummaging. I was lucky to find two wallpaper sample books for next to nothing. Now all I needed were eight frames to place the holy cards in. We attended church another Sunday and I met Joan and Kenny. I had become anxious over Amy's work schedule and her pending divorce and could feel a sense of uneasiness developing. As I talked with the couple, I learned they were part of a prayer chain. *Would you like for us to add you and your family to our prayers?* Joan asked. *"I would sure appreciate that,"* I replied thankfully.

As the days passed, I became increasingly restless and irritable. My euphoria over my craft creation and watching and caring for Kassidy while Amy was away on her long hour shifts left me lonely and blue. I would talk to my parents who would ask again, *"When do you think you're coming home?"* I only became frustrated knowing that a sitter needed to be found and I was the one who was likely going to be doing the finding. There was not much time for Amy to search the neighborhood for possible sitters. During those lonesome days I would take Kassidy for long stroller rides in Amy's subdivision. I befriended several neighbors and had potential sitters. Some nice teenage girls had very helpful parents that offered to let the girls babysit. A neighbor across the street, both the husband and the wife had attended a high school back in my hometown of Evansville. I also met a divorcee who had several children of her own. She had previously been married to an Air Force gentleman. She understood how the military demands were placed on families. We became close friends. Another family offered to have her teenage daughters help us out for three to four weeks with watching Kassidy. This was an answer to my prayers, at least for a while until Amy could find someone on a permanent basis. I invited the girls, with permission from their parents, to come over and get acquainted with Kassidy and me. The girls were friendly and very responsible. I was happy to have met them and felt they would be a great asset in the future.

As pleased as I was, the loneliness seemed to clinch even deeper into my daily affairs. Nights were long as I found myself tossing and turning. I finally asked Amy if I could find a home for her pet hamster- the squeaking wheel under its feet kept my eyes from closing. She said, *"Ask some of the neighbor kids if they'd like to give it a home."* I was relieved at her response. Now if I could just get the dog to settle down at night... There must have been much puppy still residing in this particular dog. Aaron had paid good money for it but it lacked any demonstration of control whatsoever. To feed or water it usually rendered you with bloody scratches from its endless jumping and pawing. I hated taking care of this manic pet, not to mention I could not let Kassidy outside in the yard. We were sequestered to the house, except for the occasional stroller rides.

I began to worry more about Amy excessively. She would tell me how tired she was and some nights I would talk to her and keep her awake as she drove home from the base. We had only brief encounters with Aaron, but she had to work with him daily at her job. Amy shared with me that there were two bomb threats at the base. It was unsettling to hear this news, not to mention the constant roar of F-16s above our heads as the pilots trained at nearby Luke Air Force Base.

The baby was good and could not have acted any better. She had a good routine. I wished my routine of good sleep could return. I had become more prayerful than usual. Insistently I prayed *Hail Mary* and *Our Father* prayers. I felt Aaron had become evil like the devil and felt fearful of the possibility that he might come by and cause us harm. I began to delve into a state of religiosity like never before. I made crosses with my fingers at the inside corners of the windows and doors of the house. Kassidy had not been baptized so I called my home parish and asked the priest how to baptize an infant. I felt impending doom. My bizarre actions did not interfere with my daily responsibility and caring for Kassidy. I loved her very much and remained the doting Grandma as my illness began to take hold of me.

It was now the twenty eighth of September. I had been at Amy's for nearly two weeks. I could no longer take the dog nor his banging and clanging of his dog bowls at night. I guess the simplest thing to do was take the bowls out of the yard at night, but this dog became a nemesis and he belonged to Aaron, who never stopped by to care for the dog. One night while Amy was at work, I went to feed and water the dog. This was the last time he would jump on me. I quickly walked over to the gate to the back yard and opened it. The last thing I saw was the white dogs butt running down the sidewalk as fast as he could run. *"Good riddance,"* I said aloud. Pleased at myself I closed the gate, cleaned up the dog piles in the yard and brought Kassidy outside to enjoy the fall evening. Amy became very upset with me. *"Mom, what is wrong with you?"* she yelled. *"That was Aaron's dog. He'll be upset. He paid lots of money for that dog!"* *"Well, he should've taken it with him when he left,"* I replied. *"Besides, it will probably find a better home."* My feelings were not hurt and I even felt justified in letting the dog free.

I watched the Disney movie with Kass, *The Emperor's New Groove,* and felt Aaron's behavior was like the Emperor's: self-indulgent and juvenile. It fed my mind's eye of him. I wanted to change him into a llama. My manic expressions of religion and focusing on colors increased, giving me feelings or affiliation with the devil. I removed all red things from the kitchen while Amy was at work and put them in a bag. She, of course noticed this and said, *"Mom, are you okay? Why did you take down my garland on top of the kitchen cabinets?"* She questioned, nodding her head. *"I do not know."* I stammered. Amy knew she should be concerned, but what could she do and who could she call?

XI

Off-Track

∽

All too well, I began to recognize the signs, manic signs that had finally caught up with me. I had to make a run to Target to get diapers for Kassidy. After placing her in her car seat and locking the house, I methodically mapped my way to the store several miles away. My concentration became more determined. I dismissed my anxiety and continued through the sprawling traffic. I had grown accustomed to packing Kassidy's diaper bag wherever I went with her, so I would be prepared for a diaper change or quick bottle to feed her. I arrived at Target in Sun City on a Sunday afternoon. I grabbed my purse and diaper bag as I carefully put Kassidy into the shopping cart seat and fastened her in. My mind seemed preoccupied but able to shop for the things on my list. After searching for the right size diaper, I roamed about the store and found the eight frames on clearance I had hoped to find for my Christmas presents. So I carefully picked out some that would go nicely with the holy cards that I would matte with the wallpaper book scraps. I was pleased at the creative thought and began to browse once more through the store. My mind began to race. A euphoria yet keen cautionary feeling overwhelmed me. The two feelings alternated momentarily. I panicked as I put a small bottle of Vanilla Fields perfume in the cart. A rush of intense fear took hold of my mind. Did I have too many items, I thought to myself? Had I over-shopped and had no control over my choice of purchases?

I began to take gasps of air. I quickly checked face-to-face with Kassidy and found her to be just fine. I had had these feelings before. I was not hysterical on the outside but I felt as though my thoughts were getting away from me. A flighty thought of common sense struck me if ever so briefly. *"Go to the pharmacy,"* I told myself, *"they can call the doctor and get you ordered some Ativan."* Yes, this is what I could do. Quickly I rushed to the pharmacy. My mind picked up momentum. I once again checked Kassidy and fed her a bottle while she sat patiently in the cart. I approached the overhead pharmacy sign and gained some reassurance. My heart sank as I read the sign, *Closed on Sunday.* Becoming panic-stricken once again, I knew not to get in the car with Kassidy. My fear of forgetting the way home became even more intense. How would I get help?

I quickly pulled out and unfolded the yellow paper that I had written important family names and numbers on– too many to memorize. I promptly looked up Amy's work number as another anxious wave struck me. I had to reach her. Maybe she could come and pick us up somehow. For a fleeting moment I thought, could this be happening? The phone rang and rang. *"Hello,"* Amy said.

"I do not know how to tell you this Amy, but I need my Ativan at your house. I am shopping at Target. I am afraid to get in the car with Kassidy. I won't be able to find my way back to your house safely," I exclaimed. *"They won't let me leave here now,"* she said excitedly. *"I just can't leave. Is Kassidy okay?"* she asked. *"Yes,"* I said. *"I think I am getting sick again. I need help getting to the hospital to get some meds. The pharmacy is closed."* I said. Downtrodden and disappointed, I felt shame to have let this happen. I asked again, *"Who can help me?"* She could only say, *"Call 9-1-1."* There was a long pause, *"Maybe I could get Aaron to take you to the hospital!"* She said in a half-surprising tone laden with a lack of confidence. I said, *"I do not think that is a good idea."* My problem was what to do with Kassidy. I could see both of us riding in an ambulance and my mind was racing and my heart beating faster. I feared losing complete control. Amy said, *"Make the call for help and I'll try to get some kind of answer from Aaron.*

Are you at the Target on Dysart?" she asked. *"Yes I am. I love you Amy and I am sorry for all of this!"*

Now I needed to find help. My phone had died and I was at the mercy of my ever-changing, rapid-fire mind. I approached a young man in a Target smock and asked him, *"Could you help me?"* He fully expected to help me find a camera or something else I am sure, for I was now standing in the electronics department. *"What can I help you find?"* Saying *"my mind!"* would not have sufficed, but would have at least been the truth.

I went on to explain, *"I have a mental illness and I have gotten sick since I've come to your store. My daughter cannot leave her job to help me. She's at the Air Force Base. Can you help me and call 9-1-1? I need to go to the hospital."* He stammered, quite shocked at my request for I stood beside him cool and calm and spoke in a normal tone. My mind continued to race throughout the long wait for help. I attended to Kassidy and changed her diaper. By now some of the female employees had gathered around me and offered to help. There was nothing they could do. There was nothing to help with Kassidy. She was content and was playing with her bottle as she took small sips of it. I remained calm on the outside and tried to calm myself on the inside as I went through the checkout lane and paid for my purchases. I am sure everyone was confused by now. I know I surely was. I stayed close by the pharmacy as Carlos stayed nearby with his store radio in hand. He had been so helpful. The fire department and an ambulance arrived within a few moments. I felt overwhelmed by now, but knew a trip to the hospital would surely be the best thing I could do. By now the women had taken Kassidy from the cart and were playing with her. It seemed as if everyone and their brother had surrounded me. I did not feel threatened, just overwhelmed by the out pouring of help. Quickly the firemen approached me and asked, "What's the matter ma'am?"

I began again to explain, *"I have a mental illness, I don't have my medication that can help me. I need to get to the hospital for help."* At that moment one of the firemen noticed my Maltese cross necklace. It was special to me as it held my ruby birthstone, my husband's opal, and my grandmother's opal birthstone. I held it in my hand tightly. *"Are you a firefighter?"* one asked. *"No, my husband is a captain on the City of Evansville, Indiana Fire Department."* I knew they would understand my dilemma, and would stay close to my side. One offered to take my blood pressure. The only pressure I had was that of my mind slowly slipping to a quagmire of discontent and anxiety. If only I had my medication. I thought to myself this would all go away. The ambulance people had now made their way through the store to where I was sitting. Carlos was still close by as well as the women of Target giggling now at Kassidy's baby behavior. The whole surrounding seemed surreal. Once again, I was asked *"What is wrong today ma'am?"* The gurney had now been brought inside. The crowd pushed to the side to let it through. As the briefing continued, the panic ensued on my part. I answered all their routine questions in a calm manner. Just as they were ready to load me into the ambulance, Aaron arrived. He said, *"I can take her to the hospital. My wife is her daughter."* I could not believe my ears or eyes. It surprised me that he had bothered to come. I was thankful I did not have to ride in the ambulance. My mind continued to race and I became fixated on Aaron. He now became the devil incarnate to me.

All I remember is putting the purchases in the car, locking it, and Aaron carrying Kassidy to his car. As I put on my seat belt I became tight lipped and scared to be in the same car with this young man. He asked, *"Do you want to go to Del Webb?"*

I had no idea where it was, how long it would take to get there, or what they would do when I arrived. Aaron drove silently. The drive to me was the drive to hell. I pictured him taking me somewhere and just him returning. I broke out in a cold sweat in fear of what would happen next. I do not remember arriving at the hospital, only sitting at the intake desk being asked, *"What is your problem today Michelle?"* I could barely answer coherently, *"I am bipolar. I do not have my meds. Please help me."*

The usual barrage of questions ensued, *"Husband's name and phone number?"* I fumbled for my yellow paper. Everything seemed to move in slow motion. It took every ounce of energy to reach into my purse and retrieve my insurance card and my golden paper with my life's emergency numbers on it. I had the fortitude to keep answering the seemingly endless questions. *"Doctor's name and number,"* she asked without lifting her head from the keyboard of the computer. I could hardly keep my composure and fidgeted in my seat. *"Please get me some meds,"* I said quietly to myself. By this time I was handed the phone and told it was my husband. What a relief and yet a deep feeling of remorse over the whole ordeal. *"Hello,"* I said shaking. *"How are you?"* he asked calmly.

I began to fight back the tears and incoherently mumbled *"I am at Del Webb Hospital and need to be on the psych ward. I could not get medicine at the pharmacy so I came here. Aaron is with me."* Once again my mind clicked on to the thought of Aaron being the devil. My mind flickered in and out of reality. That is why I sought help. I knew there was going to be a wait when they put me in a small examining room with Aaron and Kassidy. I sat in a chair and he perched himself on the examining table with Kassidy on his lap. It seemed to me that he was teasing her in his usual way. He would put things just outside her reach and never let her grasp whatever it was he had. I became angry and obsessed about how evil Aaron was and how much hurt he had caused my daughter, how he once again was teasing his daughter. The nurse returned with the large cup of ice water.

"Thank you," I replied. I sat seething about him. My mind became a pressure cooker ready to explode. All of a sudden I splashed the cold water on his face. *"That will cool you off,"* I said in a derogatory tone. Immediately the nurse dashed in and saw the floor drenched with water. Aaron and Kassidy gasped from the ice-cold deluge.

The nurse screeched, *"What did you do that for?"* She quickly sped off to get towels to mop up the mess I had caused. I felt vindicated in my action. What better way to cool off a devilish man but with a baptism of cool waters? The action was a surefire, quick-ticket to the upstairs psych ward. I was relieved that I finally had gotten what I had wanted all along. I felt comfort as I was quickly wheeled away from a drenched and bewildered Aaron and a laughing granddaughter. I was checked into the unit and more questions began. *"Do you have personal items that need to go in the safe?"* the nurse asked.

"Yes," is all I could say. Everything about me became inventory: one prescription set of eye glasses, one purse, one pair of sandals, one sweater. Under miscellaneous was a camera that went along with these items that went in the safe: yellow wedding band, yellow pendant with two white stones and one red stone, yellow chain, one statue of liberty pen, two car keys. Nine Ibuprofen medications secured. I signed on the dotted line next to the X that said I agreed that the belongings were mine. Now that they had my personal effects, I knew I was in for a stay. It is hard to believe the relief I felt yet I hated all the rigmarole that had gotten me there. Less fuss would have been made over a broken arm. I had caused the drama in the emergency room and had I only kept my medicine with me, maybe I could have warded off my mania. Maybe the conditions would have warranted my relapse anyway. I was welcomed to 4W, bed A414 and my roommate who lay quietly in bed. She gestured a slight hello as I entered the room.

We were introduced. *"Michelle, this is Clare. Clare, this is Michelle,"* the nurse said. I could not help but notice my personal plastic bedside commodities of a wash pan and water pitcher, were much like the color represented by my Mary Kay cosmetics. I had previously been a representative of the company. I thought the colors were especially for me and who else could have their own initials *"MK"* emblazoned on each cosmetic?

The usual stack of self-help papers were handed to me to fill out. It gave the staff a feel of where I was mentally. It also gave me a chance to express myself and provide a type of therapy that would progress each day I was at the Del Webb psych ward. One paper in particular was titled Self Talk. It asked us our own definition of self talk. *"It is the SILENT conversation that takes place in our heads all the time. Self-talk is SO powerful that we can talk ourselves into doing things.... And out of doing things,"* I answered to myself. *"There were negative and positive aspects."* Then I was asked my thoughts *"It's always something,"* I wrote. *"If I did not have bad luck, I wouldn't have luck at all!"* I responded to the negative column. The next column for positive asked, *"Can be changed to... It's life!"* I answered. *"When it gets messy..." "clean it up!" "Lucky to be here"* and *"thrilled about it."* The second page started with twenty-four affirmations. I answered seven in all. *"I feel good about....." "The future of the world." "My dogs"... "love me." "What I really enjoy most is...." "Drawing, writing, gardening, and Grandma-ing." "The person I look up to the most..." "God." "I am most happy when..." "someone else smiles."* And lastly, *"One of my many positive traits is..." "that I am highly organized."* The sheet stated at the bottom of the page, *"Genuinely liking who you are is the care of your self-esteem!"* There was not much of a problem with my self-esteem. I was brimming with it!

More papers arrived explaining safety measures in the hospital and when to ask for help. One paper I signed said I agreed to the two thousand dollar admission fee. It looked like I had better enjoy the food, room, company, and any therapy that would be deemed necessary. I fulfilled my end of the responsibility in five days. A much shorter version compared to others usually staying several weeks to a month at a time. After filling out the insurance papers I placed a call to Amy. I said hello and she asked me how she had been before I eventually got around to inquiring about Kassidy. When I asked her where she was, she answered *"with Aaron."* My heart sank. I had reneged on my promise to watch the baby. My current positive outlook at Del Webb was quickly covered by a cloud of dismay. I spoke again and asked her if she thought she and Kassidy could visit. She, thank the Lord, said they would and I asked her to bring my cosmetic bag and my pouch of colored pencils. I rarely go anywhere without my colored pencils. It provides an outlet for me artistically and releases tension when I cannot express myself in other ways. Sometimes I make artwork for my fellow roommate.

Amy arrived the next day with the items I had asked for and Kassidy in tow. It was a happy time to see them both. We exchanged pleasantries and I still felt bad about not being there for her and the baby. The guilt was quickly extinguished when she said, *"Mom it will be okay. You will be out in no time. I found help with*

Kassidy for a while." The visit seemed short but they stayed for the length of time visiting hours allowed. I said goodbye and tearfully turned away. It always seems that sometimes the smallest things trigger your brain into overdrive or "underdrive". Or, say, there is always a need to fix something that is under your skin, that you feel a need to prove yourself, to get to the bottom of a problem, to provide a solution.

It was time for my shower and I looked forward to a nice relaxing hot one to partly wash away some of my troubles of the day. I was directed to a locked door that was opened for me. I entered the shower room with my towel and wash cloth in hand. The shampoo and soap were provided. Turning on the shower, I noticed the shower head was flowing down against the wall. Of course I tried as I might to pivot it out only to have it fall back to the wall. I became perplexed as I tried to lather up. Pondering, I took the wash cloth and wrapped it around the dangling shower head. Positioning the head so I could easily stand beneath it, I tied a half-knot with the cloth around the showerhead neck so it could hang properly for a shower. The staff seemed quite pleased with my ingenuity and said the shower head had been broken for a while. *"Maybe I could get a discount on my hospital bill!"* I joked.

The ebb and flow of humor and seriousness can be experienced in most of the units. One day, as I began to prepare myself to do some drawing and printing of the Serenity Prayer, I asked to sharpen my pencils. There was an electric sharpener behind the nurse's desk. The overall seating and desk arrangement was open and the patients were free to enter or leave it while interacting with the staff. As I sat down to noisily grind the pencils to a point a distinguished man in his forties with suit and tie approached me while walking up the hall towards the desk. *"Nurse,"* he said, *"I am looking for Clare Brown."* I looked around and noticed he was directing the question to me.

"I am sorry," I said, *"I am just a patient here."* He seemed embarrassed for his indiscretion for a short while. One of the nurses at the unit desks quickly came to his side and assisted him. That was a unique experience and it taught me that you would have

a hard time distinguishing a normal person from a mentally ill one by just their looks. It can happen to anyone. A mental illness can occur at any time in your life. I happened to have a good day and had fooled someone who could generally indicate the difference between the staff and a patient.

My roommate would hardly speak and when she did it was in short, depressed sentences. I learned that she had been a nurse for thirty years and had taken care of many people in an intensive care unit in a nearby hospital. She had lost her husband recently and when I asked her what brought her here she responded with *"I cannot cry."* *"I know I need to cry, but the tears just won't come."* I understood that she knew she needed to go through the grieving process and crying was a step in that direction. We did not speak much, but I made her a small decorative card drawn with small flowers with my colored pencils. It read, *God grant me the Serenity to accept the things I cannot change, Courage to change the things I can, and Wisdom to know the difference."* I not only gave her the prayer but said it for myself.

I attempted to start to write my story. It was the beginning of at least a dozen attempts for years after that day. Usually the mania would get me off-track or some other life interruption would stop me from continuing. It just was not there. Each day the medicines took better hold of the synapses of my brain. I could feel myself diminish in the grandiose feeling and I became more *normal* in my expectations and reactions to my environment. The morning of the fifth day of my hospitalization I realized the tweaking of my medicine had finally taken and I awaited the news of being released. There was not much pressure for group therapy as I had experienced at other hospitals and it gave my mind a chance to rest. I cannot say enough about the art therapy I usually abide in. I was drawing when the doctor approached my room. *"Michelle, I think it's time for you to go home. You've responded well to the medications. I would like a follow up in a week to see how you are doing."*

"That sounds alright to me," I said happily. I could only feel sad for my roommate who lay quietly and said nothing of my

release. I bid her goodbye and felt an urgency to help her in some way. A light bulb went off in my head. I had a plan and hoped it would only bring her some relief. Amy was on her way to pick me up. While I was at Del Webb, I asked to be checked by the lab to see if I no longer carried the Lyme parasite. I was happy to learn there was no sign of it in my body. I had not shown signs of it for some time but felt assured there would be no relapses from that horrible setback. The silver and antibiotics had done their job.

I agreed to meet Amy in the lobby after I was released from the ward. I needed to help Clare and now was my chance. The gift shop was full of people shopping for their loved ones. I knew just the thing that would hopefully bring her the relief she so deserved. I got out my plastic and purchased a moderately priced and cheerful daisy bouquet. On the card, I simply wrote *Cry baby, Cry*. I gave instructions that it be delivered today to Clare Brown bed B414. The cashier took my credit card and I prayed Tim would understand my purchase. I had received flowers from one of his captains and his wife from the fire department. It cheered me up greatly and I noticed Clare had only a few visitors and no flowers, but I hoped my small card's message would be the catalyst to perhaps open her up.

I embraced Amy and Kassidy as they greeted me at the door of the hospital. We stopped at the pharmacy to pick up my medicines and sped away to her home in Surprise. The name of the town would live up to its name. I received a call from the hospital. I had accidentally left my cosmetics bag behind. We made arrangements to pick it up a day later. I arrived on the unit and asked to see Clare. Anxious I thought she might still be quietly resting in her room. The attendant said, *"No, she's gone! She went home yesterday. She cried and cried before she released to go home."* A warm glow came over me. I asked myself joyfully, had the flowers and its small message worked? I was elated to hear the news and understood what bedside nursing meant. I would always remember how important just a few words or flowers could mean to someone. It could possibly be the only one in a lifetime affirmation they so dearly needed. I left Del Webb for the final time with a smile on my face.

Amy and I decided to treat ourselves to a garden center for some flowers to plant in the front and backyard. It was refreshing to know the dog was no longer there to dig up anything we might plant. We arrived at a local garden center. There were beautiful cactus and terra cotta pots decorating its entrance. Once inside, we were drawn to the red, white, and blue petunias. I immediately thought how nice these would look around Amy's front yard empress tree. It would be another way to show our colors. The front door was already decorated with a vase of patriotic flowers. It would be a perfect match. We purchased some thyme, oregano, and a flat of patriotic petunias, as an expression of loyalty to our nation. As we were driving home, Kassidy fell fast asleep in her car seat and Amy gently turned the radio down low. A loud commercial came on, *"What are you going to do?"* said an excited woman. *"Your cat won't listen or play? Your dog is dog gone it ran away!"* Our moment of comic relief had finally arrived. We looked at one another and laughed out loud at the thought of Trevor, the dog, lost and gone. The radio commercial had broken the tension of me letting the dog go. Not another word was spoken of the canine after that.

We pulled into the driveway, carried Kassidy into her room and straight to bed. If she took a long nap, we could get some planting done. I did not know much about desert gardening, except you had to water the plants not once, but twice a day. I gathered newspapers to put in the ground to possibly help hold the moisture in. I started planting the petunias, alternating the red, the white and the purple ones that represented the blue. I dug the holes one by one until I made a complete circle around the tree. Lightning had struck the tree, so I decided to trim the tree to shape it up a bit. The tree stood royally about ten feet tall. I resumed my planting, wadding up bits of newspaper into the depressions in the ground, then planting a petunia on top and gingerly covering the soil around each plant. As I picked up another part of the paper, there was a large picture of Bin Laden. I stared back at the man's picture and saw the hate in his eyes. My thoughts were taken back to the World Trade Center towers and the plane crashes that had been caused by this diabolical man. The thought of pain and suffering of so many people became unbearable. I crumpled up his picture and felt as if I had single handedly destroyed not only his image but the very man himself. I shoved the print in the ground as a gesture of burying him. I cried and thought how I wished someone would end his evil doings. As I finished the circle of flowers I sensed someone was watching me. As I turned to the street, I saw a young man dressed in an Air Force pilot's jumpsuit seated behind the wheel of a late model red car. He smiled at me and gave me a nod. I smiled back and managed a small wave. He quickly resumed his driving and I felt in my heart a thankfulness toward his service and of so many countless others who protected our country. I inspected Amy's plantings near the rear of the house. She had a nice garden by the kitchen door.

I felt a sense of belonging to this house, a home for Amy and Kassidy. I told Amy about the pilot stopping out front and she said, *"There are many Air Force families that live in the neighborhood and they will enjoy seeing the flowers."* I smiled at the thought.

Night was closing in on the day. I became homesick for my husband and I put on a long t-shirt that read, *"This t-shirt keeps me warm when my fireman is away."* I had bought it at a previous fire chief's convention. I missed his touch and caress. I hoped to join him soon. The planes were still not flying. I had to work harder to secure a babysitter for Amy. Hopefully in the neighborhood I could find someone to trust. It soon would be time to leave. It was nearing October 14th, our twenty-third anniversary. Tim did not disappoint me, as I cried over the phone, *"I miss you honey,"* I said. *"I miss you too,"* he said somberly. On our anniversary, a knock came at the door. There stood a florist delivery man with a beautiful vase of a dozen red roses. *"Are you Mrs. Crack?"* he asked.

"Yes I am," I replied. As he handed me the bouquet, I said, *"Thank you."* As I placed the roses on the table, I buried my face into the sweet essence of their blossom. Our love had grown only deeper by our leave from one another. My heart still ached for him to be at my side. I could only imagine the heartache Amy was going through, the disappointment of her broken marriage. I filled my days with caring for Kassidy and on occasion ventured out into the

neighborhood or took a drive to the shopping mall near her home. My funds were growing slimmer so I did more window shopping than I did purchasing. My mania had totally subsided and I felt comfortable entering a store without worry of spending too much or being isolated from my medicine which I constantly carried with me. The Ativan was helpful in controlling my racing thoughts. I was thankful for how it gave my life back to me.

Kassidy was the perfect shopping mate. She drew quite a lot of attention and made it fun to share her chubby cheeks and beautiful dark hair and eyes. I loved her and Amy dearly and enjoyed their company. Amy needed a few more wall hangings so I set off on a shopping adventure not knowing what I would find. A store that showed Spanish art and décor in its window caught my eye. I found a close parking space and carried Kassidy inside. The sales clerk greeted me with a "Hello, welcome to Charros." I was caught up in the beautiful metal sculptures, wind chimes, and oil paintings of southwestern sunsets. The front of the store was nicely displayed but I had taught myself to aim for the back of the store where the clearance and bargain table and racks could be found. I quickly found a colorful sun and moon ceramic set of wall hangings. It matched Amy's natural hues of her living room. I had since removed the family picture that had hung above the couch. I had taped over the image of Aaron during my mania and Amy disliked the picture front and center of her living room anyway. The three plaster decorations would fit the wall perfectly. Amy enjoyed the southwestern sun and celestial wall hangings that were so popular.

I talked candidly with the sales lady. *"I am so happy to be shopping,"* I said, probably giving her too much information. *"I just got out of the hospital,"* and left it at that. Caringly, the woman responded, *"What was wrong?"* I felt brave in my answer. *"I am bipolar and had a manic episode. 9/11 and my family situation brought it on. I am doing much, much better now."* The woman's head dropped. She looked around and with a whisper she said, *"I too am bipolar. You are lucky and courageous to say so. If anyone here found out my boss would fire me!"* I could not believe my ears. How could someone be so calloused; she could not help what her genetic pool had dealt her. I continued to listen carefully, *"My insurance does not cover such a condition. I definitely would be fired on the spot if they knew!"* I realized how lucky I was to not only openly speak of it, but to have insurance that covered my hospitalization as well. I said, *"I am so sorry."* *"You keep telling people,"* she said. *"Maybe it will make it better for the rest of us."* She smiled as she took my five dollars for my purchase. I took her hand and gave it a firm squeeze and gave her a wink. Her words would play over and over in my mind. I indeed was the lucky one.

I began to notice Amy seemed less talkative and tired when she would return home. She would resort to falling asleep as soon as she got home and went to bed without eating supper that I had prepared for her. This went on for days. I spoke with Tim, "I am worried about Amy," I said. He was not there and could not see the daily downward spiral she began to gradually fall into. Tim reassured me that she would be okay after some rest. She had been through a lot lately. I was able to talk to the divorcee neighbor about watching Kassidy with her two small children. She said she would help Amy with little or no payment. It was nice to know a loving mother who shared the same concern. Amy had found a friend at work who worked the opposite shift as she had. It seemed like the plans for babysitting had finally been put into action.

I met Tami, a next door neighbor on a warm September Saturday as she was ready to take a bike ride with her two sons. David and Timmy, ages eight and ten. She was a nice looking thirty-something woman with her brown hair swept up in a poly tail. We became friends quickly as we would catch each other in our coming and goings, usually in the front yard. We would make visits back and forth to each of our houses. One afternoon we began to talk of our hometowns and shared a homesickness for them. She had never quite got used to the military life of moving every three to four years. Her husband was stationed at Luke AFB as a trainer for the new pilots. His days were long and you could tell she had wished him home more often, at least to spend quality time with their young sons. Each time we visited over coffee or a nice cold Diet Coke we revealed a little bit more about ourselves.

One morning while Kassidy was taking her nap, a light knock came on the front door, it was Tami. She was crying. I let her in and asked, *"Want some coffee? What's wrong?"* I asked as she wiped the tears away with her shirt sleeve. *"Ever since September 11, I've grown more worried about everything. Tom (her husband) is hardly ever at home and when he is there he's sleeping. The boys are doing well, but my depression has come back. I can hardly make myself get out of bed in the morning."* I said, *"I understand Tami. Do you have a doctor you can call?"* She became quiet and did not answer me. Her head sank down.

"If Tom knew I was over here telling you this he would die," she said. *"There's nothing to be ashamed of nor any reason you shouldn't get help,"* I said sympathetically. *"I have a doctor's number, but honestly can't call. I do not have the energy. I could barely walk over here. The boys are at school and I feel more desperate when they're not around." "Tami, can I call for you"* I said. *"Could you?"* she asked. She removed a crumpled paper from her pocket. It had the name of Dr. Nelson and his phone number on it. I asked, *"Are you able to drive or do you need me to get you to the doctor?"* She began to cry again. *"No,"* she said through her tears. *"I can drive myself."* I picked up the phone and dialed the crisis line of Dr. Nelson's office. *"Hello, Dr. Nelson's office,"* came the voice over the phone. *"Yes, yes, I have a friend who needs help." "What sort of help?"* she asked. *"It seems she has depression and can hardly do anything. She tells me she wants to sleep all the time. She cries continuously and has two young boys she can hardly take care of." "I see,"* said the receptionist. There was a pause. *"It looks like we could get her into see Dr. Nelson next week on Friday."*

Next week? Next week I thought. *"You do not understand, she needs to see someone today!"* I continued, *"I myself just got out of Del Webb for a manic episode. I can hardly take care of myself, much less my friend who cannot wait a day longer. I do not intend to go back to Del Webb over this. She needs your help today."* Once again, silence fell over the telephone line. *"Just a minute,"* she said. *"I'll let you talk to the doctor."* Dr. Nelson's deep voice answered the phone, *"Hello, what seems to be the problem?"* I once again explained Tami's problem to the doctor and my concern of both

Tami's and my mental health. We both needed an answer today. *"Let's see,"* he said. *"Can she be here at 11?"* I repeated the time to Tami. She nodded an affirmative yes. *"Yes,"* I said to Dr. Nelson, *"and thank you."* As I hung up the phone, Tami embraced me and cried into my shoulder.

"You have to go soon," I said, *"it's already 10 o'clock."* She thanked me tearfully and went home to dress and go see Dr. Nelson. She would be able to make the doctor's appointment while Tom and the boys were away. Somehow I felt better knowing she was going to get better and not worse with her depression. The medicine would help and she still had a friend she could talk to. Sometimes some of the best therapy is being able to talk about it.

Tami kept her appointment. I was proud of her and knew that things would improve. It had to get better. The Serenity Prayer came to mind. I prayed it as I got Kassidy lunch and played with her waiting for Tami to return. Tami improved slowly each day. She was able to take care of her boys, but ended her day totally exhausted. Her job was physical and demanding.

She began to smile and laugh like her old self and she looked forward to each day. The boys and Tom were lucky to have such a strong-willed woman in their lives. She never talked about whether she told Tom about the doctor's office visit but she did continue her medication. I knew all too well how lonely being at home by oneself could be. I missed my daughter terribly and knew, like Tami, our loved ones had an important job to fill first. There was hardly time to discuss matters outside of a quick hug or hello as we passed. Tami and I continued our coffee breaks and shared how important it was to stay well with our medication regimen. It was nice to have someone to talk to who understood.

XII

My Hero

୬

It looked as though Tim was going to be able to fly out to Phoenix as plans had firmed up for babysitting arrangements. There were just a few days left to stay with Amy and Kassidy. It was a relief not only to us but to many that air travel had resumed across the nation. I pondered how 9/11 had affected families like ourselves and how we were the lucky ones to have one another.

I felt people who had come to my rescue during my manic attack at Target deserved a thank you. Placing a non-emergency call to the fire department, I spoke to the captain that was in command the day of my *rescue*. I suggested a Lifesaver cake and thank you reception at the fire station. We decided what shift his crew would be working. I wrote a letter to the Target store praising the efforts of Carlos as he worked that bizarre Sunday afternoon. I sang his praises for keeping a calm demeanor and orchestrating the necessary emergency help. I also invited Carlos to the fire department reception. Thinking of the lady in the shop that had no resources or support, I came up with the idea to welcome the local newspaper as well. Here, far away from home, it was safe being an advocate for mental illness. No one knew me here but I could start a message of hope and help for those affected by both 9/11 and mental illnesses.

The date was set. Amy and I made a chocolate cake decorated with a row of Lifesavers on its border. We arrived at the station. Captain Briggs and his crew were all present. I told them, *"It's good to know there are folks out there who come to your aid. Although there was nothing physically wrong, you stood by my side during my mental anguish and upheld a professional response to my need."* I had hoped Carlos would make it. He did not show at first at the designated time, but arrived after the news media had left. The paper from Sun City arrived and took pictures of Amy, Kassidy, me, and the firefighters. The caption read: *"Michelle Krack and her family thank the Sun City Fire Department that came to her aid while she had manifestations from the 9/11 attacks. For mental illness help, please contact NAMI, the National Alliance on Mental Illness in your area."* A picture of all was printed with the caption.

I could not thank the rescuers enough that came to my aid. One of the fire department personnel, Jacquie said, *"Could you stay here in Arizona for a while, we could use you to help train our personnel during our mental illness emergency responses?"* I smiled, *"I would love to, but I am returning to my home in Indiana soon."* I hoped they would continue some form of training that would prepare their firemen to aid mentally ill patients. I am sure my emergency was not the only one they had to deal with. So many people had anxiety and illnesses that they would experience episodes of their need for mental health aid. NAMI extends intervention for police and fire personnel alike. It only takes some training and the ability to listen to a victim and their plight. The program is called *Crisis Intervention*.

It was time for the Arizona State Fair. Amy's shift was switched to evenings which allowed her more day time with Kassidy and me. We decided to have some fun and visit the fairgrounds before I left. I had been used to the activities of the 4-H Vanderburgh County Fair back home. This event was on a much larger scale. I was eager to see the different displays. Judging at my local fair in Fire Safety for years encouraged my interest in the hundreds of exhibits we would see. I loved the fair. There were many agriculture events and interesting explanations of how and why progress was made in the huge expansion of farming. We were particularly drawn to an interactive display showing cotton and its uses. A large children's plastic swimming pool was filled with tufts of cotton. It looked like a billowing cloud on the floor. We carefully laid Kassidy on the soft pillow-like cotton. She giggled and wriggled in the blanket of cotton. We snapped her picture and rescued her as she sank deep into its softness.

We passed beautiful displays of animals carefully placed in corrals shape liked Arizona along with countless other appealing displays. We ate at a Mexican restaurant and I had my second taste of authentic guacamole. We browsed around the fairgrounds and visited shops that were inside a huge building. The smells, sights, and sounds were delightful to the senses, the colors bright of vendors showing their wares. A booth that displayed flowering skirts caught my eye. I was drawn to the sleepwear where I found a flowing robin egg colored skirt with a matching sleeveless top. It was romantic and I thought it would be nice for my first night with Tim when he arrived. With just a few dollars I had left, I purchased the appealing eveningwear. In just a few days, Tim would fly in to Phoenix. I was excited but cautiously concerned and thought about the planes that had been hijacked. A flash back only made me somewhat worrisome. I dreamt of how the encounter with Tim would happen.

It seemed like a first date. I began to grow giddy like a schoolgirl. We called one another several times to make the arrangements. Amy would be at work, but Carrie and Jenny, the teenage girls that had played with Kassidy, would babysit while I would pick Tim up at the Phoenix airport. His flight came in at 8:45 p.m. It would be late when we would get home, but it was okay with the girl's parents and Amy. I got dressed, put on makeup, fixed my hair, and splashed on the perfume I had purchased earlier at Target. Nervously, I arrived at the airport and without a navigator I missed the turn for the parking garage and had to drive in a full circle around the terminal until I found the sign marked *"Parking Garage."* I carefully parked and made sure I had my keys before I locked the Subaru. Now was not the time to lock the keys in the car! My heart raced as I entered the large airport. Tim was on the Delta flight 611. I checked the electronic board and his flight was clearly shown high up on the wall. It was half an hour before his flight would arrive. I had just enough time to go to the bathroom and freshen up. I was gone for only a few minutes. Returning from the bathroom I noticed his flight was no longer posted. I panicked and wondered why it had been removed. I had hoped to see him come up the long tunnel that came up from the airplane. Security was tight and everyone waiting had to stay a measurable point back. It was sad how 9/11 changed greeting a loved one's arrival. Only a few straggles of people got off the plane, then none followed. I looked around hoping to catch a glimpse of him.

Outside the bathrooms and water fountains were walled displays of local artists. I became anxious and wondered where he was. I stepped back towards the art display, not to let anyone see the dismay I was now experiencing. Out of the corner of my eye I saw movement behind the art wall. As I turned to get a better look, there stood Tim smiling back at me as he was hiding behind the wall that separated us. We casually hugged and kissed. It felt good to finally be in his arms! We waited shortly for his luggage and I gratefully handed him the keys to the car. I could navigate better than drive at this point. As we got in the car he reached over and kissed me like he never had before. Happily we drove back to Surprise and paid the sitter and took them home. The girls were pleased at the money they had earned. It was even more of a miracle to find Angela to watch Kassidy for the long term. Tim crept in to see a sleeping Kassidy and we finally could be together for the rest of the night. I set the alarm to wake us when Amy would get home late.

Donning my new blue night gown, I approached Tim. The song, *Hero* was playing on the radio by Enrique Iglesias. As I clung to Tim, the words came alive with meaning for us lovers. I began a soft cry. He kissed me softly. The song continued. The radio faded away. We loved each other that night like newlyweds and I knew my hero was at last in my arms– forever! We fell asleep and soon awoke to the alarm. Amy would be home soon and Tim was all too glad to see his eldest daughter. We hugged and laughed when she got home. She was so happy to see her dad. We all went to bed that night knowing the next day would be a better one.

၆

We packed our bags, all the framed San Damiano crosses, my oil paintings, and luggage and prepared to leave Amy and Kassidy. It was hard to leave, but necessary for her to get on with her life. Aaron had taken all of his things from the garage and Amy was left to start all over again. She knew how to get help and knew we were all a phone call away. I hated that she lived so far from us. The time had come for us to leave. We exchanged hugs and kisses and sadly waved goodbye as we left the driveway. Forever pictured in my mind are Amy and Kassidy standing there while Amy waved Kassidy's arm goodbye. I watched them until we made the corner at the stop sign near her house. The drive was long, but seemed shorter with Tim at my side. I had forgotten how long I had been gone as we approached the trees of the Midwest. I noticed all of the trees were bare. It was now November and I had missed the changing of summer to autumn– my favorite time of year. A passing of time had magically and surprisingly taken place as a part of me had remained in Arizona.

XIII

Dogs, Darth Tater, & the Dishwasher

Arriving home in November gave me only a few weeks to prepare for Christmas. Usually there were handmade cards sent with a letter telling of all the kid's new addresses and phone numbers to share with family and friends. This ritual of the holidays would be put on hold until after the first of the year. What was wrong with celebrating Christmas through Epiphany? It was the time that the infant Jesus was presented with the gift from the Magi. No one would expect a seasonal Christmas greeting in January, but it was time that allowed me to carry on a family tradition. The kids came home for Christmas and the San Damiano crosses were well received. I shared them also with my father and mother-in-law, Grandma May, and my parents. The wooden frames complimented the colorful crosses. It was not a huge gift, but came straight from the heart.

Years later, while traveling through southern Illinois near Cave-in-Rock, Tim and I passed a sign that read San Damiano Retreat. The arrow pointed down a winding, narrowly paved road that led in the direction of the Ohio River. We backed the car up and ventured down the road. Several times we steered closer to the nonexistent shoulder of the road to make clear for rock hauling dump trucks. We passed a stone quarry. For several miles, we enjoyed the fall colors that blanketed the Illinois woods. It was once again my favorite time of year. A feeling of adventure and excitement entered the car as we approached the stucco one-story building with a fountain made of Spanish tile at its front. This was not the usual landscape you saw amongst the field, rock formation, and towering trees in this part of the country. For a brief moment I pictured myself again in Arizona. We stopped, got out, and approached the building. There was a directional sign for the chapel, gift shop, and restaurant. We followed the entrance to a gift shop at the end of the restaurant's Spanish-themed table and chairs. A young lady stood behind the counter. *"Welcome,"* she said. As I smiled at her my eye caught a glimpse of many, many crosses that covered the wall next to her. There were wrought iron crosses along with glass and crystal ones. Of course there were San Damiano crosses in all sizes. It was a beautiful display.

I was drawn to my favorite cross that was cut out and was six by ten inches. I felt I had returned to St. Damiano in Arizona and asked Tim if I could get the cross to display in my kitchen. He agreed. We did not have a cross in the busiest room of our home. It would be a reminder to us always of our past and future and of Christ's love for our family. It would be mounted on the front of an oak cabinet door piece. It turned out nicely, if I do say so myself. We ventured out onto the grounds and saw a huge towering statue of St. Francis. It must have been at least thirty feet tall. It stood opposite wooden cabins that were perched at the bluff's edge just two hundred feet above the flowing Ohio River below. We found a pet cemetery near the St. Francis statue. I wanted to stay in the cabins and enjoy this beautiful fall day with my groom of twenty-six years.

We returned to the restaurant after taking in the beautiful vista of the Ohio River and the panorama of the Kentucky banks. We learned that we could reserve a cabin and could rent it for a practical price. It was slightly furnished with a fridge, stove, and bunks. It would be like camping. It sounded like so much fun and there were places to visit nearby. Cave-in-Rock gave a view of what river pirates must have seen in years past. There were trails that led up and around the sandstone formations at Garden of the Gods and

Rim Rock. In our younger days, we would rappel over the rims of Garden of the Gods and spend an entire day taking in the fall flora and fauna and enjoying a picnic lunch on the warm rocks. These days were gone. No one was allowed to climb up or down the park rocks by rope or harness. It was heartbreaking, for they had given us so much adventure and enjoyment with our friends. For now, walking and driving would have to suffice; this was okay as we just used the time to take in the beauty of autumn. Each time I prayerfully look to the San Damiano cross in my kitchen I say a prayer of thanks for finding this cross that stayed with my family and me for years. Through good times and bad, life continues.

I have kept a variety of pocket calendars for years marking appointments, birthdays, and special events. When one looks at a full calendar year, he might imagine how I did all those things and wonder even more how I accomplished things that did not even make the calendar squares. My days at home were filled with the business that two active teenagers could provide. Carrie graduated from high school in the spring of 2001 and now entered Indiana University to study to be a teacher. I had no doubt she would make a terrific one. She had held the position of mayor of her high school where a town government was emulated, a tradition that started at the inception of the school. She led her class with new ideas. One, for instance, was a "greenie" cookout with the freshman class and the seniors. It was a hit and became an annual event. She showed much sense to detail and provided trust to her student council and government for her punctual execution of plans for assemblies and school events that needed her attention. She was a lot like me in many ways, so it was always easy to confer with Carrie over current events and life in general. Andy was still at home and had just started high school and had tried out for football. He joined the sport because of his fast running ability. He also learned he was the main object to be tackled. Both my sons and daughters preferred to run distance. Andy was no exception. He finished one season of football then joined the running teams of track and cross-country. My eldest Matt, who had graduated from the University of Southern

Indiana, helped coach Andy to many winning races and even to nationals in a 4 x 800 relay in boys' track. The first time the team had participated in a national event in the school's history. You can see the pride in this mother of all of her children. I was very involved with decorating proms and project graduation parties after Matt graduated from high school. I was still learning all the details of high school life through Matt's interests and participation. By the time the girls got there I was well established in creating themes, designs, and decorations to fit the high school's events. By the time Amy graduated from high school I figured Tim and I, including our own prom, had attended twelve in total. I guess we had a little experience with decorating and all the planning it entailed.

My calendar had been filled with dates of kids' events and their high school years seemed to fly by. I missed being around kids as Carrie and Andy progressed through their secondary years. Speaking to several church ladies, I learned the school was hiring in the cafeteria. I enjoyed the women's company that worked there and enjoyed the students and their friendly demeanor even more. There was only part-time work available, a few days a week from 10:30 a.m. to 1:30 p.m. The pay was minimal. I told myself this would be an easy job. A comfort zone had been reached. The job was not stressful and I had much free time at home and for the kids. Learning the names of faculty members and what subjects they taught came easy enough. I learned to run the dishwasher, serve on the lunch line, scrape plates, make and serve ice cream, set up and cashier for the potato bar once a month. It was enjoyable to mix the different jobs and made me accessible to Andy while he was at school. He seemed to enjoy my being there, especially when he needed extra lunch money.

There is a saying *"Fences make good neighbors."* I would like to add, *"Better neighbors are those who feed, water, and shelter their dogs."* Several years after my Great Uncle Harold and Aunt Lucy Morris passed away, their house came up for sale. It just so happened they had lived next door to us. We enjoyed having family so close, except for the time Matt drove a line drive baseball into the corner of Harold's wooden garage. We found out years later that admirable Uncle Harold had a bushel basket of the Krack kids' tennis, whiffle, and baseballs that landed near or in his garden. Aunt Lucy and Uncle Harold kept their home, yard, and garden pristine. It was nice sharing stories and passing fruits and vegetables over the fence.

One day, a young couple came to look at the house. The lady gracefully cuddled a blooming rose in her hand that grew near the split rail fence that stood between our yards. *"Oh"*, I thought, *"someone that likes flowers! I am sure we'll have lots in common."* They quickly bought the house and garage and moved in. I was anxious to meet and greet the new couple so I picked some fresh pears from our tree and presented them in a nicely decorated basket with a bow. Their names were Shauna and Jeremy. They seemed nice enough, but did not really exude the friendliness I had hoped. The gesture of pears was received and not much exchange of neighborly banter took place. I kindly said to break the silence, *"Trash pick-ups are on Thursday. I'll leave our name and number if you have any questions. Welcome to the neighborhood,"* I added.

Weeks went by when before I was saying hello to Jeremy over the fence. He was getting dog food for his two beautiful, wolfish looking dogs- as he would describe them. The mother and pup shared a small igloo home, without any shade overhead. It was late summer and the sun was hot on their thick, dark fur. I heard Jeremy say, *"If you do not feed them much, you have less to clean up."* By just the tone in his voice and the scant amount of food in his scoop, I saw that he was underfeeding the dogs. Months passed and his dogs seemed to cry instead of bark. The neighbor kids even took note of it. We could see the dogs usually had no water and both the bowls for the food and water were tipped over empty. The dogs appeared especially thin for their size and Jeremy's statement about their food kept resonating in my mind. The excrement from the dogs piled up and could be smelled from any direction in the yard. Animal Control was called a number of times by not only myself, but other neighbors as well. A bucket of water was tied to the kennel, only to be knocked over by the anxious dogs. The matter worsened as the hot days grew longer. Neighbors and I would toss milk bones to the dogs, only to have them gobbled up in seconds. The calls to Animal Control were, I am sure, constant. Jeremy liked to tinker with cars and had a huge barrel filled with fluid that he used to clean car parts in. One day he dumped its contents out at the edge of his garage and it all ran down hill into our flower and vegetable garden. Of course he was confronted about his actions but only after he had driven in our yard on a wet day with his truck. His driveway was so full of vehicles he could not back into his own drive and our yard was the closest to his garage doors. We filled in the truck's tracks in the yard the entire fall season to even out the ruts. Needless to say, the friendly, neighborly atmosphere began to diminish quickly. The dogs became such a problem, that neighbor kids were also feeding the dogs. It was learned later that this insensitive man was so paranoid that he put cameras in his back yard to guard the failing dogs. On camera he caught a young girl in the act of feeding the dogs.

It turns out that the pup died and was replaced by an English bulldog pup. The dogs had gotten into a tangle and the pup bulldog received injuries from *Maggie* that required stitches at the vet. Jeremy went door to door with his film footage until he found the culprit child and demanded full reimbursement for the damages. I had just about enough of his controlling and cruel treatment to the dogs but also his attitude toward the neighbor children for their caring actions. I felt compelled to step up and do something. The many trips to his house by Animal Control were futile. The animals continued to howl and cry so one day I made a sign and attached it to the privacy fence's other side. Our retort came in the stares and glares from the insensitive couple with a tall wooden privacy fence. It did help, but did not keep the dog from howling. My sign simply said in permanent marker on the backside of an old license plate, *"I pray for rain so your dogs may have a drink of water."* Several days went by and tacked on a tree above the fence line facing us was a sign that read, *"I pray you mind your own business."* I still do not know why I expected some other positive response. I left my sign up for weeks. It was time for a new sign after the dogs continued to cry and Animal Control did not do their job. By now, more neighbors were expressing their discontent. The new sign required a larger permanent canvas. A foot and half wide and two feet long piece of white aluminum trim was chosen. Once again, with permanent markers I printed out, *"Daily the news media passes your house. They will be inquiring about your dogs' condition. I suggest you clean out their pen, give them a bath, water and food. Expect to be on the 6 p.m. Sunday news."* Saturday morning I saw Shawna feverishly scrubbing the flea-ridden dogs. It was the first bath and cleaning of the pen any of us had seen in two years. The food bowls and water dishes were filled to the brim. Sunday came and went but the news media reporter continued to ride by on a tandem bike with his wife almost every day. I am sure there was stress and discussion between Shawna and Jeremy concerning the dogs and the events that took place. I prayed they would just surrender the dogs and let the canines have a peaceful loving home. My wish would come true.

On a fall evening after dark, Maggie and bulldog pup showed up in my yard. Shauna was in her yard and must have left them out. There was no way the dogs could gain this freedom from the double-locked pen. I quickly put them in my back yard and called Animal Control. After interacting with the dogs and waiting for the dog unit to arrive, I noticed we were covered in fleas. My dog had already gone inside and carried a colony with him. After bathing my dog, Rocky, the neighbors' dogs were picked up. I noticed fleabites on my ankles and legs. I guess my pay back came at three in the morning. I awoke having difficulty breathing. I was having an allergic reaction to the fleabites. Tim was at the fire station and I did not want to wake him, so I drove myself to the emergency room. I needed a shot of epinephrine to stop the reaction. I had to stay in the ER for several hours before they would release me. As far as my concern with waking Tim, it was later learned he was only blocks away at a house fire the same time I visited the ER. Shortly after the flea episode, Jeremy moved out and took his dogs with him. The stories followed him where he moved to. His new neighbors, who were friends of ours, said that both dogs perished that winter. I only hoped there was a dog heaven, for these animals deserved it. And, I thanked all the angels of the neighborhood who cared about these desperate dogs. I wish the next story involving canines was one that would lift your spirits, but unfortunately that isn't the case.

One particularly beautiful spring day, my children were getting ready for school when a stunning black and white husky with ice blue eyes appeared out of nowhere. It seemed that since we had a dog, other four-legged creatures seemed to gravitate to our residence. The kids did not want to go to school that day but rather stay home and play with the new arrival. The dog had no tags, only a thick, leather collar with a metal lead ring. As I put the dog in the fenced yard, he quickly bounded over the four-foot tall chain length fence. I rounded him up and secured him with a nylon rope to a nearby pecan tree. He was given food and water and seemed content to rest for a while. I placed a call to Animal Control. For some reason they gave me a number of someone and asked me to call them. I would have rather had the Animal Control people come and pick up the dog, but I called the number they gave me. There were errands to run, so I checked the dog after calling the number and briefly said, *"A beautiful black-and-white male husky was at my house this morning. He is secured in the back yard. I live near Tekoppel School."* I concluded by giving out my phone number and hung up. Quickly, I left to run to the grocery to pick up a few things. Returning with groceries in hand, I noticed the dog was now laying close up against the privacy fence. He appeared to not be moving. I thought he may be sleeping, but on further inspection I noticed he was not breathing! Panicked I quickly called Tim at the fire station. Our home was in his district and he was able to come help me. The dog had hung himself, of all things, on the bottom of the fence! He had pushed and pushed himself against the fence, allowing the metal ring to slide up a worn piece of the panel of fencing, tightening the collar as he went. I could not free him from the fence- that is how hard he had pushed himself to strangulation. Calling Tim only temporarily soothed my upset he said he would come home and help me get the dog off the fence. Before he left the station, he shared the story with his comrades. When Tim arrived I had been reduced to tears. What would the owner say or what would Animal Control do? Where were they anyway? I called them again and told them I wanted the dog's now dead body to be removed before my children arrived home. "Oh Tim," I said after he arrived, *"I can't get the dog off the fence."* He could not believe what he saw. I had to set myself in the neighbor's yard and push down on the ring while Tim lifted the lifeless dog's body up while I wedged the ring from the fence. This once beautiful dog now lay dead in my back yard. I thanked Tim as he returned to his station. Once again, a more desperate call was made to Animal Control, *"Please come get this dog's body,"* I pleaded. *"We're working on it ma'am. We'll be there as soon as possible."* Well that was not soon enough for me. Just then the phone rang. *"Is this the lady who phoned earlier about my dog?"* The man's voice questioned. *"Yes it is,"* I answered through sniffles. *"I am so glad you found my husky. We've been looking for him for days. I can't tell you what it means to me!"* No words could come from my mouth. What would I say? *"I am sorry, well your dog is here, but he's dead now."* I proceeded to tell the man the story and gave my address.

By now the fireman were rolling with laughter, for one of their jokesters had called and pretended to be the owner. I sat trembling waiting for the dog's owner to show up. Laughingly, Tim called me and said Jerry had made the call. Sobbing came easier now as I sat in the yard with a dead dog and no one to take it off my hands. It was only an hour before the kids would arrive. Slowly a blue pickup truck pulled along the alley behind the house. A middle aged, well-groomed man stepped out of the truck. He explained he had been driving around the neighborhood around Tekoppel. It seems I was not inside to answer his call for directions. I cried, *"I am sorry for your dog. I left for a short while and found him hung on the fence."* At this time I could not explain to him that the dog had mastered the execution under the fence. He went on, *"We've had Max for several years, and he has climbed the fence several times and has nearly hung himself. Luckily we were at home when he tried."* For some reason his explanation did not warrant any comfort on my behalf. He continued, *"We had a two hundred dollar reward for his return."* Later the fireman would joke, *"Is that dead or alive?"* My blood began to boil knowing of the firemen's prank. The dog's owner was calm and reassuring. He said, *"We figured something had happened to Max, like being hit by a semi. I am thankful he was with someone who cared and tried to keep him safe."* How was I to know the dog was on a suicide mission? I should have never left him alone. "I need to give you this," as he handed me a twenty dollar bill. Now I felt awful like it was blood money! I said, *"No, I can't,"* still fighting back the tears. He insisted as he gingerly picked up the limp dog's body and gently laid him in the back of his pickup. No more words were spoken, but I could feel the temperature rise toward Jerry, the mastermind dog owner.

I had to judge a firefighters' District 15 Queen Contest that night. Keeping my composure became difficult. I do not believe I told the kids the entire story about the dog for fear of crying all over again. Putting on a stiff upper lip and my dress up clothes for the judging, I headed to the fire station before my appointment with the judges. When I arrived at the station, the usual voice of the TV and firemen laughing at jokes with one another came to a standstill. You could've heard a pin drop. I came into the dining room where all the accomplices sat smiling.... at me. Then Jerry said, *"My, you look awfully nice tonight. You had a rough day today. How do you manage?"* With a long pause I said, *"I am W-O-M-A-N."* They all laughed and quietly left the room and left me with Tim and my mystery caller. *"I brought you boys some Little Debbie snacks tonight. You might say you're lucky since I did not bake them myself,"* I said with a sheepish smile. To this day, I have fire department rookies come up to me and ask, *"I hear you take care of dogs that come to your house!"* I have always loved animals as much as children. I became a little less innocent that day, and when I see a husky I think of Max and the crazy story that ensued. I guess I also learned firemen stick together, even through a bad joke.

It was a mild and sunny summer morning. I was looking forward to some yard work I had been postponing. I began to weed an iris bed of flowers when freckled-faced Ricky about age eight rode up on his bicycle. As I reached for the first handful of weeds he asked, *"Whatcha doin' Mrs. Krack?"* He was a regular visitor especially when I was out in my yard. *"Pulling weeds Ricky. What*

are you doing today?" Hesitantly he asked, *"Can I have that flag?"* Days before I had affixed a small American flag on a stick to my wrought iron gate. *"Well,"* I said *"that flag is special to me. It reminds me of my daughter who's in the Air Force and others that serve our country."* *"Oh, p-l-e-a-s-e,"* he begged, *"I promise I'll take good care of it."* I stood up from my kneeling. Facing him I said, *"If you can recite the Pledge of Allegiance I will give you the flag."* A smile came across his face and he started, *"Dear Lord..."* Before he could go any farther I gently interrupted him and said, *"Sorry Ricky, that is not the pledge."* He winked his eye and shrugged his shoulders. He made a second attempt with, *"Oh, that the Lord may bless you..."* Once again I stopped him as he prayed. *"Ricky I'll tell you what. I will say the pledge with you."* He smiled and repeated *"I pledge allegiance to the flag..."* He continued following my lead but clearly did not know the Pledge of Allegiance. After we had finished he asked again, *"May I please have the flag?"*

While detaching the flag from the gate I explained flag etiquette. He was so happy to have the flag as he waved it back and forth. About this time a late model, midsized car pulled up to the curb where we were standing. An older woman was driving. Ricky waved at her and exclaimed, *"Look Grandma, Mrs. Krack gave me the flag for saying the Pledge of Allegiance."* The windows were partly down and I could see she was having difficulty operating the electric buttons. She finally lowered the front passenger window. In a shrill voice she squeaked, *"Ricky I've been looking all over for you. It's time to come home!"* Ricky wanted to make sure his grandmother understood how he earned the flag he now was waving inside the car window. Excitedly he said, *"I said 'legiance to the flag Grandma!"* She threw the car into park and screamed at me, *"We do not pledge allegiance to the flag."* She continued sermonizing me about Jesus with inaudible sounds that blew right past me. She was terribly upset. All I had planned to do was pull weeds, but now this. Ricky stood smiling with his flag and I was bewildered as to what to say or do next. The woman was still ranting and raving about the flag. I said under my breath, *"Dear Lord, help me."* As if an answer to my prayer, I saw a low flying formation of geese almost directly overhead. Suddenly I heard a large thud hit the roof of the car. The goose mess slimily ran down the windshield. Complete silence came from within the car. After a long pause I said, *"Ma'am, it seems the geese have pooped on your car. Would you like for me to get the garden hose?"* Softly she said, *"no,"* rolled up her window and slowly drove away. By now, Ricky was pedaling down the street waving the flag in the wind. Never before was I so happy to see geese overhead. I was even happier that Ricky got to wave his flag.

Between dogs and kids, I had made myself a regular part-timer at New Hope as the main dishwasher. I was quick at the job and caught myself daydreaming about possibly getting a different job at a new department store; Gershwin's was in my nearby neighborhood. I filled out an application and tried to schedule days I would not be in the cafeteria. The store was new, so I was one of the many new hires that put up the original fixtures and displays. It was something different and I enjoyed the extra money. There were special associate discount days. When the store opened I became knowledgeable in ladies' intimates and could fit a bra on anyone that had trouble deciding from the hundreds on display. I enjoyed staying busy and quickly earned colored bracelets and pins that were worn on my nametag. I learned the proper colors and their order in display from left to right: white, pink, red, orange, yellow, green, blue, navy, purple, brown, gray, then finally black. There was rhyme and reason for this to catch the consumers' eyes and make them attractive to purchase.

I soon learned the associate's main goal was to approach the shoppers and request they sign up for a new charge card. Of course, there were dollars to save, the more you spent! Seeing that most associates got caught up in the purchase of the chintzy merchandise became the sole reason for their employment. For some, there was not much take home pay for all the in-store associate sales. A man entered the store and approached me right in the middle of the B and C cup bras one day and said loudly, *"If you can show me one thing made in the U.S.A. in this store, I'll buy it, no matter what it is,"* he added. There was nothing I could offer him that was U.S.A.

made. He left in a gruff manner. I quickly made appearances in other departments and had to listen for the announcement over the intercom, *"assistance needed in intimates please."* We were later told we were not allowed to say please or thank you over the intercom- for any reason. I was beginning to get the feel of the store's policies. I worked frantically through the Christmas season and let my part-time work at New Hope go to another cafeteria worker who wanted more hours. I was told I could still come back later if I wanted to. Quickly keeping the shelves and racks stocked, I learned the brand names and styles of every bra and undie possible. The most comical thing was trying to fit bras to two girls who only spoke Spanish. The duo finally were able to decide with much exchange of broken Spanish on my part and gesturing on theirs. That was quite an accomplishment but the customer went away happy and that was my main goal. With the holidays at hand, there was much pressure to get more customers signed up for credit cards. I felt uncomfortable mentioning it to the customers especially those who showed great negativity to being broached in the subject. Usually I kept to the policy of good customer service that would bring people back to the store for future spending sprees.

Winter turned to spring and a shipment of flip-flops arrived in huge boxes. The pairs were individually wrapped in clear plastic bags. Room needed to be made to remove all the winter socks, hats, gloves, and scarves to make space for the new spring arrivals. Following the color scheme and display cards, the spring sandals began to take shape on the intimates and apparel floor. It took several days for four women to put the China made bits of rubber and vinyl sandals into the display. I worked the job a lot by myself and for hours there was a strong sickening rubber smell that inundated the work area. Several employees complained of the odor. Headaches quickly ensued as I continued to open each package. I asked to be moved to a different department and said the flip flops were making me feel ill. I became short of breath. The assistant manager, Mark, even came over and worked with me for a while but had no symptoms as I was suffering. The more flip-flop boxes I opened, the sicker I became. By now, even entering the store affected my health. The symptoms would occur within minutes of reporting to work. I was temporarily put into the children's department but the symptoms persisted. I went to the doctor and was told I had an allergic reaction to the sandals. By now I became weak and could not perform my job. Buying several pairs of the sandals still in the bags, my husband and I thought we could have them tested for unsafe chemicals that by now were affecting several employees besides me. Customers even complained of the obnoxious odor and shopped away from the spring display. Tim started an investigation of his own trying to trace the origin of the flip-flops. He even contacted an agency in Washington D.C., the Department of Agriculture. It was learned that the making of higher end shoes, such as name brand tennis or running shoes could be traced but the lower end sandals like I had unwrapped were not traceable. There was no way of knowing what was in the packaging or sandals themselves. We even sent the merchandise to a lab for testing which turned out to be inconclusive. My days at Gershwin's became numbered. It seemed as if the odor had penetrated the entire store. There seemed to be no escaping the sickening feeling I would get each and every time I arrived at the store's door.

By now I was needed back at the high school, so I decided to leave my retail job for good. Back in the cafeteria, I was given the same duties I had before, and became cashier for the monthly potato bar the students and faculty so enjoyed. For the fun of it I started collecting Mr. Potato Head characters such as Darth Tater and other creations like Minnie Mouse Tater. The kids and teachers enjoyed the *tateriffic* decorations and usually commented on the new additions. Anytime I could have fun and bring smiles to the faces at the school, the more I enjoyed my job. The cafeteria ladies Christmas parties began to mount up as the years rolled by. My mental illness had been kept at bay for going on five years.

My life seemed to have some order to it. I continued my part-time job at school. There were workdays that caused me to be so tired I would have to come home and take a nap. I still worked part-time and failed to make the link from depression to my working environment. One day while having lunch with the other cafeteria ladies, we all expressed how tired we were. Some needed naps when they got home, older ladies had difficulty all of a sudden climbing stairs from the cafeteria. I told Tim about the discussion. He said, *"Do you think there's a carbon monoxide leak somewhere? Since you're all affected it seems like something to look into."* The next day at work Tim arrived when the majority of lunch ladies were available. The dishwasher was turned on as usual and Tim carried with him a gas detector. He slowly moved around the kitchen, there was a constant clicking at some intervals. It picked up its cadence quickly as he approached the dishwasher. He said, *"The reading is showing 100 parts per million (ppm). This is a health hazard,"* Tim said. *"It explains why you ladies have felt so tired and sluggish."* The principal and assistant principal were called to the cafeteria. There were only a few days left of school but the problem persisted until the next day when the sheet metal company fixed a vent for the gas-powered machine. The machine helped heat the water for the dishwasher. It seemed the problem was eradicated.

Summer came quickly and before I knew it, it became time for the school bells to ring again. No further work or concern was made about the carbon monoxide leak. It seemed as if everything was in working order. In February 2010, I came to work as usual, showing the girls a new apron. I felt fine and had no complaints. I even did a little skip for Rita who let out a soft giggle and nod as I modeled my new apron. The day prior the dishwasher worker had failed to tell someone of a loud muffled "boom" that had come from the dishwasher at the end of the day. Unbeknownst to me that next morning I fired up the machine I called, *Gerty*. I waited for the temperature and water to rise inside. It was about fifteen minutes before the huge lunch crowd arrived. I busied myself setting the dishwasher racks up to fill and prepared soapy water for the utensils at the scraping table. Ten minutes had passed and I began to feel faint, just out of the blue. I stepped back from the machine and caught myself from falling, grabbing onto the raised sidewall of the dishwasher. A panicky, impeding doom-like feeling, took over. I could barely put one foot in front of the other. By now, my dish-drying co-worker took her place at the end of the dishwasher.

Somehow I warned her to stay away from there. *"It's carbon monoxide,"* I said as I started to lose all sense of thinking. I pushed myself to the phone to dial 9-1-1. Confusion set in. I became irritable and began saying over and over, *"I need help. Call 9-1-1."* The dish dryer, Carol had run out to get the assistant cafeteria manager, Tina. I tried to stand and somehow while my heart was racing and my words became slurred, I managed to yell, *"9-1-1, carbon monoxide!"* Tina grabbed my flailing arms and tried to control me. My legs felt like lead and I knew something horrible had just happened. No one was listening to me. I sat in the desk chair while Ann was summoned to take my place at the dishwasher. The throng of students had arrived I was told, *"Go out and take Ann's place as a cashier for the potato bar."* Seemingly drunk, I staggered out to the waiting salad bar cashier post. I had no idea what I was doing. Kids were asking for change, which I did not offer as usual. Some kids passed me by without paying. I was in another world. I said, *"Rita, get me a stool. I can't stand up!"* I felt I was going to fall any second as she clambered to a stool near the ice cream machine. *"What's wrong with you?"* she said. I could not answer, standing there like some kind of automaton. A small part of me thought it might have been carbon monoxide. I was indifferent to what was happening around me. I managed to get through the next two lunches with my stupor and had to be reminded a number of times about my duties between lunches like cleaning off the tables. It was quickly decided it was necessary for me to perform the menial tasks. I felt awful – what had happened? Once again, my mind floated to 9-1-1. Why had not I had the forthrightness to call as I had done before when there was a carbon monoxide leak? *"For God's sake was no one listening!"* I screamed in my head.

I finally called Tim. He answered the phone calmly, *"Hello."* Frantically I brokenly told him, *"I feel sick and faint. The dishwasher.... I think it's carbon monoxide. I told them to call 9-1-1... I need oxygen! No one will listen."* Upsettingly he said, *"I can't get to you for an hour. Stay away from the dishwasher and tell them to* call *9-1-1.*" By now the ladies were busy with their own jobs for the next lunchtime. Tina said, *"It's your bipolar. Just try to relax."* I felt tingly all over and could hardly stand on my own. The last lunch was like the first two. By now a state of numbness took over my body. I could not move. There was no small talk with the teens, no smiles, no thank yous. Many realized something was wrong but said nothing. I sat down immediately and did not get up from the cafeteria table.

Tim had arrived with the gas detector. He was quickly sweeping the cafeteria kitchen and announced, *"Everyone leave the kitchen. There's a carbon monoxide leak,"* he said. The instrument indicated 250 parts per million (ppm) was present of the deadly gas. An industrial detector will alarm at 35 ppm. He walked up to me as if he had seen a ghost; he knew I had been greatly affected by the exposure. The cafeteria ladies still did not comprehend the seriousness of the exposure. The attending vice principal and maintenance personnel were summoned. Ann, who had taken my place at the dishwasher, now had similar symptoms: confusion, difficulty standing, a heart racing, and faintish. Still 9-1-1 was not called. We were told by the manager, *"You'll have to go to the workman's comp doctor's office."* Without so much of a concern she said, *"I have to go with you, but I have to count the money first."* Again the numbness came. The mapping of my brain was no longer a part of me. As I sat at the cafeteria table with the ladies, they offered me crackers saying, *"You probably did not eat much for breakfast. Eat these and you'll feel better."* How absurd I thought as I slowly ate the crackers, as I slipped further into a zombie-like state. My soul and body had eluded me. Ann joined me at the table, speechless and sharing nothing with the bewildered co-workers. The manager would scowl at us over her shoulder as she counted the stacks of bills. I could not understand her emotion and her lack of urgency in the matter. The assistant principal, maintenance man, and my husband were discussing the seriousness of the matter.

The manager drove us to the workman's comp doctor's office. Under my breath I had threatened to drive myself, soon realizing my body was not up to the task. The manager Claire was of German stock and was quite serious about the event- only in that it was disrupting her usual routine. Ann, Clair, and I arrived at the office. The room was filled with sniffling and sneezing patients. Once again the urgency of our situation was delayed as we were given a number and a seat. I became angry knowing it was too late for oxygen or any treatment that would reverse the damage that had been done. We sat silently together as we waited our turn. Claire was nervous and fidgety, now realizing the scope of our visit to the doctor. Ann and I were called back to a small room where our vitals were taken. We explained to the nurse, *"We were both exposed to 250 ppm of carbon monoxide in our school cafeteria. We are not feeling well. It happened two hours ago."* The nurse appeared indifferent to our report and said, *"The doctor will be in shortly."* We sat and discussed what had just transpired at school. I told Ann, *"We are very sick from that exposure."* I continued, *"I am sure there will be tests done to see how much of the carbon monoxide is in our systems. I do not think the others know how serious this is."* *"I feel ok,"* she said with a depressed tone. She had been exposed as long if not longer than I had. This all seemed like a nightmare from which I could not wake.

Dr. Glasglow entered the room. He was a balding man with wisps of white hair on the sides of his head. He peered over the top of his glasses and said, *"Hello, what brings you here?"* He seemed sluggish and not at all excited about what brought us to his office. Once again, I explained as Ann sat silently – she seemed to be slipping in and out of her semi-consciousness. *"Ann and I work in a school cafeteria at New Hope High School. We run the dishwasher. It malfunctioned and was tested for carbon monoxide,"* I said. *"How do you know you were exposed?"* he asked. *"My husband is a firefighter and the detector he has said 250 ppm."* I began to reel with confusion and exhaustion after my last comment. I sat quietly as the doctor gave us both a quick physical exam. He continued, *"You both need to rest and get plenty of fresh air."* He then proceeded to give us instructions for our work place. I stopped him and said, *"Claire, our manager is here. You need to talk to her."* The same sense of numbness to my brain ensued and was not going away. The doctor understood our plight but was not offering any tests or blood work to be done. He said, "*Go home. If you do not feel better by tomorrow, come back to the office.*" Claire and the doctor advanced their conversation. "*As manager of the cafeteria you are responsible for the safety of your employees. I suggest you have someone check the ductwork and machinery at your school near the dishwasher. If these ladies have continued problems they are going to see me again.*"

　　We returned to the school where my husband drove me home. He had stayed behind to ensure that something would be done to eradicate the possibility of another exposure. If it happened again, this would make it the third time for this event. I was exhausted and went straight to bed. I tossed and turned and could not sleep. I began crying insatiably. I could not control my emotions and a sense of doom became a cage. Restlessly though the night, I thought of how happy I was yesterday and how everything was going so well until this nightmare started. I arose more exhausted and unable to stop crying. Knowing I could not go to work like this, I called in sick and said, "*I am going back to Dr. Glasglow today. I feel worse than yesterday.*" Later I wondered how this affected Ann. She was in overdrive and was irritable according to our fellow employees. I made the appointment with Dr. Glasglow. We arrived early and sat out in the parking lot eating some drive through lunch. Half in tears I told Tim, who was driving, "*Could this get any worse? What will happen now?*" To the left of me I could see a slow figure exiting the comp. office. The lab coat was so long on this man that it nearly touched the ground. Between his balding head and expanding white coat, he took on the appearance of a huge white gumdrop. He reminded me of what Artie Johnson of Rowan & Martin's *Laugh-In* looked like before someone would stick it to him. He moved slowly, ever so slowly towards the parked cars. To try and humor the moment Tim and I took bets as to which car he would get in, the new model or the beat-up old Volkswagen. He finally touched the door of the old jalopy. I felt a burst of emotion. I began to uncontrollably laugh and cry. I could not stop. My mind was possessed and I could not turn off the laughing or the crying. It lasted for almost five minutes. We waited another fifteen minutes then went in to see Dr. Glasglow who had returned to the office. My husband introduced himself and explained that he was a district chief with the City of Evansville Fire Department. *"I am very concerned about Michelle's exposure to the high level of carbon monoxide,"* he said. *"Her behavior has yet to be normal since it happened yesterday. That is why we are here today."* Dr. Glasglow explained, *"Whatever happened yesterday is likely going to permanently affect your wife. Her original diagnosis of bipolar may be greatly exaggerated by this exposure. I would like for you to go to the workman's comp center near the Angels of Mercy Hospital downtown. There is nothing more I can do for you here."* My heart and hope began to plummet. What if I could not rid myself of these conditions of roller coaster emotions, sleep deprivation, waves of deep anxiety, and senseless feelings of despair over the sequence of events that had taken place on that horrible February day? Things were hard enough just trying to maintain.

My life would never be the same again. I was a mess and felt an awareness that most of my senses were being detached. I could no longer write in long beautiful cursive style. My printing and writing that I was so proud of as an artful form, had been reduced to chicken scratch. As days followed, my calendar had so many scratch-outs and white-outs, and most of it made no sense. The ledger of my checkbook was a disaster of wrong numbers and entries. I became sensitive to light and rarely felt much like embracing the sun's new day anyway. I was lost. Tension headaches dulled my thinking that resulted in crying spells and then laughter fits of insane rebuke of what had happened to me. Life was a joke. I felt like a puppet on a string with no particular rhyme or reason. The exposure to the profound levels of carbon monoxide was my puppeteer. I had no appetite or energy to prepare meals or perform the most menial tasks. What was the sense of living? My toes were numb. I had difficulty walking. My steps were broken by clumsy falling attempts to reach the next room. My hearing was dulled as well and sometimes I barely even heard people ask how I was. The family-like atmosphere at work had eluded me. I felt an outcast in my own hell that had misaligned every aspect of my life.

If this was permanent I felt it was a desperate solitary battle of my own. Tim knew all too well how serious this was and how I was affected. He pursued the medical attention I needed and tried to support my ever-fluctuating mind. We arrived at the hospital's comp. center. I had been here before when I had applied at Gershwin's. The doctor in this office quickly and mechanically scanned over my report from the previous doctor. *"Well, by the sounds of these symptoms I think it's clear to say you are having a type of mania related to your bipolar."* If I could, I would have screamed and was definitely devastated by his remarks. I had encountered enough manic episodes and this was nothing like them. This was affecting parts of my body that had nothing to do with bipolar illness. I felt absent in this whole process of medicinal intervention. Why was I even here? There was nothing that would be done for me. We needed proof and a paper trail of what had happened. The doctor wished me well and agreed to send me across the street for further testing to rule out the chance that my condition was carbon monoxide related. What did he mean? Of course it was carbon monoxide related! If I had thought it was purely mental, I would have called my psychiatrist! This had turned into a wild goose chase and I felt as if I had started running in circles like a cat trying to catch its tail. I became tearful again as we crossed the street to the hospital's emergency department.

My body was possessed. I only wanted peace of mind and someone to medically validate this experience. The emergency room was not busy. I was shown to a curtained room and sat upon the tall examining table. We waited for half an hour between the nurse's initial assessment and the arrival of Dr. Johnson. He was department head of the Angels of Mercy emergency room. He was middle-aged and had a self-assured presence. He listened to our story and my complaints that occurred since the accident. He said, *"I am very sorry for what has happened."* Tim asked, *"You don't have a hyperbaric chamber here at Mercy?"* *"No, we haven't had one for years. It was too expensive to keep,"* the doctor said, sadly. The hyperbaric chamber would saturate my body with forced oxygen. By now, as time passed, any irreversible symptoms were less likely to be reversed. The hyperbaric chamber was our last hope. Dr.

Johnson could tell I was becoming despondent over the news. After speaking to my clinical psych therapist, Brenda, she further helped by sending me to a specialist in Indianapolis whose expertise was in carbon monoxide poisoning.

Life as I knew it had come to a screeching halt. I immediately decided I would not or could not go back to work. I was fearful for a possible reoccurrence of carbon monoxide poisoning. It was my understanding that another dose could very well be my last. Self-preservation would drive my decision home. The next day I called the New Hope cafeteria and told Claire, the manager, I was resigning my position and could not come back to work due to the accident. She could only say *"ok"* and I could sense the bitterness in her response. She still did not grasp the seriousness of the situation. I immediately made an appointment with the school principal, Mr. Floyd, for the next day. I hoped to tell him what updates I had received from all the workman's comp doctors and emergency room. I slept little that night and continued to cry needlessly. I felt drained and depressed like never before. There was little improvement to tell and I hoped he would understand my condition. Carefully, I drove to school not totally trusting my driving skills. I was very nervous for no reason, as I had spoken freely to Mr. Floyd many times during the school year.

The results of all the medical visits were inconclusive to say the least, but the fact remained that I had been drastically altered mentally and physically. Mr. Floyd had arranged a time slot for me to see him. The anxiety was so much I almost cancelled the appointment. It was so unlike me to feel this way. I wanted his input and wanted to let him know why I was leaving my eight-year-long job at New Hope. He welcomed me with his big and warm smile. Before he became principal, I told him one day, *"Always keep your smile..... no matter what."* For some reason the church song popped in my head, *"We will walk with each other, we will walk hand in hand, we will walk with each other, we will walk hand in hand,"* as I approached his office door. *"Hello,"* Mr. Floyd said warmly. *"I am so sorry I was not here the day of the incident."* At least he acknowledged that something had happened! I had all faith in him that he would support my medical interventions and would support the care I needed. *"Well, first I must tell you, I had hoped to come back to work but Tim and I felt it was best I did not. Mentally and physically the carbon monoxide exposure has caused many health problems. I went to the workman's comp center– both of them– and was referred to the emergency room. The ER doctor suggested I see a specialist in Indianapolis. My psych counselor Brenda encouraged the same."* Mr. Floyd sat listening intently, *"Let me know if there's anything I can do,"* he said. At this time, I thought all the doctors and office calls were covered under workman's compensation. There was no mention that any of them were. Again, he apologized for what had happened. I did ask, *"The problem has been solved in the cafeteria with the duct work?"* *"Yes,"* he replied. I said, *"There should at least be a carbon monoxide detector to alert the ladies if it happens again. Will you promise that all cafeterias and workrooms where there are gas-powered engines have a detector? In the whole school district?"* I added. *"I would hate for anyone else to go through what I have."* Without hesitating, he said, *"Yes I will. You have my word."* He got up from his desk and we shared a mutual hug. I left his office saying goodbye to the secretaries. The girls in the office were friendly and witty when I usually came in the office. Today there was no exchange of small talk or jokes. There was a serious nature about them. I missed the good ole days. Things would never be the same again. A wave of anxiety struck me as I walked to the car. As I turned the key to the car, I cried, realizing this was the last time I would visit the employees parking lot and likely the last I would step foot in the building.

For many years, my friend and fellow grade-school track coach, Coach Terry, would joke that if we ever won the lottery we would get New Hope a track and stadium. What needed to be added now was an updated dishwasher, one safer and more efficient too! After working there eight years, I knew all the pitfalls and complaints that went along with it. I could not understand why a more direct approach and answer to the problem had not taken place since the first incident. Many repairmen that frequented our aging dishwasher said it was okay, but after the first exposure, one of the contracted repairmen said, *"This isn't safe. The dishwasher and this motor ought to be replaced. I would not want to work here with it like this."* We ladies were given a false hope for the temporary fix of ductwork added. The company that fixed the sheet metal had to be called out several times after carbon monoxide was still detected the first time. It made me nervous, to say the least, from the very first exposure. I wished there had been more money in the kitchen fund to eradicate the problem and have it done up right. We worked within our means but for now, it had cost Ann and I our health. It was a high price to pay for a wage of a few cents over the minimum wage paid for our services. I felt as I did when I worked at Gershwin's. Another environment had changed my life, only this one was more serious and had irreversible damages.

I developed a tic in the form of a slight dance with my feet when my brain would grow impatient or I would have to wait for something. Two years after the incident I saw a teacher at a local garden center. My acquired tic presented itself. She brushed by me and said, *"Do you have to go to the bathroom?"* I then realized how noticeable it was and became embarrassed by its presence. To this day it is there, but with time, lots of time, it has become less apparent. The other symptoms lingered. The anxiety was so bad on a daily basis that I called Tim at his two jobs frequently for reassurance. At night was the worst. Several times to my crying, pleading voice he would come home and lay beside me until I could fall asleep. He went through so much agony not knowing what to do or say to make me feel better. I had recently seen a new psychiatrist as my original doctor, who I had liked very much for over a year, had to leave her job for family reasons. Her name was Mrs. Pike; she was a pleasant and thorough doctor. She made me feel better with her council and good use of medications. I had now seen the new replacement, Dr. Kapoor, at least once shortly after the exposure. The relationship between she and I was lacking what I had with Mrs. Pike. The new doctor was hard to understand, as she spoke broken English. She gave the air that with no doubt she was the doctor and I was the patient. She talked down to me. This mechanical demeanor and approach to psychiatry would indeed cause me to not look forward to seeing her in the future. Too, I became increasingly agitated, terribly forgetful, and increasingly cold. I just could not get warm enough. I would set the thermostat on seventy-eight and wear several sweaters in the house. It was March and quite cold outside.

Fifteen days had passed since the carbon monoxide incident. Never before had I encountered this type of reaction with my previous manic episodes. Usually, my medications would make things tolerable within five days of hospitalization. It was agreed we would call Dr. Kapoor for another appointment. I felt the world was slowly slipping from my grasp. I argued constantly with Tim and could cry and curse again the next minute. Perhaps the right regimen of prescriptions would help my symptoms. We saw the doctor on a rainy Tuesday in March. It was agreed Tim would meet me there from his work, so I would drive separately. I drove like a nervous sixteen-year-old. It was only a short distance and I knew the directions, but the anxiety it caused in getting there was unbearable. Tim and I met and waited our turn at the doctors' office. We sat down in her small office and faced her. I glanced across the shelves in her room and became fixated on a picture of her daughter with a sock monkey. My daughter Carrie and I had fun with the new Kia car commercial that featured a song by The Heavy entitled, *How You Like Me Now?* The idea of the commercial is that the kids' toys left in the Kia came to life when the passengers were gone. They used the tune to rock out as they cruised around the city. Carrie was able to find a life-sized sock monkey at a local Goodwill and gave it to me for my birthday. We had fun driving around shopping that afternoon with the sock monkey's arm and hand waving from the car's back window. We had fun, lots of it, from all of the stares and laughing we got from shoppers in the parking lot.

Unfortunately, sitting in that office with Kapoor was not nearly as fun as the sock monkey afternoon. I came back to the reality of where I was. Tim began to explain the carbon monoxide story. I felt like the doctor listened, but she surmised it was mainly my bipolar acting up. She emphasized that was the main culprit. I disagreed with her and did not hold back. I began to curse her and tell her, *"You do not know what the hell you're talking about!"* She leaned back from her desk in great surprise. Tim said, *"Michelle, settle down."* Something snapped in me after she said, *"Maybe you need to go to the hospital."* I had prided myself in keeping out of those places if at all possible. This would not be one of those days. By now Tim and Dr. Kapoor were standing because I was standing and screaming at the top of my lungs. *"Hospital, hospital!"* All I needed was medication. *"I do not need your damned hospital!"* I screamed. By now the whole situation was out of control. I picked up her phone and yelled, *"Why don't you call me an ambulance. Yes, an ambulance!"* I stammered. I became more furious and dialed 9-1-1. *"I need an ambulance at Dr. Kapoor's office stat!"* I said. *"Where are you calling from?"* asked the operator. *"Dr. Kapoor's office!"* I snapped. *"What is the address?"* Hell, I don't know, I thought to myself. That was the only thinking that was taking place. I yelled at the doctor who was now vacating the room along with Tim, *"What the hell is your address?"* She answered back, *"10 Division Street."* I curtly told the operator then slammed down the phone. I grabbed pictures of her family from the shelves and stuck them under my coat. By now the entire office and waiting room was hearing the maddening display. I pushed back Tim and the doctor and headed for the door. I pulled my keys from my purse and ran to the car. As I tried to put the keys in the locked door, Tim grabbed them and took them away. *"I just want to go home,"* I sobbed. *"I just want to go home."* My mindset was torturing. I had lost all control. I had never been like this except for the first time I ever got sick, really sick before my bipolar diagnosis. I pulled away from him and walked quickly to the street. I had on open-toed dress shoes.

The cold rain dampened my feet as I walked. I became more furious with the rain and how wet I was becoming. As I walked north, I began to place the framed pictures one-by-one in people's yards along the way. I have no idea what possessed me to do this. I just did it. Later, Dr. Kapoor would be glad to retrieve her family photos. I marched in the rain determined to go home. I knew the way and there would be no stopping me now. Looking both ways, I crossed the street but was still dangerously close to the traffic. It must have horrified Tim. He ran out ahead of me to stop traffic. His actions infuriated me even more. I began to run in the pouring rain. The droplets made it hard to see where I was going. By now I had entered the backyards of residents along the way. This had been going on for about eight long minutes. An ambulance and police car now added to the parade of Tim, Dr. Kapoor, and some staff from the office. A friggin' parade in the rain. They were all damned fools I thought. I just wanted to be left alone. I found some shelter in an old, rickety wooden shed with its door open. I could see Tim standing about twenty yards away. *"Leave me alone,"* I screamed. I began to cry *"E.T. go home– go home,"* over and over. I bounded from the shed and cut back into a side street that led back to Division Street. I stayed alongside the rocky shoulder. By now the police car was rolling up closely behind me. He nearly bumped me with his car. *"Crap! Now the police were involved,"* I thought. I became angry and took off my rubber-soled shoe and slammed it into the police car's front window. It bounced off and the next thing I knew I was lying in a deep puddle of water with my hands being jerked to my backside. My arms wrenched with pain as my hands became locked with the snap of handcuffs. I began to sob again uncontrollably. What had I done to deserve this?

Well, for one, I had called my own ambulance and had screamed at my doctor in her own office. But, I threatened no one no had intentions of harming myself. I was loaded, soaking wet, in to the ambulance. I began to yell obscenities at Tim and the officer. My arms and wrist burnt with pain. As the ambulance attendants covered me with a blanket, one said, *"You might as well stop yelling. It won't do you any good."* So I did. I kept perfectly quiet all the way to the emergency room. As usual nothing was done. I lay there shivering from the drenched clothes I was wearing. Every time I saw Tim peer around from the nurses' station, it infuriated me all over again. He was out there with his buddies devising a plan as to what to do with me. What would he do with me? I was a raging lunatic and only wanted to go home. It was decided I would go to Dymphna Hospital. I had never been there before. Dymphna is the patron saint for the nervous and mentally ill. It was a psychiatric hospital and was in the same area as the workman's comp. centers I had already visited. The staff was unfamiliar with my lengthy history of hospitalization at St. Clement's. I settled down quite a bit in the emergency room and it was agreed that I could go home and change my clothes. Meanwhile, Tim called my parents to devise a way to get me to go to Dymphna's. It was agreed that Dad would say he wanted to check out the facility for future reference. I have no idea why I went along for the ride. I should have obviously seen it coming. I felt like a derailed train loosing contact the tracks that were reality. All they needed was my signature to agree that I would take treatment at St. Dymphna's.

Somehow I signed a paper and the next thing I knew I was in a scanty hospital gown with no belongings. I was introduced to a group of young people in their twenties. My demeanor had changed and I felt safe, dry, and cautiously calm for the moment. A bit of realism hit me and I knew I needed psychiatric intervention. I expected to stay my usual five days, do what was expected of me, and then be on my way home. The group was pleasant enough as they were offered sugary snacks and Cokes by the staff. Crayons and coloring books were at the table. We colored and spoke in normal tones to one another. *"Hi, what's your name"* a pretty, young, brown hair and brown-eyed girl asked? I told her, now realizing how tired I was. Exhaustion had set in, but there was an underlying anger and mistrust that soon bubbled to the surface. I tried to keep my composure and did for several hours. I grew tired of listening to the young group go on about their last fix, which was mostly just a cigarette.

I lost total interest and noticed the game shelves and how messy everything was. *"Why can't people put things away,"* I thought. I began to arrange things neatly in stacks. Coloring books and crayons stacked next to one another, then playing cards. I was happy with my organization and felt compelled to push some responsibility on the rest of the group. Without saying a word I took a black crayon and outlined the color book and crayon stack on the wooden furniture and then proceeded to write in front of the playing cards and the other stacks their corresponding titles. I then went to the side of the wooden cabinet and wrote *"To Sanity,"* and onto the wall, *"and beyond."* I was perfectly content with my artistic endeavor. It would be hours later before the hotheaded nurse's assistant would be literally screaming, *"She defaced the furniture and wall! She messed it up,"* pointing to me.

Needless to say, I was whisked away to another unit without a word or further reprimand. I soon realized the mistake I had made and landed in a noisier and more obnoxious place. There was loud television and many people aimlessly roaming around. I was surprised no one asked me for a cigarette here. There was a patio designated for smoking and I wanted no part of it. There were always people gathered at the locked patio door when the hour struck so they could fill their lungs with nicotine. Someone checked my wristband that I had forgotten about having. My gown was thin and cold. One covered my front, the other my back. They stayed together with strings tied around the neck. I was so cold I shivered. I asked for a blanket after I was shown to my room and was given medication. I am still not sure what it was that I took, nor did I really care. Whatever it was it seemed to calm me down a little.

My room was dark and faced the west side of the building. The view was of a paved street that ran along the side of another nondescript, gray building. I had a beautiful panorama of the west sky. As I sat on my bed I saw a red, glowing light about the size of a teardrop in the corner of the room. I knew it was a camera and I hated being watched, especially while undressing with male nurses possibly watching. I later realized I had complete privacy in the thick walled bathroom. I entered the bathroom and looked in the mirror and smiled and said aloud, *"How do you like me now?"* I would take three or four showers a day in attempt to warm myself. I walked around the unit wrapped in two heavy blankets around my head and shoulders. They must have thought I was a real nut case. Later Tim would find out through his research in carbon monoxide that the body's core temperature is actually lowered. It affects the temperature gauge of the brain; I drank many cups of decaffeinated coffee and hot teas when possible. The showers helped a lot if for only a temporary fix. I sat in my room staring at the glowing red light.

Something came over me. An impish impulse to cover the obnoxious glow seemed like the thing to do. I let myself back in the bathroom and got handfuls of toilet paper and wet them at the sink. I then stood on my chair and flung the wadded wet mess at the menacing orb. After several trips to the bathroom and about six flings, I had the thing covered thickly with layers of wet toilet paper. I was pleased with my efforts and would see how long it took them to realize they could not see me. At least a half hour passed before someone showed up at my room with hands on hips shaming me, *"Girl, what is wrong with you?"* No one had asked before nor did they seem to really care. I was not receiving the usual attention I had gotten at St. Clement's Hospital. I was told, *"You are not allowed to have a chair anymore!"* Big deal I thought as I watched the maintenance man scrape the mess clean, teetering on a tall ladder. He laughed in spite of himself that he sounded like Santa Claus. *"Never seen anything like this before,"* he chuckled. I was allowed one phone call a day. There were about twenty people, street people, as I would call them on the unit. Most of them were there because of drug abuse and they were rough speaking and tougher acting than I was used to. Oh, how I missed St. Clement's. Journaling was usually a healthy way for me to deal with the passing time.

Journaling 3/15/10

Michelle May Belle is given daily papers from staff that are collected at days end. No discussion, no therapy.

Just fill out the same papers every day for what would be ten days. Who cares? Who reads them? Do they know how tormented my brain and thinking are? Here is an example of Dymphna's "therapeutic" papers:

What is goal setting?

-Goals are set to improve your life or achieve something

-There are two types of goals:

-Short term– a goal you want to see take place day to day or week to week.

-Long term– a goal you want to see happen from month to month or year to year.

-Short term goals can be integrated into long term goals. The goals should always be realistic to the doer. Remember, the point of setting a goal is to improve one's self, not make one feel like a failure. Do not give up if your goal is not achieved, just continue to try.

-There are three parts needed to set a goal:

-TASK what do you want to achieve

-TARGET what you are doing to achieve it

-TIME SPAN when you want to achieve it

I live in only the moment. I take paper out and begin to doodle artwork and affirmations on it with multi-colored markers. I make a crossword of fellow patients names of Lisa crossover with Tammy connected to Mallory.

GREAT FOOD, GREAT SMILES, THANK KITCHEN, GOOD LUCK, THANKS TO YOU.

(3 blue ribbons flowing from each other marked each with 1st CLASS and outlined in blue)

Parts needed to set goals are

-TASK – I answer "Yes, We do it."

-TARGET – "Yes" I draw the bull's eye target with arrow through the middle.

-TIME SPAN – I answer "NOW"

My interpretation was juvenile to say the least and no one told me different. As days passed I wrote more. Sometimes I was making sense, sometimes my pen seemed to have a life of its own. Once again there was no interest in any of my expressions. *"What was the use?"* I asked myself. My actual task was to find medications and ask for those medications that would help me sleep and lessen my anxiety that had become insurmountable. My target was and should have been to gain sanity and have expectations to go home. The time span should have been a minimum of five to seven days.

In all actuality it would take two years until I felt as good as I did the morning before the carbon monoxide accident occurred. The time frame St. Dymphna's was asking was longer than they could keep me in their care. More profound was the daily handout titled "Preventing Relapse." It explained that relapse is *a process of gradual decline in function proceeding or leading to the recurrence of a particular disease.* I had reached the outer rim of unhealthy behavior– beyond any mania I had or would ever experience in my entire life. Further it read, *relapse is preventable if individuals are aware of their condition.* Tim also knew my condition was a result of the carbon monoxide exposure. No one at St. Dymphna's seemed to take his information or address my simplest concerns. Between the anxiety and the inability to increase my core temperature, I was a bundle of nerves and regressed into a child-like state. Out of all sixteen symptoms of relapse, I had managed to have a positive check by each and every one. What treatment or interaction would or could Dymphna's have provided? I experienced the following sixteen listed; depressive mood, lack or loss of confidence, denial of symptoms, poor judgment, compulsive behavior, confusion- with a capital C, difficulty making decisions, easily irritated or agitated, unhealthy eating patterns– that varied day-by-day, lack of organization of daily routine, feelings of helplessness, unhealthy sleeping patterns- there was no sleep, apathy – my writing expressed this, withdrawal from usual activities- there were no activities except for eating so this was hardly applicable, and inability to concentrate or focus attention – my flits of ideas wondered and flew at high rates of turnover.

There was so much verbiage on these papers that they were a perfect joke to anyone who was mildly, much less acutely, ill. The papers were filled with pages of my incoherent rambles and I usually had to ask for more lined paper. In a way, I suppose it was therapeutic and was the only positive conditional treatment I received. The day would not be complete without being handed a Dymphna's "Review of the Day" paper to be filled out before sleep meds were given at approximately ten o'clock.

Dated March 9, 2010: here are the questions asked and my answers. My cursive happened to be readable that day and my mania was high. There were seven questions.

#1. Identify one positive thing you did today. *Made a stand for myself.*

#2. How do you feel now? *Much better than in the morning (my anxiety and severe headache had lessened.)*

#3. What was the most important event that happened to you today? *Loving my husband Tim.*

#4. Did you accomplish your goal for the day? How so? *"Yes. Saw it coming- the two of us meeting in the middle."*

#5. Did you learn anything today? *Ask, tell, ask, tell, bitch- originally thought. Ask, ask, tell, tell then bitch- there is a difference.*

#6. Are you experiencing any suicidal thoughts? *No. Except for destroying this delicious cake, hats off to the pastry!*

#7. Are you having thoughts of harming others? *Watching "Friends" TV show about pranks – harmless means of diffusing anger. Wish that the staff at Dymphna's could join the "Ooga Booga Club" my family hosts.*

My family found humor in just about everything. This place was too sterile and impersonal. I felt like a part of the furniture—how does furniture have feelings? The answer to this would probably be somewhere in the same realm as understanding my answer to question seven from above. I did endorse my bookcase art work by signing it M. K. L. P. N. You would have thought that being a nurse and now a patient would have given me some control. I doodled art and played word games on pages and pages of lined paper. From *T-I-M-O-T-H-Y* printed across the page I cross-worded *M-I-C-H-E-L-L-E* and *H-I-S-T-O-R-Y* from Tim's name. From history I printed crossway *H-E-R-S-T-O-R-Y*. From Michelle down I crossed *S-P-I-R-I-T-U-A-L*, *V-I-C-T-O-R-Y* and *T-H-A-N-K-S*. I guess even then they were words that would encompass how I am doing today.

On the same page, I wrote in beautiful cursive: *The future belongs to those willing to sacrifice and believe in the spirit of Christmas and dreams.* An icon of a peace symbol and two Christmas bells surrounded the words. Hours upon hours of positive affirmations filled three folders that were written in white toothpaste. One read, *Paper, A League of Jesus*. The others titled *Games and Friends* and the final one *Unit*. My routine daily was writing, drawing, or collage building with occasional artwork drawn on Styrofoam cups. By now the word was out that I decorated the cups. I wrote pages of disappointment of the uncleanliness of the dining area on the unit. Obviously it was never read. Bits of food would lie in the same place and would dry up after days of neglect. Black scratch marks etched the walls and appeared dirty and unclean. These housekeeping infractions just tormented me. What else was there to do or places to go?

There was one time I began to hallucinate and fixate that my husband was a zombie with another fireman he had lunch with. The shells of their bodies would remain sitting at a booth in a restaurant while terrestrial slugs would drop to the floor from their pants legs. They had infinity for food morsels on the floor. I wrote a note, *Lunch is waiting, pretzel, Cheetos, a snipple of dried noodle, cornbread, hair, a little cake or apple.* Also added was this little verse, *some may belch and some may fart, I get my goodies from the wheels of a grocery cart.* The delusion was only temporary and lasted for only a few hours. I did not express this to anyone who would listen. Who would care?

It was not out of the ordinary for Tim to make the local evening news or morning paper for his account of a recent fire in the city. A newspaper article describing a house fire on Cherry Street was given to me by family. Tim was mentioned in the article. It was bizarre how reality mish-mashed itself into my overactive brain. I can offer more humor by some of the poetry I gleaned from my current condition. *I sit, I stand, I sit, sit, sit, mostly on this upside down trash pit. My desk, the bed is just the right height. My knees come equal to the light. I am not complaining as you see, to the cold that is deep inside of me. So a look, a stare, while I wear, a bound-up towel upon my head, I look like the other guy who worked with Ed.* Since the chair had been removed from my room because of my escapade, I now used an overturned trashcan for a chair next to my bed now being used as an art table.

I received many cards from immediate family and close friends. I was luckier than most in this regard. Many did not have family or friends. If they did, they had been alienated from them. I too left thank yous to not only kitchen help, but the nurse that complimented my room decorating. A roommate wanted more information about NAMI so I wrote her a little note that read, *Dear Jessica, Keep the old friend (like me) and make a new psychology. Do the best in all that you do! It doesn't matter your name, success, or fame. Just laugh out loud when you see, Michelle May Krack, the name, and help all that you can. Contact NAMI.org. National Alliance on Mental Illness.*

Mealtime was noisy and the other patients were seated too close for comfort. Table manners were lacking and most of the people acted like hogs at a trough. How had I gotten into such a place? Food went on the floor and stayed there for days. I would make bets with myself about how long those three peas would lay there in the corner before they would be swept up. They would stay there for days until I could not take it any longer, so I would pick them up out of disgust. The dust bunnies in my room could have choked a horse. If you blew a strong breath you could watch them roll across the floor. I sat at my window on an upside down trash can. I would watch the cloud formations for what seemed like hours. It was like hallucinating but there were actual clouds and my imagination was the limit. No one offered me a kind word or comment even when the meds were passed out. I began to collect my medicine cups to recycle and later use for craft projects.

One day, a storm brewed up and I watched a lone pine tree from the dining room, just outside the smokers' patio. The wind blew the branches fiercely to and fro. I could see a long face of an old man in its boughs and he seemed to be snoring. The wind blew open his mouth. It seemed he was startled during his nap only to go back to the rhythmic rolling of the branches that lullabied him in his sleep. There honestly was nothing to do. I knew that asking for art supplies was out of the question, given what I had created in the first unit I visited. By now Tim had brought me some clothes and no pajamas. I was not happy with his choice of mix-matched outfits either, only adding insult to injury. Mom sent along some nice garden magazines. They were well received and were a sight for my sore eyes that longed to be outside to see real plants and flowers. I preferred to stay in my room most of the time. The television was so loud in the common area and most of the *inmates*, as I would call them, were acting as if they belonged in prison.

One of the ladies saw me looking at her and our eyes met; she said, *"What's your problem bitch?"* I had regular street clothes on and she only had the gowns on that the hospital provided. It was plain to see she pretty much ran charge of the television and everyone around it. When there were outbreaks amongst the patients no one on staff bothered to intervene or try to keep the peace. Some of the staff even acted indifferent to each other and their wards. By the third or fourth day, I felt sure I would be going home soon. I was allowed makeup and the constant two blankets that partially made me feel warm. The chair to my room was never returned so I kept the metal trashcan turned upside down and continued to use my bed as a desk. I began tearing colorful garden pictures from the magazines and made beautiful collages by gluing the slick pages together with my white Crest toothpaste. They could not take that away from me.

I learned that Amy and Kassidy were coming home for my other daughter's bridal shower. I could not wait to see them during visitation. It would be another day before they arrived. Tim came to visit me one day after supper. I was allowed to follow single-file off the unit with others to the cafeteria line. You needed to be careful who you sat near or looked at or all hell would break loose. I kept to myself mostly and spoke only to one other young woman, Katie. I felt so out of place and longed for my family at home. The woman that had called me a bitch circled me in the dining room and raised her voice. By now I had learned her name was Barb. She had it in for me. I had not said a word to her or even given her a glance. She kept picking on me, *"You think you're extra special don't you?"* she said with a snicker. I paused and said, *"My name is Michelle."* *"Well lottie da,"* she said. She walked around me as if to catch any imperfections she could use against me. I stood silently and tried to ignore her. She would have several more altercations with me at meal time about the salt and pepper and about my makeup. I soon learned she had no personal effects with her and no visitors. It was no wonder she bullied everyone around her. How sad I thought.

While in the small dining room on the unit, I started to doodle my name and some flowers with an ink pen onto the soft Styrofoam surface of my water cup. The artful display started to get the attention of the others on the unit. Barb walked over and sat down without a word. I continued drawing names and doodle art on the cups as everyone took turns handing me their cups for a new personal creative design. Finally Barb approached me. *"What is your favorite flower?"* I asked her. *"Roses,"* she said quietly. *"Would you like your name and a rose on your cup?"* *"Yes,"* she said in the softest tone I had ever heard. I would not call us best friends at this point, but the encounter did help simmer down the yelling on the unit.

During a visit with Tim on the fifth day of my stay, he stopped long enough to talk to the mealtime supervising attendant.

I grew impatient with Tim and told him he was wasting my time with a total stranger. I had a few ounces of water in a Dixie cup and I threw it at Tim. I was furious and we quietly argued as I walked to the guarded doors. Little did I know that this altercation would buy me five more days in that hell-hole. Sometimes you just never knew what was going to set me off. The next day the news came in. I heard there was a fireman injured at a fire scene. I knew Tim was working that day on the fire department and I began to worry. Worry turned into anxiety and I into a begging patient wanting to use the phone to see if he was ok. It was overwhelming and the anxiety completely took over. I asked the nurse's assistant if she could call his number and check to see if he was ok. *"No,"* she said. *"Take your turn in the phone line."* There was only fifteen minutes left for the phone time and six people were already in line. If I had been at St. Clement's someone would have called for me. I could feel myself taking fear like a person on a hijacked plane. I do not know where I was flying off to, but was preparing for a plummeting crash. I frantically paced up and down the hall imagining Tim was hurt.

No one was paying attention to me until the huge male nurse's assistant noticed my agitated state and my pacing. I kept crying to *"Call Tim, please call him."* I became transfixed over the now real thought that he was injured. I was surrounded by five assistants and nurses. They gathered me up and drug me into a tiled floor and walled room. They held me tightly while someone gave me a shot to settle me down. I lay there on the cold tile asking the gorilla-sized attendant, *"What will you do to me next?"* I was not sure but I feel as if the anxiety that day was brought on by the day's previous event. Even after being hospitalized I could not sleep entirely through the night. I roamed the silent hallways, took another hot shower, picked peas off the dining room floor. I became obsessed with cleanliness of the surrounding unit. I would clean for a lack of anything better to do. Late at night I would hang my collages in the walls of my room with dust bunnies. I would wedge the corners of the artwork carefully under the used oxygen knobs or defunct emergency buttons along the walls. Then I would wad up the dust bunnies and press them in the void to hold the art display in place. Who needed tape and glue? I found my own resources.

The fifth night I was up at two in the morning putting the stack of twenty or so puzzles in order in the dining room. When you are sick, one of the most trying things is to find a single puzzle piece on the floor and try to decide what box it belongs in. I think puzzles are overrated for mental wards. Who stays long enough to finish one? Others take it apart before you could possibly finish it. It is all another form of mental warfare. Finally, I started to see a crying woman sitting by herself in the TV room directly across from the nurses' station. The room had about twelve upholstered dining room chairs and two small couches pushed closely to the walls. The TV was in a corner of the room and to sit and watch it one had to crane their neck around the next person to see it. One day, several of us tried to make several rows of furniture to watch TV. You would have thought we had committed a crime. Quickly the chairs were put back against the wall. The nurses' station was a wide door that led back to a room of small lockers and beyond that the tiled room where I was dragged and drugged.

No one was around this woman. I cautiously approached her. She was in her fifties and was a large woman. She kept crying out loud, *"I am going to kill myself. I am going to kill myself."* She did not notice me standing there. I got enough courage to say, *"Hello, my name is Michelle."* She stopped crying for just a moment and said, *"I am Carol."* Sobbing, she stated, *"I am going to kill myself."* I asked *"Do you know why?"* *"No,"* she said. *"Can you tell me more?"* I asked. I wondered where all of the nurses were. Shouldn't someone be with her? She had two hospital gowns on front and back and gathered by ties around her neck. I sat with her for a while. She began to tell me, *"My kids won't let me see my grandbabies. I just want to die."* There were no words to offer her, only my presence seemed to slightly calm her. After a while I decided I was getting tired. I said, *"Goodnight"* and walked back towards my room. She began to wail again, *"I am going to kill myself,"* over and over. I got back to my bed and could not sleep due to her loud crying. Laying there for minutes more, I could not sleep. Then there was the sound of nothing, pure silence. I thought they must have given her something to quiet her or found a distant room for her. Restless and tossing and turning, I got up again and walked towards the TV room where she had been sitting.

About a half of an hour had passed since I last saw her. As I approached the chair where she once sat there was one string from a hospital gown. I began to get a sick feeling in my gut and a sixth sense told me something was wrong. I looked around and saw no one or heard no one except a small *thud* sound coming from behind the large door next to the nurses' station. Through my confusion, I began to pray The Prayer of Jabez, *Oh Lord, bless me indeed enlarge my territory, that your hand would be with me, and that you would keep me from evil, that I may not cause pain.* My heart beat faster as I came nearer the wide door. Through a four inch crack I could barely see her lying on the floor. Her body was pressed against the door. She was gurgling and her face was a plum purple. The door began to close shut. I knew if it did, it would lock as it had done before. The nurses needed a key to unlock it. I pushed my foot against the door and was able to pound simultaneously on the barely reachable nurses' station door. This woman was trying to kill herself by self-strangulation. I did not know it possible. The sight of her was frightful. She was trying to make good on her mantra of suicide. I could see the nurses through the wide window of the door. *"Help!,"* I yelled while pounding my fist as hard as I could. *"Help!"* I screamed this time. Not one nurse so much as lifted their heads in my direction from their computer screens. For the third time I yelled, *"She's killing herself!"*

By now I had let my foot go from the door that began to slowly shut with her body pressing quickly on it. A nurse finally broke her concentration and heard me. I kept pounding and yelling, *"Help! Help!"* She quickly moved towards the nurses' station door and fumbled with her keys until she could open the door. *"What is going on out here?"* she said, perplexed. Well I am so sorry to have bothered you, I thought doggedly. *"Carol,"* I gasped, *"is lying behind the door!"* The door was just closing and clicked as the nurse pushed passed me, *"Quick, get the stethoscope, BP cuff,"* she yelled. As a nursing reflex, I grabbed the equipment from a nearby hook. By now, the nurses were clamoring over one another. This dire situation was also one of chaos as they bumbled out of the station. Eventually three nurses were pushing on the big door after the first nurse unlocked it. Carol was dead weight at this point. The nurses could now easily hear the gurgling and witnessed her horrid facial expression. I am sure their adrenaline was what helped them open the door. They dropped to the floor and began to unwind the tightly wrapped hospital gown string from her neck. She had used it as a tourniquet in her attempted suicide.

Her limp body lay cold on the floor; she was barely breathing. Someone got the oxygen tank and mask, another took her blood pressure, and another kept calling her name, *"Carol, Carol...."* I stood back and watched and became anxiously angry for their nonchalant handling of Carol from the beginning of this horrific affair. Now, she was an emergency because they had waited so long to hear our cries. Carol began to catch her breath as she slowly turned from purple to pink. She began to moan and roll back and forth on the floor. *"I want to die,"* she kept saying over and over as she cried. This episode would be ever etched upon me. A nurse looked at me and said, *"It's time for you to go to bed!"* No one counseled me or even said thank you. They should have thanked me. I did their job.

There was no sleeping that night. It was now my fifth, going on sixth day in this nightmarish place. I was better off at home in my own bed. At least at home I would not have had to witness an attempted suicide and have to feel threatened with almost every encounter on the unit. The pink of dawn slowly filled my room and I watched out my window as the pink turned to gray, full of clouds. They took some particularly interesting shapes: an elephant, then an airplane, then a cherub. I would not and could not forget the night before and wondered how it all was possible that the carbon monoxide poisoning had turned my world upside down.

I dragged myself to breakfast. I could hardly eat. I could only think about what would happen next. I prayed for peace and going home soon. There was no treatment. I felt like I was being warehoused, my crafting was lost in storage. After breakfast I went back to my room, my makeshift chair, and bedded desk. I poured myself into my artwork. I went to retrieve my toothpaste from my drawer and noticed someone had taken all the medicine cups I had collected. It was pretty sickening that the staff was playing head games with me. I could not wait to leave. I humored myself every time I entered my mirrored bathroom. Saddened, I drew a soft smile and said to the mirror, *"How do you like me now?"* I took a shower to try and warm my chilled body. For fifteen minutes I would be left alone and could retreat into a womb of security. It was all the sanity I had. I dressed warmly with layers of clothes and a hat Tim had brought me. I felt like the bespectacled man in *One Flew Over the Cuckoo's Nest* that always wore a sock hat. I did not really care what I looked like as long as I could be half warm. I wondered what else I could do within my means to add warmth to my cold core. Cayenne pepper or hot sauce could help but I had no access to it. Why not try black pepper? It was an experiment and I would have plenty of time and resource to practice on myself. At lunch I added two teaspoons of black pepper to my Dr. Pepper. I gulped it down. It was not that bad; I imagined it raised my temperature just slightly. Every time I was offered a Coke, I administered the peppered treatment. When the others witnessed this, they cringed and writhed as if in pain. *"No way are you going to drink that,"* Barb said. For once I would out tough her. I took gulps, smiling all the way. No one would try it. I was indeed crazy and they would start to leave me alone. I began to feel safer and more secure in my environment.

The cleaning lady was changing the sheet and making an extra bed in my room. There was no further cleaning activity to notice although the room needed it. An extra trash can was getting full so I dumped it in her trash cart outside the room. Marge was not big on conversation but told me I was getting a new roommate. I had enjoyed the private room and wondered what the new arrival would be like. I continued to tear out landscapes of flowers and even pasted the silver seal from my breakfast cereal to my window, behind the curtain and elusive red eye of the security camera. I wanted my family to know what room was mine. There was nothing saying I could not wave from my window and blow kisses through the glass to my sadly smiling family. My action at the window was stopped by the entrance of one of the staff. Linda, my nurse said, *"I need to talk with you Michelle. I am sorry you had to witness what Carol did."* I just sat there and waited for more of a response, like, *"How do you feel? What can we do for you?"* There was no further discussion except for the business that brought her to my room. *"We have tried different ways but none are possible. You are the only one that can have Carol as a roommate. The only other room that has an extra bed is Jack's room."*

Could you believe it? As if it was not enough to see this woman try her hand at suicide; it was over the top that now I was to be her roommate. Another wave of anxiety began to provoke me. I took a deep sigh. What could I say? I do not recall uttering any kind of negative response aloud, but felt a sense of responsibility for Carol and the staff that was using me to watch over her. I would be on alert to her every move. If they were expecting me to act as staff, I sure as hell was well enough to go home! Carol was quietly ushered into the room. There was no exchange of words. She went straight to bed, her back to me. She slept for hours. The nurse checked on her only once. I never left the room. I continued to hang floral pictures in my room and place the rolled up, wedged dust bunnies behind the hangers of knobs or fixtures on the wall. There were about six collages and pictures of birds and flowers. The sunflowers, roses, and red birds were most prominent. I took a short nap and made no noise for my roommate.

When she finally woke, she looked straight at me and said shyly *"I am sorry about the other night."* I paused and said, *"I understand. I have a granddaughter too!"* We began to talk about her situation. Her family had estranged her but she never said why. She went on, *"It's unbearable not to see your grandkids."* I did not want to upset her and merely asked, *"What will you do to get out of here?"* *"I am waiting to hear from my doctor,"* she said. We exchanged names and addresses after a while. She seemed perfectly calm and lucid as if her previous behavior had never taken place. At best, it seemed as if she just needed someone to talk to – someone who would listen. It was nearly lunch time when my nurse Lynn, came in and said excitedly, *"You girls are lucky! Well I've never in all my twenty years here have seen a room decorated like this. I could sure enjoy staying in here for a while."* And she did. It was the most attention and dialogue I had received from any staff. It was now becoming my seventh day. I now felt like my roomie's nurse, art therapist, and friend.

The time had come for lunch. Carol would have to stay in the unit due to her recent suicide attempt. I lined up as if in a chain gang and waited for the doors to open to the long, ramped hall to the dining room. I was told that Dymphna was keeping me longer because of the two ounces of water I had thrown at Tim in the hallway. How absurd, I thought, over such a petty action. No one asked my side of the story. I was being ignored and resented it. It had not taken much, especially for Tim to set me off. Today Amy and Kassidy would arrive by plane from Phoenix for Carrie's bridal shower that weekend.

XIV

Michelle, Are You in There?

ℒ

    I had planned for months to give Carrie the perfect vintage themed shower. I prided myself on the made up games of guessing what items of old might be. The person with the most guesses would win the game. I had many artifacts handed down from my grandparents. I wondered if they were still alive what they would think about my hospitalization. I daydreamed more, playing out the shower's events through my head. The introductions, the games, the opening of the gifts, the perfect cupcakes in green, yellow, and orange arranged on my Granny Koressel's beautiful glass cake pedestals. Carrie and her maid-of-honor were going to wear vintage dresses from the 1940s. I would wear a more matronly dress of small, red checkers with a matching hat. Guests had been encouraged to wear old hats that were furnished for their donning pleasure. A shower like this would never be heard of. I could not wait. Realizing I may still be in here that day made my heart sink and I could only pray that Tim could get me out of here in time. He was agreeing with me that it was time for me to leave, but his request was falling on deaf ears. His calls were not returned and he became more perplexed with the situation. He was unable to catch staff he needed to talk to during my visitation. There would never be nurses available, only assistants. He called and called but to no avail.

The door opened for the day and I carried a small gesture of thanks in my hand for the cooks. I had made them a decorative collage that said, *World's Greatest Cooks*, torn out of magazine letters. I appreciated their tasteful food and they were always pleasant and helpful. They squealed with delight as I showed them the special artwork. The next day it was hanging behind their register in the food line. No money was exchanged but a tab was kept for each of us. I had no idea how much the meals cost. I ate like a bird for I had no appetite ever since my arrival. I filled my large Coke cup with Dr. Pepper so I would have a reserve going back to the unit. I added black pepper to my Dr. Pepper as usual. It did not taste bad at all and gave the drink a little extra zing. By now Tim was doing more research on his own. He had ordered two books on special delivery so he could have them in his hands. The author was Dr. David G. Penny, he was a specialized Ph. D in the study of carbon monoxide. He represented people in court cases to prove how carbon monoxide altered their lives and he had the scientific proof to win his cases. Tim became a quick study and realized by his findings through Dr. Penny that I was not only showing physical signs of carbon monoxide poisoning, but mental ones as well. I was an exact personification of the typical carbon-monoxide-exposed person. There was proof of my symptoms that exacerbated my once relatively undisturbed diagnosis of bipolar disorder. Tim so wanted to have an exchange with my caregivers that he pressed on until he finally arranged a hearing on my behalf. It would take place on my ninth day at Dymphna's. I passed the time by pacing in the short, black-and-white hallway to give myself exercise. By now, I was decorating Styrofoam with a black ink pen for every single person on the unit. It passed the time and gave me a good feeling to make others smile.

The patio was open for smokers or who ever wanted to go outside. I did not care for the smoke, but at least to have had the sun and wind touch my face. I happily followed the short line of patients that clambered at the outside door that was tightly locked. The assistant carried a radio and turned it to a soft rock station. It was a relaxing moment and I soaked up as much sun as I could on this particularly warm spring day. I began to talk to Jeff, who took quick puffs of his cigarettes and quickly exhaled during his jittery words. He had a lisp and seemed very self-conscious about it. I listened as he told his story. *"I am recently divorced and alcohol got me in this place. Been here 'round two weeks. I hope I haven't lost my job,"* he said. *"What do you do?"* I asked, interested. "I am a roofer for a local company. I sure hope my job is there. I need the money. The only clothes I have are what I wore here." I sat for a moment to first think through my idea before I spoke. *"What size pants do you wear?"* I asked. *"32 34,"* he answered. I thought about all the old firemen uniform pants Tim had accumulated. *"Jeff, my husband wears your size. I can give you some pants perfect for your roofing job!"* "Th-thanks," he said. *"I have some shirts I can give you too!"* He later told me he was getting out in two days. This was the news I had also hoped to hear. We made arrangements and exchanged phone numbers. He later would be called and picked up four pairs of pants, four long sleeve flannel shirts, socks, and underwear from my porch in sacks marked, *"To Jeff. Good Luck!"* I had not seen Tim for several days and it was reassuring to see him. All thoughts of anger at him were gone. We held hands as we waited outside the door where the hearing would take place. It was just beyond the cafeteria. I sat nervously but kept myself on high alert to keep calm and collected. I said not a word as two men and a woman walked into the room. We all sat down together, they at one end of the long table and us at the other.

I already felt a barrier between us. Tim began, *"I am Tim Krack, Michelle's husband."* The others returned. *"I am Dr. Luigs, the chief administrator."* *"I am Dr. Ingle, Michelle's doctor"* and *"I am Karla, Michelle's nurse."* I swear I had never seen or talked to these people until I just laid my eyes on them this day. Obviously, all they knew about me was what was written about me on the unit nurse's notes they now held in their hands. *"It's my understanding Michelle acted out the other day towards you. Is this true?"* asked the nurse. *"No,"* Tim said. *"It's hardly a reason to keep her here. It was just water and she was fooling around."* *"We do not take things like that lightly around here,"* stated the administrator. He added, *"It seems Michelle has a condition that needs much attention."* *"What have you done for her that we could not do at home?"* Tim asked. There was complete silence. The doctor spoke up, *"We could let her go home on trial. You could attempt to care for her, but agree to bring her back if need be."* Tim knew how important it was for me to be at Carrie's shower. It looked as if things were going my way. I would have to not let anything bother me or act out in anyway. I just hoped my fellow patients, some new friends even, would not cause a scene and pull me into something. Tim gave each of them a handshake and it was agreed I could go home the next day. It would take that long for the paper work. Luckily I had planned for the shower and all my props, supplies, and needed materials were staged on my dining room table. All that was needed was me. I could look forward to going home.

It was now the dawn of Friday morning. All the paperwork was in order. I sat patiently in the TV room waiting for my freedom. This jailbird was about to fly out of dreaded Dymphna. Barb approached me and sat down in the overstuffed chair next to me. She had been a rebel rouser on the unit. *"Please do not bother me,"* I said under my holding breath. *"Your makeup looks nice. Are you going home today?"* she asked. *"Yes,"* I said. *"I really like your makeup. You know, I do not have any here. What do you say I have yours."* I did not care about giving her the makeup, and I just could not afford a scene now, especially not now. *"You can't have it now,"* I said, *"but when they bring my things I'll be sure you get it."* I said firmly. I did not let her know how nervous I was, but I was shaken clear to the bone. Just a few more hours and I could leave this hellhole. I thought it best to keep a low profile and return to my room. Once again, I entered the bathroom with the decorated mirror of miniature flowers affixed with toothpaste. I smiled a happy smile and said, *"How do you like me now?"* The night before my family came to visit, the house rule still held. I was allowed no visitors due to the water escapade. These people were unreasonable and took their authority a bit too far. They were more barbaric in actions than the people they took care of.

I fashioned a collage that said, *"Hi,"* and toothpasted it near the already displayed round, silver cereal seal that I had placed on the window days before. My family agreed to come visit me, all by finding my special window. I sat patiently and watched. The time slowly ticked by as I watched a free rabbit run from here to there on the grassy yard. There were no plantings, no cheery flowers, just green grass and a lonesome rabbit. I felt like the mad hatter and the bunny was the nervous rabbit character in Alice in Wonderland. Was I crazy? Just a bit, but I thought I could feel a sense, if only a small part, of me returning. I watched the beautiful sunset. My family drove up in the small, brown minivan. They all looked happy and pointed at me in my window. The stickers helped them find my room amongst six other windows that faced them. We blew kisses back and forth. I hid myself partially behind the curtain away from the eye of the camera and kissed the cold glass. We exchanged hand signals for a few moments and they drove away to get a pizza... without me. I felt cheated and lonesome. My image in the mirror had grown sad as I again said, *"How do you like me now?"* I told myself: just a few more hours, just a few more hours.

I slept in my clothes that night. They were warm and comfortable. I almost felt warmer than I had in all ten days that I had been at Dymphna. What a name for this place I thought. What was the point of calling it by a saint's name? They gave no mercy and they definitely were not saintly, except for the one nurse that complimented my room. My roommate had been gone now for several days. I could not imagine her leaving so soon after her suicide attempt. She must have been extra good at convincing the doctor and nurse that she would be okay. She called me up about a month later. She had cleaned her purse out and came across my name, *"Michelle May Krack,"* scrawled on a piece of paper with my home phone number on it. *"How are you?"* she asked. *"Just fine,"* I answered. *"Things have settled down quite a bit. It's good to hear from you. Are you okay?"* I asked. *"Yes,"* she answered. *"I've been able to see my grandkids."* Not much else was said except she did thank me for being there for her. We hung up and I never heard from her ever again.

It was the final day I would grace the breakfast table with my presence. I could not forget my promise to Mary, my only obligation to this place. There was no counseling and no one ever asked me what I felt about anything. They did not even hear Tim out of his concerns. I am sure they did well getting my hospital insurance money- at least that is what it seemed like was their main objective for my long stay. I left Dyphmna Hospital at eleven in the morning, March 19th. It felt good to be back home again. The smells and sights of the house were so comforting. My dogs- Jake the Dalmatian and Lil' Bit the Boston Terrier- were so happy to see me. I stayed awake the entire day although I had not slept as much as I should have. I began to recheck my supplies for the shower. Everything was in order. I gave my family hugs and kisses as they arrived at the house. Everything seemed perfect. As the day wore on, my patience dwindled. I began to act out fits of rage towards Tim with just less than twenty-four hours before the shower was to take place. I lost control. I did not know why. It is as if the jabberwocky had taken over my brain, like a car on a cliff about to go careening down a steep slope. There was no returning. I slowly lost grip with reality and the carbon monoxide grasp had once again come in waves to quickly claim my sanity. I cursed Tim. I shoved Amy into the doorway, I told Carrie, *"You're just a spoiled brat."* What was happening to me? I became the drama queen in a badly acted movie. The script was getting worse and there would be no applauding my role. Tim hailed the ambulance for me and with some coercion I was strapped to the cart. I insisted my two white folders that held the shower plans go with me. I knew I would sit for hours in the emergency room before someone would decide what to do with me. I had a bridal shower to plan and no one was going to stop me.

Because of the workman's comp, the Angels of Mercy staff decided to take me back to Dymphna Hospital. The whole care plan at Angels of Mercy clinic had started by asking questions about my initial visit. I needed to allow a wave of anger to subside as I entered yet another typical emergency room cubical aligned with all the lifesaving gadgets. None of them would be of assistance to me. It was a part of my body that there was no treatment for. No one could put a band-aid, a cast, or a thumb on what treatment plan to take. I lay quietly on the bed now unrestrained. I paged through my notes rehearsing to myself what I would say at the shower. I was the master of ceremonies. I had to pull all of this together- somehow. I became more agitated with Tim, so the nurse asked him to go to another room. When in an irritated state it seems your closest loved one becomes your worst enemy. This was no exception. I watched the time tick away: a half hour, an hour. It was a good thing I thought that I brought something along to pass the time.

For nearly two hours I lay untreated and unchecked by the nursing staff. I was just outside the nurses' station with the curtain pulled. The only time they bothered with me was to bring me a cup of water when I was able to get their attention. Carrie had since joined Tim in the waiting room. The shower was just twelve hours away and here we all sat in this circus, this horrible nightmare. Now, like Alice and the rabbit hole, I just wanted to wake up. I heard mumbles from the nurse that they were waiting for a consult from Dymphna staff to arrive. *Oh my God!* I thought, *I can't go back there.* I did not want to die, but I felt compelled to run away as fast as I could from this place. No one was paying attention to me, no one at all. I had taken off my sandals earlier and now I carefully placed them on my feet and lowered myself to the floor. I looked both ways down the emergency room corridor; there was no one around. The nurses were busy with an accident victim that had just arrived. There was a nursing student that walked in front of my cubicle as I quickly picked up my folders and with my best effort, I followed her out of the emergency room door, past the security guard, out into the cold night air. That was easy, I thought to myself. Now, where would I go and how would I get there? I was not for sure but saw a group of people standing near the parking lot west of the emergency room. I bravely walked up to them, without money, identification, or much of anything. I had left my purse at home. My religion told me to pray. I prayed, *Dear Lord, help me through this night. Help me do what's right. I can't go back to Dymphna. Please hide me in your care. Amen.*

A new sense of purpose and determination empowered me. The group was standing by their cars. About three of the five turned to me as I approached them. I guessed they must have been with the accident victim who had just arrived. If I had money I would have been successful calling the cab which I had tried on the phone in the hallway before I decided to leave my room. Damn, if I had a credit card I could spend the night in a hotel and be safe for a while from the clutches of Dymphna's. By now it was noticed that I was missing. I know exactly where I wanted to go: to my sister, Marty's. She lived on the westside about two to three miles away. I asked one of the strangers, *"Could you give me a ride to my sisters? It's an emergency,"* I pleaded. *"Sorry lady,"* he responded. *"We're from Illinois and we don't know our way around here."* Damn again, I thought. This plan was not going as I had hoped. I needed to hide until it was time for the shower, an unrealistic thought. You know, like everything would magically be okay by then. I set out walking with sandals on. Why had I not worn regular shoes? By now I was practically running from the hospital. There would be no catching a ride in a nice warm car. I had only jeans and a long sleeve shirt on and there was a crispness in the air. A cold night would ensue.

I decided to take off my sandals; I could walk quicker without them. I filled the shadows along the way, mainly staying in alleys that dotted my westward route. I came to a fire station and thought for a brief moment I could get help there. No, you fool! They would call Tim in a heartbeat! These firefighters were like family, but there would be no rescuing me this night. I was smart to stay out of harm's way. I felt no fear of the dark street and the occasional passing car. By now it was just after midnight. I crossed a well-lit double boulevard. I stood behind telephone poles as cars approached as if to hide or at least attempt to. By now, Tim probably had every police car on the westside looking for me. I had now walked almost a mile and was getting cold. I dodged behind a large clump of decorative grass as a police car slowly drove by heading west. I was thankful that I was not detected. By now I was crossing railroad tracks and decided to put my sandals back on. I found more dark alleys that zig-zagged back and forth from block to block. I had no fear except for trying to escape. I knew I would have safe haven at my sister's house. It had taken me an hour and a half to reach St. John Avenue. I felt colder than ever and lamented how unprepared I was for this trek. As I walked a darkened street near the trailer park I saw a rug covering a manhole cover. I picked it up and gave it a shake. It did not seem all that dirty, so I held onto it. Someone must have covered the vents to keep the sewer smells at bay. I did not care. It did not smell and it was large enough to cover at least my shoulders. A few steps later I found an orange lying on the street. I picked it up and found it was soft and near rotten. I thought it my only defense if someone tried to stop me. They would get a halfway rotten orange in the face.

I felt safer now as I crossed Maryland Street. There was no traffic so I headed up the long hill of the last leg of my journey. Only six blocks to go! If someone was going to see me, it was on this street. There were no direct alleys that ran east and west of here. Marty lived atop the hill. Luckily I only saw one car and was able to hide behind bushes that were in front of a house. Now, I only had a block to go. I threw the orange deep into the woods and clutched my folders and my rug close to me. It was the home stretch. Tim and Carrie were beyond themselves for fear as to where I was. God forbid something had happened to me. It was now three in the morning and there was no sight or sound of me anywhere. It is as if I had disappeared into midair. Tim was furious with the hospital staff and began to look at other options for me. If he found me he had to get help somewhere other than Dymphna's Hospital and Angels of Mercy. He contacted St. Clement's crisis hotline for an emergency admission. He still had to find me. The shower was now ten hours away and I was certain no one would be finding me.

I reached Marty's house and walked up the long concrete steps next to her house. There was lawn furniture under a lone pine tree with thick pine needles beneath the tree. I curled up in the Adirondack chair and pulled the rug up over me. I felt a slight bit of warmth and satisfaction in my choice of resting places. The flower bed restricted anyone from seeing me directly from the street. I was not quite content with my arrangements, so I began to think about going to her shed for better protection from the cold night air and better concealment. As I opened the gate to the side of her house, I was greeted by her two dogs, Bunny and Jersey. They were happy to see me. They did not bark but jumped up and down on me in excitement. I got to the shed door. I knew Marty would be getting up in a few hours. Hopefully it would be alright to let her know I was in her tool shed and that I was safe. Luckily I had a pen and loose leaf paper in my folder. I wrote her a note. *I am sorry to bother you, but I am okay. I had to get away from the horrible hospital. I am in your shed.* I signed it, *Love, Michelle.*

I pushed it through the doggy door so she would see it. The dogs had settled down as I let myself in the tool shed. It was still dark, so I had to feel my way around. I found a lawn chair. It felt good to sit down. I began to fumble around for more warmth. The rug was not enough. I needed something on my head, shoulders, and legs. Marty had a large canvas umbrella. I used it to wrap around my arms. I found a half-clean, black plastic flower pot you get at the garden centers. I placed upon my head for warmth. It worked nicely. I used the rug to cover my legs. I finally began to feel warm and fell asleep for several hours. Eight hours until the shower. Marty had woken up to go to the bathroom and get a drink of water when she noticed the scrawled note on her kitchen floor. She read it in disbelief. She looked out to the dark shed and could not tell if I was there or not. She carefully came out to the shed and while opening the door said, *"Michelle. Michelle, are you in there?"* She had awakened me and I began to cry. *"Something's happened with this dammed carbon monoxide. I lost it and Tim took me to the emergency room. You have to promise me you won't call him. I cannot go back to Mercy or to Dymphna's. I have to go to Carrie's shower. Please help me sis!"*

She insisted that I come inside and warm up. I did not decline her offer. She gave me a blanket and some hot tea. *"This has been a nightmare Marty, a complete nightmare!" "How did you get here?"* she asked. *"I walked and ran from Angels of Mercy. What time is it now?"* I asked. *"5:00 a.m."* she said. *"I need to call Tim,"* she said calmly. I knew I could not stay away from him forever, but he had to promise and keep the promise there would be no Mercy! She called Tim and he arrived a few minutes later. He told Marty that he promised that he had made arrangements for me at St. Clement's. All I could think of was how this state of mind would rob me again of Carrie's shower which was so dear to me. Tim looked tired and scared as he stepped in the front door. I was in no shape for mind tricks or attempts to send me back to that godforsaken place. Tim once again told me he would do it all my way. He could not afford for me to take off again, and knew I would definitely do it.

It was now mid-morning. My daughters were cautious about me. I acted as if nothing had happened that night. We had to go on with the shower. I was good at putting on events and so my mind was still very active. We arrived at the school cafeteria where the shower would be held. I began to decorate the room with a wooden screen that held all the old antiques for the games to be played. I helped Carrie set out the beautiful cupcakes. I put Tim in charge of music. He plugged in the radio and sat on a stool near the kitchen. He looked as if he felt drained and exhausted from worrying all night long. I have a picture of him to prove it. The guests started to arrive one-by-one. They signed in so we could draw names for prizes. I had invited my friends, even some of my best friends from NAMI. They had no idea what had transpired in the last twenty-four hours. I thought I had somehow masked my mania and fully enjoyed the shower. I was in my element, covered, and comforted with family and friends. The games and refreshments went on without a hitch. Everyone seemed to have a good time. As we carried the gifts to her car, Tim said, *"Remember what we agreed upon?"* We had discussed me going to St. Clement's after the shower was over. I was relieved that I was able to attend and orchestrate the shower but it was now time to pay the piper, as the saying goes.

I was still irritated, not at Tim, but at the hold that this carbon monoxide had on me. Nothing was like me anymore. I seemed to hate everything about everything. It was all a huge mess. I once again felt like Alice, but this time like I was in a shrinking machine not knowing who or what size of event would be next. The waves of sanity and insanity had to stop. St Clement's was my only hope. I had been there before and the environment was much more relaxed. I did not care for some of the staff, but for the most part, I felt safe there and they listened to me and my family as well. Amy and Kassidy had packed their bags to leave to go back to Phoenix and I had packed my bags too for my little visit. I threatened Tim that I would buy ten pairs of pajamas so I would not have to wear those crappy, thin hospital gowns that tied around my neck. I kept my promise and when I got out of St. Clement's I went straight to Target and bought ten pair, one for each night I would spend at Dymphna's. They were on sale of course. If I was going to stay that long in a hospital, I would be prepared and I would feel good and look good in doing so. Several pairs of the pajamas were of the sock monkey. Well, *"How do you like me now!"* This repeated message became clearer. I had some control over my behavior and the prescription of Ativan seemed to calm me even more. I do not recall being given any at Dymphna or at Mercy; this could have prevented a lot of my anxiety. A lot of unnecessary drama could have been prevented, like the administration of the hypodermic during my anxious moments about Tim's safety.

I resented those ten days at Dymphna's and, two years later, told a representative of Dymphna at a Health Fair what had happened to me. Regardless, I told him, "I doubt I would ever go there or send someone to your hospital." He said, "I am sorry for what happened to you. Did you fill out a questionnaire after you got home?" he asked. I could not remember if I did or did not. It did not matter. I said, "You have no treatment plan for someone with carbon monoxide poisoning." He felt uncomfortable with my accusations, but I felt a need to advocate just the same. A fancy name and four walls do not a good mental hospital make, and he needed to hear it. He would remember this day and hopefully prevent the same occurrences for someone else's diagnosis like mine. I told him I had a mission in life, and had planned to execute it. He shook my hand and thanked me. I took a piece of paper and pen from his booth and wrote my name, Michelle May Krack. "I thank you too," I said. I moved onto the next display about high blood pressure. Hopefully this man was in some capacity to pass the word about my situation. Maybe the staff and their policies had changed. I cared not to entertain the possibility of me going there ever again. It was my closure and I needed to do it, to move on and forget the supposed treatment and hope for better prospects for those individuals with mental illness and carbon monoxide poisoning.

I needed a referral to go to St. Clement's and set up communications with Southwest Behavioral Health. I was able to get it over the phone with my regular nurse practitioner. I peacefully went to St. Clement's, where I stayed for my usual- five days. The medicines seemed to be working better for me. At this point we had no idea what or how the bills would be paid. We had hoped all the Dymphna bills would be covered by workman's comp. There were no calls from New Hope. There was the stigma that my bipolar was fully to blame. I still had much of the physical symptoms that occurred that had nothing to do with bipolar disorder. I could not walk a straight line, sometimes I would practically fall over while standing perfectly still. My vision was terrible- it had become so bad I could never see without my glasses. I had not used glasses before the incident. Floaters in my eyes were so huge I saw large black spots peripherally that resembled the passing of a small animal. I would have numbing in my feet and hands. But, namely my demeanor and typically pleasant disposition were completely altered. Dr. Penny's advice from his book read, *"Due to high levels of carbon monoxide exposure some or all symptoms or conditions are more likely irreversible."* I decided to take supplements for the brain. B-vitamins, black cohosh, and fish oil were added to my daily regimen of psychiatric meds. It was a handful of pills to take every day but I felt it was my way to have some control of my life. I had no idea if it would help but at this point it surely could not hurt anything.

I felt extremely lucky having a husband that knew he loved me and could separate my condition from the real me. We had just started on my recovery or what I had hoped for in a chance to be normal again. Tim decided he would cheer me up by getting new counter tops and a new top to match on our kitchen table. The original counter tops were put in poorly in 1986. It was time for a change. The old oak table was longer than it was wide and fit perfectly in my kitchen that had six doors and two windows. The table had been salvaged before the old St. Thomas school building had been torn down. Its top had many cut marks in it and had been used for many years to make dumplings and kuchens for the annual Fall Festival. It served us well for our growing family of six. We just now had to add an extra chair for Kassidy.

❧

I spent much of my days lying on the couch watching movies. Be it depression or direct result of the carbon monoxide, life was much slower and I could not have cared less about its ever-changing days or seasons. I use to revel in activities and family events. They all brought anxiety and hopelessness to me now. I could barely remember what normal was like. My short term memory was horrible. I made myself take walks and tripped many times in doing so. Cleaning that needed ladders to reach our ten foot tall ceilings remained untouched. Ladders and long steps up and down were off limits to me. My sense of balance was quite affected. I learned to live with my restrictions and hoped for a better tomorrow. For several months I continued the brain-nourishing supplements I had started. For a year prior to the carbon monoxide incident, I took three thousand milligrams of fish oil daily. I wondered if taking this would have protected my brain somehow from the exposure. There was very slight improvement but as I had learned from taking new psychiatric medicines, it took time and when that is all you have, it seems to take even longer.

St. Clement's was a quiet place. If there were any outbursts they were quickly quelled by the staff usually with soft dialogue. It felt safe, safer than Dymphna for sure. My kids made me a card for *Momma Gong.* I have no idea where that came from, but it fit the nicknames they had for one another with three letter words like Mai, which was Matt's nickname. They had a language of their own and marveled in their extreme croquet games that Matt usually set up in the yard. My kids did not lack a sense of creativity or humor. I guess they got it honest enough.

Mom, Dad, Tim, and the kids were always good about visiting me in the hospital. They did not have to. It was definitely an effort on their part to support me in these difficult times. I only wished and prayed for the better ones. The anti-anxiety and anti-psychotic meds seemed to help immensely. During my stay at Clement's, one of the staff tried to convince me that I was a candidate for EST- electroshock therapy. I felt the carbon monoxide had complicated things enough and I did not wish to experience shock therapy. The tech often insisted I watch the video that explained the procedure. She did this day after day. Until I agreed to watch it just to get her off my back! While watching the *professional* film, I caught a glimpse of her in the film peeking around the corner of the room where the video was being taped. It appeared amateur in nature and I felt compelled to never be candidate for this kind of treatment. No thank you.

There were more activities to attend. Group therapy usually bored me and I grew restless waiting for other fellow patients to slowly answer questions. I took to art forms of Styrofoam cup decorating and had made a suitcase out of a paper sack. It opened in the front to make it very practical for carrying home my personal effects. In one group session we were asked to write down on a piece of paper what we liked about one another. These are the following statements from fellow mental health unit friends about me: *"creative and caring"* from Jason. Sharon wrote *"funny and smiling all the time. A way of finding the good out of somebody"* added Tim. *"Just met her"* said Mike. *"Helped Michelle make a collage. That was pretty special"* exclaimed Jimmy. Clare wrote, as I was ready to leave after five days, *"Have a good ride home!!! Do not come back!"* My toothpaste, glue, and newspaper collages brought smiles to many faces.

One day before leaving, John, a new guy, made his way onto the unit. He was ranting and raving and slamming chairs under the dining room tables. It was a flash back to Dymphna for me. He made everyone uneasy and you could feel the tension mounting. The staff was not getting through to him. He yelled, *"I need a smoke. Get me out of this damned place."* He sat down grumbling to himself as I approached him. *"Hi John,"* I said. *"I understand you got trouble."* *"Hell yes I do,"* he slammed. *"Can I show you something?"* I asked. *"What?"* he said loudly. *"Well, you think you have trouble, just read this."* I had written my name Michelle May Krack, on a piece of paper. He snatched it from my hand and at once yelled out loud, *"Michelle May Crack."* Starting to laugh, I said, *"That is my name and I am bipolar."* By now he had found some humor. *"No way,"* he said chuckling. *"Way,"* I said smiling. It seemed his dynamite mood had now made a complete 180. We sat and talked. We did not discuss his problem, but I felt a sense of accomplishment and had a natural way of counseling the most difficult patient on the unit. I had met my calling. I doodled affirmations. I had left, *How do you like me now?* or *You are a star!* A beacon of light and inspiration to others. We were given handouts at some of our sessions. One was, *Follow-up Care.* The steps were listed one through six:

1. *Keeping a Routine*

2. *Doctor's Appointments*

3. *Medications*

4. *Having Balance*

5. *Support System*

6. *Plan B*

I knew the importance to all these steps. My routine was minimal but attainable. I mostly rested, watched television due to the malaise the carbon monoxide created throughout my body. I steered clear of social interaction, even church, so that my anxiety would not be fostered. I was religious about taking my meds and keeping doctor's appointments. I had seen too much self-medication and non-compliance with doctors in my own family. I knew what the ramification would be if I did not follow step two and three perfectly. Balance was like a tightrope walker with no net and I never knew how the fall would happen and how long it would last. Balance meant once again minimal activities that would provoke an episode. My support was God and my family. There was no doubt. As far as Plan B was concerned, I had already encountered the plan through X, Y, and Z. I tried writing but could never get past a few pages. There was no flow or connection between my words. It was nonsensical. I played my flute and sang songs like Patsy Cline's *Walkin' After Midnight.* I hummed bars of that song when I walked after midnight the night before Carrie's shower. I was always, *searching for me.* Arts and crafts seemed to settle my nerves and I could still provide painted welcome signs of slate and wood for church socials and card parties without directly involving myself.

We were given daily affirmations at St. Clement's. I tried as I might to relate to each one. One in particular was, *Problems have only the size and the power that you give them.* I have no idea what God had or has in store for me. It is all in a plan greater than I can imagine. I need to go with the flow even though the tide is rough. The card further read, *I will not make mountains out of the molehills of my life.* I could always find someone in therapy that had it worse, and at times, much worse than I had. I tried to squelch any pity parties. My regimen of medications seemed to help marginally. Many of my family and friends would bring up the possibility of a lawsuit regarding the carbon monoxide. I had lost employment and it looked as if any possibility of any further employment was out of the question. We kept our faith that things would improve.

Meanwhile, we arranged for a meeting with the school district's Superintendent. We wanted to make him aware of all the treatment and current conditions I was having. Eighteen months had passed since the carbon monoxide exposure. Not only was I concerned about my future, but too the safety of those who still worked with the antiquated machine that had poisoned me. We arrived at the school's main office building to talk to Mr. Lilly. He was a middle-aged man and greeted us with a hand shake and a smile. Tim brought along files consisting of all my medical history. We had also reports from the Indiana University toxicology lab that unfortunately resulted in inconclusive test results. As we sat and talked with Mr. Lilly, he listened carefully to all the details of the two incidents involving the dishwasher. I made mention of the meeting I had with Mr. Floyd, the principal. I brought up his promise be made good to install a carbon monoxide detector in each of the school's cafeteria's and anywhere a gas powered engine is used within the buildings. Mr. Lilly assured me that a detector had been placed in New Hope. There was no mention of other schools participating. I later called a cousin who managed the cafeteria at another school within the district. She neither saw nor heard of any carbon monoxide detector in her kitchen. We explained the course of following through with the workman's compensation doctors and their referrals. Tim showed Mr. Lilly all of the thousands of dollars that had accrued as a result of my injury while on the job. He said he would take them under advisement. I felt a great letdown in how this whole story was unfolding. It was obvious that I was unable to work and the symptoms would remain. I was so unsteady at walking that bruises filled my arms from falling into things. I usually wore long sleeve blouses to hide the bruises as I did this day, visiting Mr. Lilly. My memory was horrible. I had to write down everything, every day to remember the slightest of tasks. Unlike me, I missed several doctor's appointments. I wrote some appointments on the wrong days in my calendar. My vision was very poor and the floaters in my vision were so big they drastically impaired my vision. I became easily agitated and was anxiety ridden most of the day. I took Ativan for the anxiety at the end of every hour it was possible. It helped, but did not alleviate the problem as a whole. Nights were sleepless so I was put on Temazepam for sleep. All these factors, as explained to you the reader and to Mr. Lilly were put on the table.

I suppose by just looking at me he could hardly believe there was anything wrong. We explained that we wanted to know what to expect from workman's comp. as we had each treatment through their specifications and had approval of each action. We still to this day have not heard back from Mr. Lilly concerning our plight. It was now becoming apparent after several weeks that we were not going to have cooperation from the school's Superintendent. We entertained the possibility of a lawsuit. It made us almost physically ill to know that a devoted employee of eight years would suffer an accident on the job and would not be compensated.

Further, other schools were not being protected and the original machine that caused the problem was still in operation. We contacted a number of attorneys in the area and were told they would not handle the case due my preexisting bipolar disorder. Another factor was the Statute of Limitations, the two-year bench mark was fast approaching. We prayed on it and put it in God's hands. A friend of mine told me it was the Year of Faith in the

Catholic Church. It was all I needed to hear. I felt let down by the school's lack of support. I poured myself into my church's projects as much as I could with my limitations. I felt the real faith was in the people that worked in the church and not the people who ran the school. I prayed that no further injury would happen to the kitchen ladies or worst yet, the children.

It has been three years since my life was changed by carbon monoxide poisoning. I have worked diligently to regain my steady walk, steady hand, and balance in general. My handwriting has returned to its beautiful style. I can now climb stairs and even small ladders or chairs without falling. From time to time I have to take a sleeping pill to aid my much-needed sleep of eight to ten hours. I finished taking Ativan for anxiety after a year and a half ago. I still suffer anxiety attacks, yet they are more manageable with medication. Sometimes I choose to refrain from social events and I am okay with that as long as it lets me stay well. I have no need to call Tim at work and cry for him to be at my side. I drive freely and keep my routine without fear of any kind. I have been fortunate in that the most obvious side effect I have is the small tic in my little dance when impatient or waiting for something. Tim said he does not notice it anymore but I can still tell. I began writing of this journey in July of 2012. The medication I started in the spring of 2013 has also helped. It has replaced the previous medications I had been taking. I opted to change medications completely. It took about three months for the headaches, increased anxiety, and physical side effects to subside. I have been blessed with the ability to write my story so that it may help my children and others. I thank those for making it possible, my husband, children, parents, and friends. This has indeed been the Year of Faith.

XV

There is Hope and Will Always Be Hope

⊱

There is hope and will always be hope in the recovery process. My appointments with my doctor had stretched out to six months. I now had a female doctor that soon understood my goal of staying on the medicine regimen and trying to live as normal a life as possible. It was too bad my original doctor did not have the information about the induced mania from antidepressants. Unfortunately, I followed my medicine routine to the proverbial T and it explained the repeating behavior that was definitely not normal. I have learned that in psychiatry, the doctors *practice* medicine like any health professional. That style of doctoring seems to fit perfectly. No two people are alike and the perfect cocktail sometimes takes years to develop. It has taken thirty years of perseverance and testing to come to the conclusion that a combination of new medications work for me. This was only made possible by my current doctor, Dr. Whitehead at Southwestern Behavioral Health. I owe much of my diligence and sounding board techniques to not only my family but to Brenda Meyer who councils me at Southwestern. She probably knows my mental status as well as my husband. She is quick to pick up on any behavior that is out of the norm and helps me keep on track by collaborating my treatment with Dr. Whitehead. One is lucky to find a doctor and clinical counselor that listen and are willing to take the steps to make their patient's life stable and fulfilled. I appreciate their sense of humor and it has helped me in countless ways. Both are most serious about my condition but they are always aware that a smile and laugh go a long way.

In January 2013 I attended a NAMI soup supper. During the meal there was discussion of the opening of a new recovery center. I became very interested as I learned a job opening for a peer recovery advocate was available. An introduction was made to Lori Rivera, the recovery center's coordinator. I learned the position required someone to be in recovery with a mental health issue. I welcomed the chance to be back in the work place again. It had been two years since my job at New Hope High school. Symptoms from the carbon monoxide poisoning had diminished. I spoke with Tim about the part time job at the recovery center. He supported my decision to try this new opportunity. After several weeks I had a scheduled job interview. I met with Lori and her supervisor Beth Barchet, the Programs Director at Southwestern Behavioral Healthcare. One of the questions that I was asked was, *"What long term goal do you have?"* *"To stay in recovery. To stay well,"* I responded. Happily, I accepted the position as a peer recovery advocate.

Before the recovery center opened Lori asked if I would be willing to give an interview on *The Trend* radio show on NPR with Micah Schweizer and I accepted. The live show aired February 8th, my Dad's birthday. I shared what my early symptoms of bipolar disorder were during the manic episodes. I emphasized how important adherence to medications should be to maintain recovery. I applauded the success of my current medications along with following the guidelines of my psychiatrist and counselor.

The doors opened February 28th with Lori and me greeting our peers. Soon after, an advisory council was formed from frequenting peers to help decide how the recovery center would operate. A name needed to be created. After a number of meetings it was determined the name would be the Peace Zone. Peace stood for Peer Empowerment & Advocacy in the Community of Evansville. We also needed a logo to go with our new name. Several ideas were submitted on paper. I put my creative thoughts to work and created the chosen design. Simply put it was a fashioned sixties peace sign with the word *zone* printed across its center and a dove holding an olive branch perched on the Z of Zone. Blue-green colors were chosen by the deciding group to render the new design. It was an honor to have my idea chosen. I felt a real sense of belonging to the cause. This job fit my creative nature and filled my desire to help others.

December 2013 was an exciting time as we witnessed over three thousand visits to the Peace Zone since the February opening. The Zone offers peer support for those who suffer from mental health issues. Group discussions provide positive support with an emphasis on recovery and coping skills. More specifically, we empower members so they can become self-advocates for their own mental health and recovery. Other programs include job-readiness, community education and outreach, arts engagement, billiards, music instruments (guitar, keyboard, drumming circle, and lap harps). Physical activities include stretching classes, an indoor walking track in the gymnasium, and Wii games. There are also opportunities on how to use a computer with everything from basic usage to Facebooking and resumé-building.

One day, a gentleman surprised our group as he answered the question, *"What has the Peace Zone done for you?"* He told us he had been stricken so greatly with anxiety that he could not go into Wal-Mart to shop with his family. After visits to the recovery center he found it easier to accompany his family during their trips to the store. He now frequents the store by himself. Lori and I could hardly imagine what impact the Peace Zone had on this young man. This is just one of the many positive changes we have witnessed in peoples' lives.

As our doors welcome more visitors, another part-time peer recovery advocate position opened. Lisa Cheatem was on board when we planned and held a successful Christmas party with sixty peers in attendance. Every day is a joy as Lori, Lisa, and I work well together. It is nice knowing that one's life work and passion can make a job not seem like that much of a job at all. During a recent visit to Dr. Whitehead he greeted me at the door of his office. We exchanged smiles. Before I spoke, he said, *"You look satisfied."* I could not have agreed with him more. My life has come to a time when I could enjoy simple things again. A good night's sleep assures me a level of recovery that I so desire. I have been blessed with a new job that brings a sense of fulfillment. That feeling has been missing for a long, long time. I have surpassed the fear that Michelle may crack!

Update

Life has moved forward since this book was published in 2014. It's hard to believe that so much time has passed by. My medicine has kept me stable now for seven years. No meds have had to be altered. I am lucky in that regard.

About a year after I was off lithium I became very anxious. After seeing my therapist she came to the conclusion that I was inadvertently overdosing on thyroid supplements. My thyroid was working now so I no longer needed the Synthroid.

One of the reasons I was taken off the lithium was the effect it was having on my kidneys. I now have stage three kidney disease. I was seeing the nephrologist every six months, but since my condition remains stable I now I see him once a year. If you are on lithium it is important to have routine blood work done.

I'm sorry to say that in 2015 I lost both of my parents within six weeks of each other. Mom became ill and required two surgeries. The heart surgery was too much for her. I miss her dearly. At her funeral everyone in the family was given a butterfly pin from her collection and wore them in her honor. She loved butterflies. I've planted a butterfly bush in my front yard to bring butterflies as a reminder of Mom.

Mom loved to play the organ at St. Philip. She had done so for forty years. The electric piano at her home was donated to the Peace Zone. It brings merriment and happiness to all when played. One of my peers loves to sing the blues and play the piano.

Dad would say many times that he wanted to take Mom out of the hospital and to the French Lick Resort. The resort is frequented by many and is known for its historic mineral springs.

Dad said it could help Mom. It became his mantra as he became more ill.

My dad's decline after Mom died was sudden. He was suffering with the mania and became a failure-to-thrive patient. There were many days no one could communicate with him. We were blessed with two days that we were able to talk and understand each other.

The first of those days was when Dad called me to his beside and said, "Michelle, can you forgive me for how I treated you while you were growing up?" I choked back the tears and responded, "Dad, it's all about forgiveness. Yes, I do."

A week before dad died my siblings and I spent an afternoon rubbing Dad's feet and brushing his hair. He was relaxed and enjoying himself. We listened to him tell us about his Marine Corps days. It was a good day with Dad. A lasting memory.

Family was at his side during his last hours in a hospital in Washington, IN. While sitting with him I looked on the wall in the small room and saw a splendid picture of the French Lick Resort. We found out later that there were local pictures hanging in the rooms, but this was the only one of the resort. We pictured how Dad and Mom must now be united at the grandest hotel of them all.

My medications carried me through these days from my parents needing my care to heartbreaking loss and finally their funerals. I stayed on my meds and prayed that I would stay well. My family looked on expecting me to have a breakdown. It never happened. My mental and physical health was tested. Enough can't be said about how well the prayers and medications have sustained me.

The Peace Zone has been open for six years. During that time I've become a Certified Recovery Specialist/Community Health Worker. I have also continued my peer mentoring at the Peace Zone Recovery Center. I lead outreach at the local hospitals on their adult mental health units as well as at a drug and alcohol treatment facility. I've also shared my story with NAMI Family to Family participants and at CIT (Crisis Intervention Team) training classes. I've also had several book signings. My book is now available at the University of Evansville, the University of Southern Indiana, Ivy Tech Community College, Willard Library, and Evansville Public Library.

My family is growing! I now have a total of three grandchildren, one girl and two boys. My kids are spread throughout the United States. There's always an excuse to hop on a plane or into a car. I'm very proud of my family and happy for their successful lives.

Tim and I celebrated our 40th wedding anniversary in October 2018. I married my best friend and it's fun to watch our family grow!

It's good to dream. Writing this book was a dream come true! My current dream is that my story be made into a movie and spread the message of hope in recovery of mental health issues. I also wish to make an audio-book for those who can't read the printed page.

I am so blessed by all the people that I have met since this book was published. New friendships have been forged.

Often I tell others that everyone has a story to tell. The more people who struggle with mental health issues share the more we're not isolated and struggling all alone. My hope is that we can rightfully pursue and reach recovery in our lives. We deserve a happy forever after.

Acknowledgements

A special memory to those we will never forget.

To my loving husband Tim, my children Matt, Amy, Carrie, and Andy. My parents, sister, brothers, grandparents, and granddaughter Kassidy, daughter-in-law Paige, cousins, friends, mother-in-law, and father-in-law.

To my son-in-law Brock Harris for his patience and hand at editing my story. To my daughter Carrie for her assistance in the editing and with formatting the revision.

To my son Matt for being my marketing director.

To Sara Grubb for typing my story from long hand. To Jon, her husband, for allowing her time to do so.

To Tracy Wheatley and Matt Wagner for the cover art.

To my former psychiatrist, Dr. Willard Whitehead, and current therapist, Brenda Meyer LCSW, at Southwest Behavioral Healthcare for their years of mental health care.

To my current psychiatrist, Dr. Greg Unfried, for helping me maintain my wellness.

To Lori Rivera, Lisa Cheatem, and Beth Barchet for being wonderful people to work with.

To Daniel Knight, Studio B, for author photography and family photographs.

Where do I start to thank all of those who have made the Peace Zone possible? Without grants and donations the Peace Zone could not operate. Thank you!

Peace Zone was founded in 2012 by Beth Barchet and Rick Paul of Southwestern Behavioral Healthcare, Inc. which secured funding from the Indiana Division of Mental Health and Addiction for the start-up of a peer-run recovery center. With this grant, Southwestern Behavioral Health received the seed money to start a recovery center. Southwestern donates facility space to the Peace Zone. Peace Zone has submitted all of the necessary paperwork and has become a 501(c)(3) non-profit tax-exempt organization.

City of Evansville Endowment Fund Grant: Southwestern Behavioral Health, Inc. recently received a grant from the City of Evansville Endowment Fund to be issued for the Peace Zone for the addition of a wheelchair accessible sidewalk and additional lighting in the courtyard.

Author Biography

Michelle May Krack, whose name is frequently mispronounced *Crack,* was diagnosed with bipolar disorder in 1989 when she was thirty-one.

Her memoir, *Michelle may crack!,* is written for her immediate family and extended family and those dealing with mental health issues.

She believes recovery is possible with mental illness.

Michelle has lived in Evansville, Indiana all of her life, sixty years.

Currently, she works at the Peace Zone, a peer-based recovery center as a Certified Recovery Specialist(CRS)\Community Health Worker (CHW). Michelle also leads outreach programs at the local hospitals, including a drug and alcohol treatment center.

In 2014, Michelle received the Consumer Advocate Heroes for Recovery Award from Mental Health America of Indiana for her work.

She has been married to her husband Tim for forty years. They have four grown children, one granddaughter, and two grandsons.

Her hobbies, besides writing, include gardening and art in various mediums.

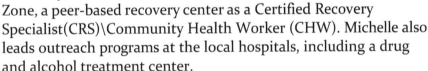

Contact   Michellemaycrack@gmail.com

CPSIA information can be obtained
at www.ICGtesting.com
Printed in the USA
FFHW020815190319
51111205-56572FF

9 780578 451732